BRIDGES OF POWER

Women's Multicultural Alliances

Edited by
LISA ALBRECHT & ROSE M. BREWER

Foreword by Caryn McTighe Musil

Published in cooperation with
the National Women's Studies Association

New Society Publishers

Philadelphia, PA   **Santa Cruz, CA**

Gabriola Island, BC

Inquiries regarding requests to reprint all or part of *Bridges of Power: Women's Multicultural Alliances* should be addressed to:

New Society Publishers
4527 Springfield Avenue
Philadelphia, PA 19143

ISBN USA 0-86571-183-6 Hardcover
ISBN USA 0-86571-184-4 Paperback
ISBN Canada 1-55092-002-2 Hardcover
ISBN Canada 1-55092-003-0 Paperback

Printed in the United States of America on partially recycled paper by Wickersham Printing Company, Lancaster, PA.

Cover art is derived from the logo of Break the Silence Mural Project, by Miranda Bergman. Cover design by Tina Birky.

Book design by Tina Birky.

New Society Publishers gratefully acknowledges permission to reprint the following:
1. Pheterson, Gail, "Alliances Among Women: Overcoming Internalized Oppression and Internalized Domination," originally appeared in *Signs: Journal of Women and Culture,* Autumn, 1986, Vol. 12, No. 1, 146–160.
2. Bunch, Charlotte, "Making Common Cause: Diversity and Coalitions," appeared in Charlotte Bunch, *Passionate Politics, Essays 1968–1986, Feminist Theory in Action,* St. Martin's Press, New York, 1987, and originally in *IKON,* No. 7 (Fall 1986).
3. Parkerson, Michelle, "Did You Say the Mirror Talks?" A slightly different version appeared in *Hurricane Alice: A Feminist Quarterly,* Vol. 4, No. 2, 1987, as "No More Mammy Stories."
4. McDaniel, Judith, "Taking Risks: The Creation of Feminist Literature," appeared in *The American Voice,* No. 17, Winter 1989, pp. 102–109.
5. Giacaman, Rita, and Johnson, Penny, "Palestinian Women: Building Barricades and Breaking Barriers," appeared in *Intifada: The Palestinian Uprising Against Israeli Occupation,* ed. Zachary Lockman and Joel Beinin. A MERIP Book, South End Press, Boston, 1989, pp. 155–70.
6. Lorde, Audre, excerpts from *A Burst of Light,* Firebrand Books, Ithaca, NY, 1988, pp. 56–7.

To order directly from the publisher, add $1.75 to the price for the first copy, 50¢ each additional. Send check or money order to:

New Society Publishers
PO Box 582
Santa Cruz, CA 95061

New Society Publishers is a project of the New Society Educational Foundation, a nonprofit, tax-exempt, public foundation. Opinions expressed in this book do not necessarily represent positions of the New Society Educational Foundation.

Acknowledgments

This book, which has taken us two years to complete, is rooted in a much longer history of thinking about women working together and struggling for social change. As early as the Spring of 1986, a group of women at the University of Minnesota began networking with the National Women's Studies Association (NWSA) and other women on campus about the possibility of bringing the annual NWSA conference to the University of Minnesota. In fall 1986, the University of Minnesota and NWSA agreed to work together to bring the conference to the Twin Cities campus in June 1988. By winter 1987, as both of us were working with the National Program Committee, we began to think of possibly doing this book. In the midst of sorting thousands of index cards tied to the program and arranging sessions, we knew that we should put together an anthology of the rich material before us.

With a great deal of euphoria following the conference and NWSA's expressed interest in an anthology generated from the gathering, we began to seek out potential contributors from those who presented. For the next year, we alternately worked on the book and sent it out to publishers who expressed interest. By this time, the hard-core reality of getting out such a collection hit us. Work we saw as highly important was getting undervalued at the University and sitting on publishers' desks for many months. We had to maintain the energy and commitment to the book and each other in view of this. Our rather unconventional alliance tested us more than either of us ever articulated. Given the lives we've chosen to lead as feminist academics and activists, we juggle a number of writing projects, community projects, and personal commitments, yet, we managed to keep the energy to see this through. It wasn't until fall 1989, that we connected with New Society Publishers. We thank Barbara Hirshkowitz for believing in the book and sharing her enthusiasm with her colleagues at New Society Publishers. We also thank Tina Birky for her editorial assistance and Marie Bloom for her imagination and energy. With their guidance, we have kept our initial vision of this book intact. Of the eighteen essays here, thirteen were presented at the 1988 gathering. We've added five other essays to fill in what we felt were critical gaps in the collection.

Many people besides New Society Publishers were involved in bringing this anthology to fruition. Without the National Women's Studies Association and the following people, it would not have been possible for us to make this book happen.

- *NWSA Minnesota Steering Committee:* Sherrole Benton, Alicia Del Campo, Sally M. Gordon (NWSA National Conference Coordinator), Lori Graven (University of Minnesota Professional Development and Conference Planning Department), Judith Hence, Sophronia Lui, Pam Marshall, Jessica Morgan, Naomi Scheman, Ann Truax, and Ann Veverica.
- *NWSA National Program Committee:* Elinor Lerner (Chair), Bonita Hampton, Diana Brandi, Diane Finnerty, Sophronia Liu, Lois Helmbold, Lorraine Ironplow, Lynn Gangone, Pat Clarke, Pat O'Reilly, Rosemary Curb, Tania Ramalho, Wilma Beaman.
- *Minnesota Local Program Committee:* Lisa Albrecht (co-chair), Rose M. Brewer (co-chair), Terri Carver, Sharon Day, Judith Hence, Becky Kroll.
- *International Plenary Committee:* Becky Swanson Kroll (chair).
- *Lesbian Plenary Committee:* Pam Marshall (chair).
- *Community Outreach Committee:* Judith Hence (chair).
- *American Indian's Advisory Committee:* Margaret Peake Raymond (chair).

A number of organizations helped to fund our conference, providing necessary support for bringing plenary speakers and writer who joined us. Audre Lorde, Gloria Anzaldúa, Beth Brant, Rayna Green, Michelle Parkerson, Judith McDaniel, and Roxanna Carrillo all came to NWSA thanks to these funds. We thank the Minnesota Humanities Commission, the Minnesota Women's Fund, the Elizabeth Quinlan Foundation, First Bank Systems, the Caroline B. Rose Memorial Women's Fund, and the Central Administration of the University of Minnesota, Minneapolis-St. Paul.

The University of Minnesota supported both the conference and this book in various ways. Lisa Albrecht's single-quarter leave in fall 1988 helped us move the book ahead. In General College we thank the Division of Arts, Communication and Philosophy, Terry Collins (Division Head), Principal Secretaries Charlene Allert and Annette Digre, and student workers Jennifer Wesson and especially Linda Juang. We also thank Jim Dillemuth for technology assistance. In the Department of Afro-American and African Studies, we thank principal secretary Mary Chisley.

There are several women to thank for their wisdom, comments, and help. Liz Kennedy, SUNY/Buffalo–Women's Studies, gave a wonderful reading to our manuscript. She was generous in her time and wisdom. Beverly Sorensen and Gloria Anzaldúa also gave us their insights at crucial moments during our writing. Several anonymous reviewers gave us very useful feedback on the text as well.

We especially want to thank our families: Walter and Sundi, and Bev, for living with many missed weekends and for their love, support, and encouragement, and good will about this book. We also want to thank one another for persevering despite many obstacles. Not only have we completed this book together but we have created a friendship and an alliance.

Lisa Albrecht
Rose M. Brewer
Minneapolis, Minnesota
February 1990

Foreword

Caryn McTighe Musil

When there is no vision, the people perish. —Proverbs 29:18

There is a special urgency to this book. Bridges. Power. Multicultural. Alliances. All of these are concepts that are fundamental to our collective survival as women, as people of many races, as nations, as a fragile planet preserved or destroyed by the vision we are capable of mustering and the actions we are brave enough to take.

Bridges of Power: Women's Multicultural Alliances brings together many diverse voices challenging assumptions and urging a bold course of action. This book emerged because of the thinking and work of the National Women's Studies Association, which has a thirteen-year history of being unafraid to grapple with these urgent, exciting and difficult issues. Feminism offers both a necessary critique of what is and a transformative vision of what we can become. Both perspectives are embedded in the collection of essays in this volume.

If the seventies were dominated by the exhilaration of discovering and naming ourselves as women, bound together in sisterhood, the eighties have been dominated by the discovery and definition of our differences as women. A button at our 1985 national conference that read, "Sisterhood Is Trying," captured both the enormous commitment to forge unity and the emotional and intellectual weariness of the process. The eighties, however, grounded us irreversibly in the particularity of each woman's life, in the rich and complex diversity of our multiple identities marked most notably by race, class, ethnicity, sexual orientation, and age.

The challenge of the nineties is to hold on simultaneously to these two contradictory truths: as women, we are the same and we are different. The bridges, power, alliances, and social change possible will be determined by how well we define ourselves through a matrix that encompasses our gendered particularities while not losing sight of our unity. A number of contributors to this volume address that complex but essential task directly.

The collection of voices speaking to us in *Bridges of Power* draws upon a richly diverse community of women, one that gathered at the University of Minnesota in 1988 at NWSA's national conference. These voices expand the boundaries of knowledge, stretch the notion of what is possible, and speak proudly in their mother tongues, challenging us to connect.

The volume reminds us, too, that as women we have learned a lot together about power. Where to find it, how to wield it, and how to transform it. We have learned about power that has always been ours and power that has always been denied us. Most importantly, we have begun to ask ourselves two questions about power: power to do what? and for whom? In asking those questions, we have sought greater alliances with other women, women with whom we may share differences but through whom we discover our common heritage as women and our deeper connection to all humanity.

"When there is no vision, the people perish." But when together we can dream a world of collective survival, we all flourish. That is the urgent challenge that is before us as feminist educators, workers, activists, mothers, artists, community organizers, dreamers, doers, survivors and sisters: bridging our differences and finding our power. That is the task we must turn to quickly, with all our collective energies.

April 27, 1990

About
the National Women's Studies
Association

Founded in 1977, the National Women's Studies Association functions as the national clearinghouse for information about feminist research, curricula, Women's Studies program development, pedagogy, public policy, and feminist education in the community. Through scholarship that unites women, curricula that include women, and quality education for all, NWSA seeks to influence national and global policies that affect women's lives. Believing that knowledge is a form of power, NWSA thinks feminist education can lead to social transformation. Recognizing that education occurs at all levels both inside and outside of classrooms, NWSA brings together educators and community activists as well as researchers and public policy makers.

A multiracial and multicultural organization with a diverse membership committed to education, NWSA provides curriculum resources and scholarships, hosts national and regional conferences, and publishes *NWSA Journal,* an academic scholarly journal, and *NWSAction,* a quarterly newsletter. It has established an Archival Resource Collection on Women's Studies programs, is issuing a national report on the Women's Studies major, and is in the midst of a three-year project to look at what and how students learn in Women's Studies courses. For further information, write to the National Women's Studies Association, University of Maryland, College Park, MD 20742-1325, (301) 454-3757.

Contents

I
Foundations

II
Women's Leadership and Power

III
Building Women's Multicultural Alliances for Social Change

Appendix

To Sundi and the children

I
FOUNDATIONS

Bridges of Power
Women's Multicultural Alliances for Social Change

Lisa Albrecht and Rose M. Brewer

In June 1988, over 2,000 people gathered in the Twin Cities for the tenth annual National Women's Studies Association (NWSA) conference, "Leadership and Power: Women's Alliances for Social Change." Initially our goal was to provide a historical record of this gathering. Just a year earlier, the NWSA annual conference had convened at Spelman College, in Atlanta, Georgia; it was the first time an NWSA conference was held at a historically Black institution. In 1987, record numbers of women of color attended the conference. In 1988, the NWSA conference organizers were strongly committed to retaining the diversity that we had at Spelman. It was in this spirit that we in Minnesota, along with NWSA, planned our conference. We saw this meeting as an opportunity to look more carefully at the connections women make with one another. We were especially concerned with bridging the gap between community and academic women. In the planning, programming, and actual conference, large numbers of women from many communities—locally, nationally, and internationally—came together to look at women's leadership and how we build alliances.

Working on this book has given us the opportunity to look more

---

We have decided to use both *Black* and *African-American* in this book, even though there is some discussion about how people of African descent want to describe themselves.

closely at these issues. The 1988 NWSA conference was a springboard for many of us who think about the issues associated with alliances and coalitions. What is a coalition? What is an alliance? How are they different? Many people use these terms interchangeably, including many of our contributors. Let us take a closer look at these meanings. How do we define leadership when working in coalition? And how do we define power in alliances?

Coalitions have traditionally referred to groups or individuals that have come together around a particular issue to achieve a particular goal. These groups operate autonomously and are usually not connected to each other; most organizations have different agendas as well. Upon completion of the shared goal, coalitions often dissolve and organizations go back to their own work (Brown, 1984).

As Bernice Reagon has stated, coalition is not not meant to be a safe place. "You don't go into coalition because you just *like* it" (1983:356). She tells us that coalition work is not something that happens at home in a safe space. Working in a coalition is about survival, and coming together makes individual groups stronger. Reagon's words connect to the theoretical position taken by Bonnie Thornton Dill, in "Race, Class, and Gender: Prospects for an All-Inclusive Sisterhood" (1983). Dill argues that women of color must come together before forming broader alliances with white women. This shatters the myth of the past three decades that the women's movement/sisterhood is based predominantly on the notion that women share a common set of experiences based on gender. Until white women acknowledge that white is not the center of all experience, and women of color have their own agendas, coalitions will not be easy to establish. This leads us to the work of Gail Pheterson, whose important article "Alliances Between Women: Overcoming Internalized Oppression and Internalized Domination" is included in this collection.

Pheterson helps us to see that we must recognize and interrupt how we internalize both oppression and domination if we are to create successful alliances among women. Pheterson, studying Black-white, Jewish–non-Jewish and lesbian-heterosexual alliances, found that "in every group, past experiences with oppression and domination distorted the participants' perceptions of the present and blocked their identification with people in common political situations who did not share their history." Manifestations of internalized domination for many white women include their inability to understand and accept all but a narrow range of white experience. On the other hand, internalized oppression often causes marginalized women to feel angry, isolated, and defiant. Compounding these differences, some women experience internalized oppression and domination simultaneously, since their identities include both oppressor and oppressed in different situations.

Building alliances

We would like to move beyond coalition; we see the concept of alliance as a new level of commitment that is longer-standing, deeper, and built upon more trusting political relationships. This is tough to achieve given the multifaceted issues confronting any coalition: Who sets the agenda? What are the power differentials? What different skills do we bring to the table? What different visions of social change do we have? And what different leadership styles do we use and do we value? Out of our vision of alliance formation we see allies as people who struggle together on a number of progressive fronts, not just on a single issue that might emerge in a short-term coalition. We see coalitions as short-term solutions and alliance formation as ongoing, long-term arrangements for more far-reaching structural change.

This collection breaks ground with a critical discussion of women's leadership and power in the context of alliance building for social change. As we cross the threshold of the 1990s, diverse groups of feminists appear ready to seriously engage in alliance formation to create social change. To forge these kinds of practical connections, we need to embark on theoretical investigations that aid us in our understanding of coalitions and alliances. We also must look at models of successful alliances to try to analyze why they have succeeded. If we are to understand alliances, it is critical for us to develop alternative conceptions of leadership as well as power. The crux of alliance building is a credible model of leadership that will account for differences and the re-visioning of traditional conceptions of power.

Feminist perspectives on power and leadership

We believe that power in alliance building involves something other than a top-down, imposition-from-without model. We must look at the concept of power in both the private and public domains. The classic western patriarchal view of power is defined in terms of domination and control, that is, power-over (Macy, 1983). Power is, therefore, a property or quality that particular people possess situationally. Those who have acquired power work toward maintaining it by attempting to be invulnerable and closed. Following this view, reality exists compartmentalized to support the separation of the self/the personal, from the public/institutional, and the continued view of these individuated domains of power.

Contemporary feminist perspectives on power differ. Power is not viewed as a property possessed by those who dominate, rather it is seen as process in which people transform themselves personally and collectively (Hartsock, 1981). Power, derived from energy and strength in people, requires an openness and vulnerability. It involves linking the personal domain with the public domain to redefine the self as a whole and as vitally connected to others. Thus, when feminists speak of power, it is often that we speak about power-with, rather than power-over (Hartsock, 1981; Macy, 1983). This synergistic framework recognizes the interdependency of the private and the public domains of reality.

Power differences between groups and within groups are also an important issue for consideration in alliance building. In a society divided along race, class, and gender lines, white people, men, and middle and upper class people monopolize a disproportionate amount of power. The issue for women's alliances is recognizing power differences and overcoming these divisions. We cannot presume that a particular group can be viewed monolithically. For example, over the past twenty years, new class divisions within the Black community have emerged (Wilson, 1978). Despite the historical alliances between Black middle class women and poor women, today their common ground, built on racial oppression, is complicated by new class differences (Landry, 1987). The assumption by most women, including many Black women, that all Black women share the same material and social interests must be re-examined. Many middle class Black women are no longer rooted within the Black working class community and are not a part of the day-to-day struggle of poor Black women. In her essay in this collection, Audre Lorde demands that we move toward structural change; she urges us to do more than educate ourselves through observation and the absorption of knowledge. She challenges us to take action by supporting those radical institutions that connect us to global social change. For Black women, specifically, it means making alliances across the diaspora.

The implications of this definition of power upon women's leadership models is dramatic. We need to ask, have women developed alternative leadership strategies? If so, how have we gone about developing these alternative leadership strategies? And, most significantly, have these strategies worked toward the building of alliances among women? We hope to address some of these questions in this collection.

Drawing on Pheterson's concepts of internalized oppression and domination, it becomes even more critical to ask these questions. If women, indeed, carry the histories of our past experiences with oppression and domination, does it become impossible for us to identify with others who are different, yet share in a common political situation?

Indeed, the most striking models of feminist leadership involve decentralization and shared decision making in both the public and private domains. Is it possible for women to practice the power-with model of leadership in a world dominated by leaders who assert themselves using the power-over form of leadership? Are power-with models of leadership sustainable over time? And do they allow us to generate social change? What are our essayists saying about this question?

Judith McDaniel reminds us that we need to be "taking risks." Mediation is a dialectical concept; essentially it is the idea of brokering: the bridge or connective through which social change occurs. Feminist leadership and power through alliances for social change occur through a number of mediated relationships: self-transformation, transcending otherness, and shattering institutional boundaries. In "Taking Risks: The Creation of Feminist Literature," McDaniel tells us that risk is not merely about danger and loss but about a "profound change in our landscape, both the personal emotional landscape of our lives and the physically present landscape." In the context of building alliances, risk involves the utilization of each woman's personal power to effect change at various levels. Individually, women must take responsibility for breaking down their own barriers of internalized oppression and domination. Women must also come to understand that the cultural, racial, class, generational, sexual, ethnic, and religious diversities among us create different leadership styles. We believe that the boundaries of doubt, pain, and fear can be overcome. If we are to successfully mediate these boundaries, it is critical that we listen and respect each other, learn about our differences, and make ourselves vulnerable.

We believe that women's alliances do inform contemporary feminist leadership models. Davida Alperin's feminist notion of alliances focuses upon an interactive, rather than a pluralist or separatist model of coalition. Her analysis emphasizes the importance of interaction among various types of oppression and that this interaction "can generate a more effective political action for long-term social change." She also cautions us not to assume that "leaders who excel in building inner group solidarity [will be] effective coalition builders." This is critical. Autonomous women's groups need to continually self-examine their own leadership.

Michelle Edwards' all-female communities offer us a model of leadership based on a version of separatism. Her women musicians opt out of their dominant communities because their voices have been suppressed. Certainly separating off is one model of leadership and change that is not talked about enough but is important to women's growth and development. Within her examples of separatist music communities, alliances had to be built, particularly among members of the interracial swing band. As a result of these separatist coalitions, women gained a sense of empowerment. This is, then, a different reading of separatism. These alliances were more than a permanent separation from the patriarchal society of the music world. The women's musical communities served multiple purposes. Women gained skills and learned to work together; as a result, they then acquired the power to create their own places, either remaining within the women's communities or making larger change in the male-dominated musical communities.

Michelle Parkerson echoes the power of Black women filmmakers in "Did You Say the Mirror Talks?" She speaks poignantly of how women who are clearly on the bottom in terms of societal resources have turned this situation around. Black women filmmakers are not to exist. There is nothing about making film in the traditional fashion that embodies their existence. Rather, the mainstream film industry has negated Black women's lives through stereotyping and gross distortions. These women are truly on the edge of established filmmaking but have gone on to create in the context of shared support and networking. African-American women coming together creatively offers a model of resistance and change that is well worth considering. A small number of Black women filmmakers might not be able to dismantle the film industry and the pervasive institutional racism and sexism of that industry, but they can create an alternative institution of independent filmmaking. Taking the initiative to create a space to practice their craft is a kind of leadership that can lead to broader alliances and the potential for changing a dominant cultural apparatus like the film industry.

It is also important for us to look briefly at the historical context in which we discuss women and leadership. Bunch (1987), in an article that originally appeared in *Ms.* (July, 1980), looked at what she called the leadership crisis among women. Besides society's inability to view women as leaders, we compound the problem by often seeing feminist leadership as antileadership. In our attempts to create a female-defined form of leadership that is less hierarchical, we have sometimes practiced leadership as sharing power so totally that we bury any form of individual female talent. Feminist collectives, as Janice Ristock notes in this anthology, often blur over differences among women, creating further problems. Both of these issues have led to conflict in many women's organizations. Bunch reminds us of Jo Freeman's 1973 remarks on "the tyranny of structurelessness," (p. 125) and the detrimental effects that little structure can have on women's groups. It therefore becomes critical for us to make distinctions between validating the role of a feminist leader as a woman who has the ability to act and who uses her power for effective interaction, rather than for manipulation or control. Bunch articulates three functions of feminist leadership: (1) leadership must build movements by enlarging its own organizations; (2) leadership must reach beyond its own constituencies to others; and (3) leadership must work within traditional institutions in order to transform them. We would also like to add that we see leadership that occurs outside traditional institutions as vital for social change as well.

If we apply this framework to the building of women's alliances, we recognize that feminist leaders need to move outside their own particular set of experiences in order to work together successfully. In doing so, we must recognize that women of different backgrounds bring differing styles as well as different levels of expertise to coalition. All of us are grounded in different cultural traditions. For women whose cultures have been marginalized, culture becomes an even more powerful force. For example, African-American women see leadership reflecting collective change. This comes out of a cultural tradition of communalism, which means the survival of the individual is dependent on group survival. Many American Indian women see leadership as intricately related to family and Indian community, no matter what sphere this leadership emerges within. How these multiculturally diverse women exist in the world often flies in the face of dominant ways of being. Feminist leadership for social change must take into consideration these different traditions and heritages. Sharing leadership, therefore, involves developing strategies to utilize individual expertise without undermining any one woman's experiences.

Given racism, homophobia, antisemitism, and class privilege in America, it is not uncommon in coalitions that women have different kinds of expertise. Feminist leaders must combine ways to highlight skills while also figuring out how to share them. Many of us come out of traditions that have stressed networking and collective approaches to survival at the grassroots level. Other women work toward change through legal and political channels of established institutions. Leaders in our alliances must create pathways that allow different women to learn how to travel these diverse avenues for social change. In doing so, women should be simultaneously confronting their own internalized patterns of oppression and domination.

For example, some of us come to the table knowing how to negotiate bureacracies as well as having contacts within them. When we work within established institutions, we must recognize that people come to these systems with different sets of skills. Clearly, class differences affect who works from within dominant systems. If you cannot articulate and speak the language of the oppressor, you are often excluded. If you do not have the resources and money of the oppressor, you go up against tremendous material disadvantage. It is our sense that when working within bureaucracies like the university, there is a constellation of accepted strategies for accomplishing goals. For example, we often write grants for start-up funding for programs beneficial to women. The grants from inception to final write-up require a great deal of time, energy, and follow-through. White and middle class women, in coalition with women of color and working class women, may take the initiative to do this work and support each other to take the lead, while clearly not recognizing the necessary input from all people in the coalition.

The dilemma is that women of color and working class women often bring other skills that are not so directly tied to the bureaucractic workings, which gives the appearance that these skills are not so essential. This is a fundamental misreading. Women of color and working class women often have the ability to put issues on the table directly and in a straightforward manner. Given long histories of marginalization, these women know how to strategize and act and not just talk an issue to death. Culturally, within their own communities, they have been required to develop resources when none seem to exist. Because of cross-cutting identities, historically disenfranchised women often bring a level of sensitivity and attunement to the complexities of decision making. Yet the constellation of accepted skills that work within the bureacracy definitely privilege many white and middle class women, enabling them to accomplish certain coalition-related goals. As a result of this privileging, they presume that completing bureaucratic tasks are equated with significant individual accomplishment and expertise. How should people be recognized? We often amplify the bureaucratic contribution and turn it into *the* contribution. Our recommendation is to create structures from the start that are responsive to group members. We need to move away from the "I can control this" mentality to a genuinely multicultural context. It is a conundrum: Do we break the circle of privilege by opening up to a range of possibilities, or do we accomplish the goal with the tools that work given the existing order? If the latter, white women and middle and upper class women will continue to dominate alliances.

We want to reiterate how important it is that women come to alliances on equal footing with each other; however, it is critical that women who have privilege come to terms with the implications of it. White women cannot set the agenda and control alliances, nor can middle class people expect to do so in alliance with working class people. We are specifically looking at race and class here, not the entire range of dominant versus oppressed relations. But we encourage the reader to look at the constellation of oppressed/oppressor relations that fit their material conditions.

Beyond our different skills, we also have stylistic differences. Cultural diversity means that we must acknowledge that women do indeed act differently to reach particular goals based on the historical impact of racism on their lives. For example, both Rayna Green and Beth Brant highlight how American Indian women's leadership reflects home, community, and family in ways that are unique to various tribal histories. In looking at the lives of American Indian women and how racism has affected them, it is important for us to recognize that the forced inclusion of Indian peoples into U.S. white society is significantly different from the forced exclusion of other people of color (Day, 1989). Indian people, despite their sovereignty, have historically been coerced off their tribal lands by the U.S. government and pushed into white society, whereas African-American peoples have a history of segregation from the white dominant system. We must never assume that racism has affected all people of color in the same way. Nor should we assume within any group that racism has a uniform effect on its strategies for change.

We believe this has implications for forming alliances. For example, in working on our conference, American Indian women met as a *separate* planning committee within the conference structure. These women shaped the participation of Indian women throughout the conference. Another kind of example centers around the need for us to recognize the diversity among Black women. For example, Gordon (1985) argues strongly against alliances with white women. She believes that short-term coalitions are in the best interest of African-American women, who should be devoting their best energies to the self-determination of Black institutions. Clearly this is a different position from the one that Reagon (1983) takes.

Certainly, the road toward social change through feminist alliance is and will continue to be rocky, but not impassable. The articles we have gathered demonstrate not merely our hopes, but concrete examples of successful social change built through coalitions among women.

Understanding intersections of oppression: Why now for women's alliances?

In reviewing articles for this collection, we often found ourselves asking the question, Why now? Why are the conditions for alliance building more apt to occur at this historical juncture? The narrowness associated with the second phase of the women's movement that emerged in the 1960s is being transcended for what we see as *three reasons*: (1) autonomous movements of women of color, especially viewed in the context of the United Nations Decade for Women; (2) the intellectual critique of white feminism by feminists of color, particularly its impact on Women's Studies; and (3) the impact of the global political economy on women internationally.

Autonomous movements of women of color and the intellectual critique

First, movements of women of color internationally and nationally have represented an independent and autonomous mobilization that has strengthened and gained major visibility during the eighties. The autonomy of U.S. and international women of color activists and writers has put these women in a position to work in coalition with white women from their own power base. This power base did not simply happen, but reflected the international growing pains of a global women's movement. In her essay in this collection, "Feminist Alliances: a View from Peru," Roxanna Carrillo gives us a good history of contemporary Latin American feminism as she describes the various *encuentros* that have given women the opportunity to network and build alliances. It is this emphasis on diversity and the interconnectedness of oppressions that characterized the movement from the periphery to the center. The interplay between women's activism and the intellectual development of a feminist theory came hand in hand. U.S. women of color and international feminists have also been at the center of a remarkable outpouring of stringent intellectual critiques of white feminism. In the early eighties, with the publication of *This Bridge Called My Back: Writings by Radical Women of Color* (1981/1983), *All the Women are White, All the Blacks are Men, But Some of Us are Brave: Black Women's Studies* (1982), *Ain't I a Woman?* (1981), and *Women, Race and Class* (1981), among others, the racism of the U.S. white women's movement could no longer be swept under the rug. No longer could gender alone be the defining element of the women's movement. White feminists had come to define gender as narrowly as the white woman's experience. What emerged from the critique of feminists of color was the simultaneity of multiple oppressions in women's lives.

What is also critical to remember is that many of these writings came on the back of intense community political struggles. For example, in Boston, following the murders of a number of Black women, the Combahee River Collective organized to act and articulate a position on Black feminism (1977/1986). The American Indian community in the Twin Cities in the late 1960s was very much at the core of the formation of the American Indian Movement (A.I.M.). Indian women were visible in leadership during this time and helped to develop community activities and theoretical positions taken by A.I.M. (McIntyre, 1990). As the Chicano movement also grew in the late 1960s, it emerged simultaneously on university campuses in the Southwest and among working class people, especially farm workers. Early Chicano Studies courses, however, presented women as passive makers of culture. The work that emerged from Chicana feminists placed women at the center and examined Chicanas as history-makers and women who resisted (Zavella, 1990). Asian-American women's groups have also organized across the country since the late 1960s. Given diverse ethnic backgrounds, these women tend to form regionally around their own identities. Groups like the National Organization of Pan Asian Women, Asian American Women United, the Vietnamese Women's Association, Filipino American Women Network, and Cambodian Women for Press, Inc., are examples of such groups (Chow, 1989). It is also important to note that many lesbians of color formed their own groups, sponsored conferences, and started publications that specifically address intersections between race and sexuality. Two such groups are the National Coalition for Black Lesbians and Gays, which publishes *Black Out*, and Gay American Indians, which sponsors yearly conferences.

On the global level, the United Nations Decade for Women (1976–85) was responsible for three conferences—in Mexico City, Copenhagen, and Nairobi. We must not minimize the impact of these global gatherings. The purpose of the Mexico City meeting, held in 1975, was to organize women globally for the first time. The agenda included peace, all forms of political, economic, and social equality for women, and the eradication of underdevelopment. There were two forums. One consisted of 1,300 U.N. delegates chosen to represent their countries by their own governments. The U.N. forum worked to develop a World Plan of Action with recommendations for governments to adopt. The second forum, known as the Tribune, included close to 6,000 women from nongovernmental organizations (NGOs). These women did not officially represent their governments, but they did represent the range of issues that the U.N. delegates took up. Despite the power of bringing together all these women, the Mexico City forums only emphasized the divergent priorities of women from the North and South.* There was much controversy, especially over the redistribution of wealth and power as a means to improve the status of women (*Connexions*, 1985).

In Copenhagen in 1980 U.N. delegates and over 8,000 NGO participants gathered again. Their purpose was to assess the progress or lack of it made over the past five years for women and to evaluate a program of action for the remainder of the decade. The problems

---

* The terms *North* and *South* are used rather than *developed* or *underdeveloped countries, Third World, First World,* or *industrialized,* which all imply ethnocentric labeling. We choose to use the term *South* to refer to Latin America, Asia and the Pacific, and *North* to refer to the U.S., Western Europe, and Canada.

that had emerged in Mexico City intensified in Copenhagen. The North-South split grew; women from the North argued that the critical issue was gender, with nationality, race, ethnicity, religion, and class subsumed under it. Women from the South argued that we cannot separate gender from all other forms of oppression.

By 1985, in Nairobi, the atmosphere changed. Women from the North came more prepared to listen, and women from the South, in large numbers, put forth a woman-specific agenda that integrated nationality, race, ethnicity, class and religion. Women from the South formed autonomous organizations to address their specific needs. Women also began to create alliances within and across national boundaries to further network and share their resources (*Connexions*, 1985). Virginia Cyrus' article in this collection offers a rich list of global Women's Studies resources, many of which emerged as a direct result of these international gatherings.

The impact on Women's Studies

It is not surprising that the academic arm of the women's movement, Women's Studies, has had to confront many of these same issues. An area that we as academics want to investigate is the impact of this global critique upon the academy and Women's Studies. We are interested in looking at how these critiques are currently shaping Women's Studies, as well as how feminism affects all disciplines. We also want to address the nature of alliances between Women's Studies and Black/Ethnic Studies and, lastly, how community alliances must also continue to be made.

As the discipline of Women's Studies enters its third decade, we are faced with the challenges of diversification. Women's Studies has been, for the most part, white women's studies. Faculty members have predominantly been white, and the curriculum has been eurocentric, with token efforts made at understanding race and class from a global perspective.

Clearly one of the offshoots of this critique has been the transformation of the curriculum to be inclusive of not only women, but multicultural concerns, especially the voices of women of color (see *Radical Teacher* No.37, 1989). We see real limitations with the way curriculum transformation projects have been posed as the linchpins of institutional multicultural/gender change. Curriculum change alone is often cosmetic if other change doesn't occur simultaneously. We need to address the uneven and incomplete way in which transformation occurs. Curriculum transformation needs to be one point in a larger map of change, not the central focal point. Of late, Women's Studies-initiated curriculum transformation projects have linked gender and multicultural integration while building only limited alliances with Black or Ethnic Studies departments, often with limited knowledge of the literature of multiculturalism or Black or Ethnic Studies. This is a suspect model, since alliances must start from the inception of any project (Guy-Sheftall and Bell-Scott, 1989). If Women's Studies scholars are to be serious about multiculturalism, then they must become fluent in the work of people like James Banks (1989, 1988, 1987), as well as Peggy McIntosh (1984). It is clearly time for a new paradigm that builds on both Banks' and McIntosh's works.

The reality today is that there are conservative counter-forces pushing for a white male western curricular core (Bloom, 1987; Hirsch, 1988). We believe that it is imperative that both Women's Studies and Black and Ethnic Studies find ways to work together. Black Studies and Ethnic Studies people need to confront their fears of Women's Studies. Often, white women's gains are viewed as losses for people of color. The deeply rooted patterns of institutional sexism within Black and Ethnic Studies set up a dynamic where it is difficult to think in terms of alliances with Women's Studies, which has traditionally been racist. On the other hand, Women's Studies often dismisses potential alliances with Black and Ethnic studies programs because they don't treat these programs seriously.

Women's Studies and the community

It also seems essential to us that Women's Studies academics rebuild connections with communities outside the university. Initially Women's Studies came out of a revolutionary women's movement tied directly to communities. However, today, its insurgent roots are increasingly institutionalized in the academy. The emphasis is on being a Women's Studies scholar. We see this happening at the expense of women no longer being connected to grassroots communities. Rewards within the academy do not go to social change researchers or to individuals who want to work within grassroots organizations as well as in the academy. Academics get rewarded for presenting papers at professional association conferences and publishing in scholarly journals, not for working for social change in community and grassroots struggles. How does change occur in this context? We see the need for multiple pressure points of change. Multilayered strategies must unfold on a number of fronts if the academy is to become credible as an institution where diverse voices and perspectives are heard and where community input and involvement is not only recognized, but encouraged.

Conferences can be vehicles for social change in forging community-academic coalitions; however, we have to recognize that conferences in and of themselves are not alliances. They are usually moments in time when people come to get renewed, share ideas, and network. As a case in point, the National Women's Studies Association is an organization that attempts to foster alliances between academic feminist and feminist grassroot organizations, yet there are few scholarly organizations that attempt to bridge this gap.

There are other ways that we must continue to make community links. Community education is essential, whether academics move into the community to teach or whether we engage community activists in teaching roles on our campuses. If we say we take community involvement seriously, we have to fight against bureaucratic policies that prohibit non-Ph.Ds from teaching at the college level.

We need to take a close look at participatory research models in which researcher and participant come together to determine the nature of the project from its initiation to its conclusion. There is a co-equal relationship that develops which determines the design of research, its methodology, and policy implications. We see the community and the researcher empowered through this alliance (Maguire, 1987).

Global economic and political transformation

The final point we want to make about why now is the right moment for alliance building is tied to looking at the larger global political climate during the eighties and into the nineties. In studying the global economic and political picture, we want to focus on the internationalization of the economy, the dramatic plunge in power for disenfranchised peoples who made gains in the 1960s, and the climate for racial hatred and intolerance that has emerged during the eighties.

The internationalization of the economy during the last decade generated profound consequences for women of color and white women globally. Internally in the United States, Black women, Chicanas, American Indian, and many Asian American women lost ground as firms left the U.S. and went abroad for even cheaper labor (Fuentes and Ehrenreich, 1983). The servicing of the economy within the U.S. means that the new American working class is predominantly female. White women are increasingly making up a low-paid labor force of service workers, as are women of color. Black women are disproportionately represented as private household workers, cooks, housekeepers, and welfare aides; Latinas as agricultural workers, housekeepers, sewing machine operators, and electrical assemblers; Asian American women as dressmakers, launderers, electrical assemblers; American Indian women as child-care workers, teachers' aides, and welfare aides, while white women are more likely to be dental hygienists, secretaries, dental asistants, and occupational therapists (National Committee on Pay Equity, 1988). The average service sector wage is $13,000 per year (Williams, 1988). Many of these jobs have few if any benefits and no retirement plans (Rothenberg, 1988). Within this context, U.S. women of color are more disadvantaged than white women because of a split within the service sector. Women of color who are nurses' aides, cafeteria workers, and home workers make even less than many working class white women. Yet it is important to recognize that there is a good deal of common ground. Alliances around working conditions, wages, and unionization are possible.

Internationally, U.S. multinationals have set up free trade zones where they continue to exploit the labor of women of the South (Fuentes and Ehrenreich, 1983). The new employment patterns of women differ from an earlier period (Beneria and Roldan, 1987). Labor-intensive production is transferred to the South from more developed areas. One form of such transfer is subcontracting. Beneria and Roldan point out:

> In Mexico, vertical subcontracting is normally referred to as maquila, or "domestic maquila" in the case of homework. It consists generally in processing work or production for another firm under very specific contract arrangements, with design and other product characteristics included. It affects mostly labor-intensive tasks resulting from fragmentation of the production process so that different parts can be carried out by different firms (1987:32).

Mexican women are heavily involved in this aspect of the international division of labor. High numbers of women workers are found in the garment and textile industries, as well as in electrical/electronics, metal, chemical, and other industries (Beneria and Roldan, 1987). Over one-half million East Asian women work in export processing zones, earning subsistence wages. Many move to urban areas, leaving their families for the first time, looking for excitement and a higher standard of living. Most find poor living conditions, and, especially in the electronics industry, occupational health hazards that are frightening (Fuentes and Ehrenreich, 1983). In various places globally, women are similarly paid extremely low wages and find dangerous working conditions. It is quite apparent that women are contributing to multinational profits as well as being exploited personally and socially.

It has been difficult for us to find examples of cross-national alliances that seek to link labor struggles of women in the U.S. to global labor struggles. We do have examples of national struggles for political change where women have built alliances within their nations. The essay by Rita Giacaman and Penny Johnson about Palestinian women addresses how these women have risen to leadership positions during the *intifada* within the national liberation struggle. Chi-Kwan Ho's article outlines the differences among women activists in Hong Kong, and historical developments that are bringing women of different backgrounds together.

In one of the most dramatic examples within the U.S., poor women who are viewed as pariahs by street-level bureaucrats, sociologists, and public policy officials move to empower themselves through the welfare rights struggle. In "Conflict and Cooperation Among Women in the Welfare Rights Movement," Guida West discusses class and race tensions, which when dealt with in coalition ultimately lead to a significant social change movement built on the leadership of poor women and women of color. This is not an easy empowerment, but it is an example of women's resistance that is essential to social change.

The globalization of the economy, the loss of high-paying industrial jobs, and the growth of the service sector reflect the economic underpinnings of inequality for women of color in the 1990s (Skolnick and Currie, 1988). The loss of economic ground of large segments of the American population continues. Writers such as Kuttner and Thurow have labeled this loss of economic ground a "decline in the middle class" in the United States (Skolnick and Currie, 1988, p.119). The number of families earning between $20,000 and $49,999 in 1984 dollars has dropped. While this was happening, the number of families in both the low and high income categories has increased (Skolnick and Currie, 1988). Citing Katharine Bradbury, an economist for the Federal Reserve Board, Skolnick and Currie note, "the proportion of American families earning less than $20,000 increased by over 4 percent between 1973 and 1984, while the proportion earning from $20,000 to $50,000 dropped by more than 5 percent" (p. 119).

We believe it is also important to recognize the dramatic plunge in power for historically disenfranchised people in the U.S. For example, Omolade (1986) informs us that between 1960 and 1980, the number of female-headed Black families grew to nearly 50% of of all Black families, and that one-half of these families live in poverty with a median income of $7,425 for a family of four. As well, white female-headed households have grown, and these families have lost economic ground, too. Given these intolerable conditions in women's lives, it is not surprising that movements for social change have arisen that acknowledge the intersection of race, class, and gender. In the Twin Cities, one such organization—Women, Work and Welfare—reflects the intense cross-racial economic pressures faced by women. In Women, Work, and Welfare's Bill of Rights (n.d.), this multiracial alliance of women states:

All people shall have the right to the financial resources by which to purchase goods and services to meet their basic needs. This should include but not be limited to: a) an adequate variety of nutritionally balanced food products; b) decent, safe, and sanitary dwellings for all individuals; c) adequate clothing to protect against the elements; d) quality health care; e) the right of parents to provide full-time childcare of their choice.

This is just one local example of the kind of organizing that is happening today. Clearly, now is the time for alliances, given the movement of women of color, the intellectual critique by women of color, and the changing global political economy.

A final point we want to address is the climate of intolerance that has grown during the 1980s, particularly in relation to hate violence. The white supremacist movement took a new turn as Klan membership decreased, while more militant revolutionary groups emerged. Hate violence expanded beyond anti-Black and anti-Jew activities to a focus on a variety of issues, including taxes, immigration, foreign aid, crime rates, the farm crisis, and antigay violence in conjunction with the AIDS epidemic (Hate Violence and White Supremacy, 1989). While neo-Nazi skinheads have been at the center of the worst racial assaults in both rural and urban areas of the U.S., white supremacists simultaneously have garnered an unusual amount of media attention, and, like David Duke, some have even been elected to public office. There is a clear convergence of tactics: the paramilitary training and revolutionary indoctrination of groups like the Posse Comitatus; the unadulterated ideological hatred and violence perpetrated by some skinheads; and the mainstream media focus and cable access television recruitment campaigns of the Aryan Resistance (Hate Violence and White Supremacy, 1989). Paralleling these developments has been a devastating rise in racist, antigay, anti-Semitic, and sexual violence on college campuses (Shenk, 1990). The 1980s proved to be a fertile decade for the growth of this kind of bigotry. It seems to us that the 1990s must be the decade when we build the necessary alliances to end this alarming trend. Legislators, educators, and community activists need to work together to pass laws, promote channels for understanding diversity, and support the development of bonds among people to reject hatred and violence (Hate Violence and White Supremacy, 1989).

One way in which these powerful alliances might be built is organizing across race, class, and gender lines to address the AIDS epidemic. Now in its second decade of devastation, this health crisis is touching all of our lives. We can see that the initial efforts of most AIDS-related organizations and agencies were focused on a gay, white, middle class, educated male clientele. This is not to denigrate the remarkable ability of gay men to mobilize (Hammonds, 1986). However, communities of color and women have not benefited from the services provided, and more and more today we are finding new task forces and agencies developing around the particular needs of women and people of color. Given the competition for limited funds and the barriers of racism and sexism, it seems to us that brand new alliances are needed if we are to successfully educate a broad spectrum of people and lobby for an acceptable response from federal, state, and local governments.

Building women's multicultural alliances for social change

The key questions we raise in this collection include: What insights do feminists bring to the traditional perspectives on social change? Are feminists seeking social change at the local, state, national, or international levels? Are we looking at personal or institutional change, or both? Are we looking at creating social policies that effect social change? If the answer is yes, feminists are working toward social change at all these levels—and we believe it is—it seems to us that feminists are also trying to re-conceive leadership roles and how we utilize our power. We are also seeking transformatory perspectives that move beyond the singular, monist models of social change prevalent in the 1960s. Essential to this reconceptualization process is a perspective developed in *Liberating Theory* (Albert, et al., 1986): complementary holism. This means that "parts which compose wholes interrelate to help define one another, even though each appears often to have an independent and even contradictory existence." Our common struggle for social change is propelled forward by the recognition of unity in diversity. This interconnected reality is the core element in emancipatory struggles where alliances occur.

In shaping the theme of the National Women's Studies Association's 1988 conference, and in reviewing and selecting papers for this collection, we have found a rich body of work that addresses an unresolved issue in the global women's movement. For us to change those structures that give rise to our multiple oppressions, we must recognize the interlocking nature of the self and the institutions that impede our alliance work. We must engage in a two-pronged strategy of transformation: changing the institutions while recognizing and transcending our differences. The multiple issues regarding alliance building cannot be resolved by simply giving lip service to women's diversity. There are hard-core issues around power, privilege, and leadership that we all must address as we build women's alliances for social change.

New organizing is the key to women's multicultural alliances. Leadership and power do not flow to unorganized masses of women and our allies without hard work. New strategies of organizing include recognizing the interplay between work and family for many women and organizing within and across our different communities. We need new grounds from which to work together, both on and off bureaucratic turf.

We hope the following chapters offer new visions of leadership, holistic perspectives that reconceive power, and new strategies for social change. Within these contexts the recognition of profound differences in history, resources, and cultural moorings are essential to the women's alliances we envision.

References

Albert, M., Cagan, L., Chomsky, N., et al. 1986. *Liberating Theory.* Boston: South End Press, p. 18.

Banks, James A. 1988. *Multiethnic Education: Theory and Practice,* 2nd ed. Boston: Allyn and Bacon, Inc.

Banks, James A. 1987. *Teaching Strategies for Ethnic Studies,* 4th ed. Boston: Allyn and Bacon, Inc.

Banks, James A., and McGee Banks, Cherry A., eds. 1989. *Multicultural Education: Issues and Perspectives.* Boston: Allyn and Bacon, Inc.

Beneria, Lourdes, and Roldan, Martha. 1987. *The Crossroads of Class & Gender.* Chicago: The University of Chicago Press.

Bloom, Allan. 1987. *The Closing of the American Mind.* New York: Simon and Schuster.

Brewer, Rose M. "Race, Gender, Class and the Women's Movement: The Role of Black Feminist Intellectuals." In N. Alarcon, L. Albrecht, J. Alexander, S. Day and M. Segrest, eds. *The Third Wave: Feminist Perspectives on Racism,* New York: Kitchen Table: Women of Color Press, forthcoming.

Brown, Cherie R. 1984. *The Art of Coalition Building: A Guide for Community Leaders.* New York: The American Jewish Committee.

Bunch, Charlotte. 1987. *Passionate Politics: Feminist Theory in Action.* New York: St. Martin's Press.

Chow, Esther Ngan-Ling. 1989. "The Feminist Movement: Where Are All the Asian-American Women?" In *Making Waves: An Anthology of Writings by and about Asian-American Women.* Asian Women United of California, eds. Boston: Beacon Press, pp. 362–76.

Cole, Johnnetta B. 1986. "Commonalities and Differences." In Johnnetta B. Cole, ed. *All American Women: Lines that Divide, Ties that Bind.* New York: Free Press.

Combahee River Collective. 1979. "The Combahee River Collective: A Black Feminist Statement." In Zillah R. Eisenstein, ed. *Capitalist Patriarchy and the Case for Socialist Feminism.* New York: Monthly Review Press. Reprinted in *The Combahee River Collective Statement: Black Feminist Organizing in the Seventies and Eighties,* Freedom Organizing Series No. 1, New York: Kitchen Table: Women of Color Press, 1986.

Connexions, 1985. *Forum '85, Nairobi, Kenya.* Summer/Fall, 1985, No. 17-18 (special issue).

Davis, Angela. 1981. *Women, Race and Class.* New York: Vintage Books.

Dahrendorf, Ralf. 1959. *Class and Class Conflict in Industrial Society.* London: Routledge & Kegan Paul.

Day, Sharon. 1990. Personal conversation, St. Paul, MN. (Also see Alarcon, N., Albrecht, L., Alexandar, J., Day, S., and Segrest, M., eds. (forthcoming) *The Third Wave: Feminist Perspectives on Racism.* New York: Kitchen Table: Women of Color Press.

Dill, Bonnie Thornton. 1983. "Race, Class, and Gender: Prospects for an All-Inclusive Sisterhood." *Feminist Studies* 9:131–148.

Friedan, Betty. 1963. *The Feminine Mystique.* New York: Dell Publishers.

Fuentes, Annette and Ehrenreich, Barbara. 1983. *Women in the Global Factory.* MA: Institute for New Communications and South End Press.

Gay American Indians. c/o Lee Staples (612) 870-4848.

Gordon, Vivian V. 1985. *Black Women, Feminism, and Black Liberation: Which Way?* Chicago: Third World Press.

Guy-Sheftall, Beverly, and Bell-Scott, Patricia. 1989. "Black Women's Studies: A View from the Margin." In Pearson, Carol S., Shavlik, Donna L., and Touchton, Judith G., eds. *Educating the Majority: Women Challenge Tradition in Higher Education.* New York: Macmillan Publishing Co.

Hammonds, Evelynn. 1986. "Race, Sex, Aids: The Construction of 'Other'." *Radical America* Vol. 20, No. 6, pp. 28–36.

Hartsock, N. 1981. "Political Change: Two Perspectives on Power." In Charlotte Bunch, et al., eds. *Building Feminist Theory: Essays from Quest.* New York: Longman Press.

Hate Violence and White Supremacy: A Decade Review, 1980–89. 1989. *Klanwatch Intelligence Report,* December 1989, No. 47. Montgomery, AL: Klanwatch Project of the Southern Poverty Law Center.

Hirsch, E.D., Jr. 1988. *Cultural Literacy: What Every American Needs to Know.* New York: Vintage Books.

Hooks, Bell. 1981. *Ain't I A Woman: Black Women and Feminism.* MA: South End Press.

Hull, Gloria, Smith, Barbara and Bell-Scott, Patricia, eds. 1982. *All the Women Are White, All the Blacks Are Men, But Some of Us Are Brave: Black Women's Studies.* New York: Feminist Press.

Joseph, G., and Lewis, J. 1981. *Common Differences: Conflict In Black and White Feminist Perspectives.* New York: Anchor Books.

Krauthammer, Charles. 1990. "Education: Doing Bad and Feeling Good." *Time,* Feb. 5, p. 78.

Landry, Bart. 1987. *The New Black Middle Class.* Berkeley, CA: University of California Press.

Lefkowitz, R., and Withorn, A., eds. 1986. *For Crying Out Loud: Women and Poverty in the United States.* New York: The Pilgrim Press.

Lorde, Audre. 1984. *Sister Outsider.* New York: The Crossing Press.

Macy, J. R. 1983. *Despair and Personal Power in the Nuclear Age.* Philadelphia: New Society Publishers.

Maguire, Patricia. 1987. *Doing Participatory Research: a Feminist Approach.* Amherst, MA: The Center for International Education, School of Education, University of Massachusetts.

Marx, K., and Engels, F. 1962. *Selected Works* (2 vols.). Moscow: Foreign Languages Publishing House.

McIntyre, Shelly. 1990. Personal conversation. Minneapolis, MN.

McIntosh, Peggy. 1984. "Interactive Phases of Curricular Re-Vision," in Spanier, Bonnie, Bloom, Alexander and Boroviak, Darlene, eds. *Toward a Balanced Curriculum: A Sourcebook for Initiating Gender Integration Projects.* Cambridge, MA: Schenkman Books.

Moraga, C., and Anzaldúa, G., eds. 1981. *This Bridge Called My Back: Writings By Radical Women of Color.* MA: Persephone Press. Reprinted by Kitchen Table: Women of Color Press, New York, 1983.

National Coalition of Black Lesbians and Gays (NCBLG). P.O. Box 50622, Washington, DC 20004.

National Committee on Pay Equity. 1988. "The Wage Gap: Myths and Facts." In Rothenberg, Paula, ed. *Racism and Sexism: An Integrated Study*. New York: St. Martin's Press.

National Women's Studies Association. 1981. "Women Respond to Racism." Annual Conference, Storrs, CT.

National Women's Studies Association. 1987. "Weaving Women's Colors." Annual Conference, Atlanta, GA.

Omolade, Barbara. 1986. *It's a Family Affair: The Real Lives of Black Single Mothers*. Freedom Organizing Series No. 4. New York: Kitchen Table: Women of Color Press.

Parsons, Talcott. 1951. *The Social System*. New York: Free Press.

Radical Teacher. 1989. *Balancing the Curriculum*, No. 37 (special issue).

Reagon, Bernice Johnson. 1983. "Coalition Politics: Turning the Century." In Smith, Barbara, ed. *Home Girls: A Black Feminist Anthology*. New York: Kitchen Table: Women of Color Press.

Rothenberg, Paula. 1988. *Racism and Sexism: An Integrated Study*. New York: St. Martin's Press.

Shenk, David. 1990. "Young Hate." *CV: The College Magazine*. Feb. 1990, 34–39.

Skolnick, Jerome H., and Currie, Elliot. 1988. *Crisis in American Institutions*. Glenview, IL: Scott Foresman and Company.

The State of the World's Women, 1985. 1985. Oxford: United Kingdom: New Internationalist Publications. Reprinted by Women, Public Policy and Development Project, Hubert H. Humphrey Institute of Public Affairs, University of Minnesota, Minneapolis.

Williams, Rhonda M. 1988. "Beyond Human Capital: Black Women, Work, and Wages." Working Paper No. 183. Wellesley, MA: Wellesley College: Center for Research on Women.

Wilson, William J. 1978. *The Declining Significance of Race*. Chicago: University of Chicago Press.

Women, Work, and Welfare. n.d. *Bill of Rights*. (310 East 38th St., Minneapolis, MN 55409.)

Zavella, Patricia. 1990. Talk, given at *Las Mujeres Institute*. Ford Foundation Incorporating Feminist Scholarship Concerning Gender and Cultural Diversity into the Curriculum. St. Cloud, MN: St. Cloud State University. (Also see Zavella, 1987. *Women's Work and Chicano Families: Cannery Workers of the Santa Clara Valley*. New York: Cornell University Press.)

Social Diversity and the Necessity of Alliances
A Developing Feminist Perspective[1]

Davida J. Alperin

Introduction

Within the last two decades feminist activists and theorists have increasingly recognized and been forced to take into account the great diversity that exists among women.[2] Even if we limit our attention to women in the United States, such differences include characteristics of class, race, ethnicity, ability, and sexual preference, among others. Women's movement organizations and feminist theorists have reacted to this great diversity in a variety of ways. In reading about and participating in discussions of this issue, I have found one emerging conceptual model to be particularly valuable. This model is based on ideas presented in essays by Audre Lorde,[3] Bernice Johnson Reagon,[4] and Charlotte Bunch.[5] This new way of thinking about differences stands in sharp contrast to a number of other theories of social and political life. It also implies methods of organizing that are very different from those that have been traditionally incorporated into movements for social change. In particular this new model has important implications for thinking about and organizing political alliances.

After describing the model I will explain why alliances are a necessary component of political action based on such a model. This argument draws upon Nancy Hartsock's writings in which she integrates the Marxist notion of "standpoint" into feminist thought.[6]

Three models of social differences and political action

Lorde, Reagon, and Bunch do not necessarily have a uniform vision of diversity and coalition. Their articles do share a number of features that distinguish their thoughts from what I shall call pluralist and separatist models. Each of these models represents one way of understanding social differences and the implications of those differences in political organizing.

The issues of social diversity raised here have been part of a great many debates centered on political theory and action that have occurred within academia, as well as in the women's movement, civil rights movement, old left, new left, and labor movements. To fully understand the nuances and subtleties of the various positions, one would need to discuss them within the contexts in which each of those debates arose. My purpose here, however, is to highlight on a more abstract level some of the main points of disagreement within those debates. Each of the three models I present is, therefore, a simplified composite of a number of positions taken by various scholars and activists.

The pluralist model

Pluralism is one model of politics in a society of diversity. Political scientists developed it to explain political processes and interest group activity in the United States.[7] While some of its propositions have been discredited and a number of its former advocates have proposed revisions to it, many of pluralism's assumptions have become a part of our country's popular political culture.[8]

Pluralists argue that social groups, including those representing economic, ethnic, racial, religious, and regional interests, among others, compete for resources and beneficial policies that are under the control of government. They predict that this competition will be moderate and will not create demands for radical transformations in our society. Pluralists insist that conflicts are not likely to become irreconcilable in the United States because they believe that each interest group sometimes wins and sometimes loses in its competition with other groups. This adds legitimacy to the process, even though groups may not approve of every governmental decision.

Pluralists also contend that the degree of conflict in the United States is moderate because the economic and social divisions in our society are cross-cutting rather than overlapping and because no single social division overrides all others. When divisions are cross-cutting it means that within each ethnic group, for example, there are many different religions, occupations, and other types of groups represented. In contrast, overlapping divisions would exist if most members of a particular ethnic group also shared similar religious affiliations and economic status. Pluralists argue that nations such as the United States with cross-cutting divisions are less prone to system-threatening conflict than places such as Northern Ireland, where most divisions overlap the overriding religious division. This is because in the numerous political conflicts that occur in the United States the contending sides are not as consistently composed of the same sets of citizens as they tend to be in the case of Northern Ireland. Thus in a nation with cross-cutting divisions, two laborers who lobby together to strengthen occupational safety laws are just as likely to oppose each other on an abortion issue because of differing religious beliefs. Because each citizen's interests correspond to a changing variety of other citizens' interests, and because no group consistently wins or loses, societal conflict can usually be managed without basic transformation of the political or economic system.

Pluralists disagree among themselves as to the best strategy to use in order to promote the interests of groups who traditionally have had less status and fewer resources in society. Two different strategies developed by pluralists are the *assimilationist strategy* and the *cultural pluralist strategy*.[9] The assimilationist strategy corresponds to what has been called the "melting pot" theory of ethnic relations. Assimilationists believe that traditional ethnic affiliations recede in importance in modern industrial societies as economic and contractual relationships become more important. They wish to speed up this transition so that individuals will be judged on their personal achievements and not on the basis of such characteristics as race, ethnicity, or gender.

Another group of pluralists advocate a strategy called cultural pluralism. In contrast to the melting pot image used by assimilationists, cultural pluralists use the images of a crazy quilt or a symphony orchestra to describe their ideal society. They suggest that just as different colors in a quilt and different sounds in an orchestra can be part of a larger harmony without losing their distinctiveness, so too can different social groups maintain their distinctiveness within a broader social harmony. Cultural pluralists stress that citizens should maintain their distinctive cultural traditions and that prejudices can be reduced by exposing individuals to the many rich cultural traditions that exist within American society.

The separatist model

In contrast to both versions of the pluralist model stands what I shall call the separatist model. This model encompasses the views of some thinkers within Marxism, feminism, and various nationalist movements who make the following two claims. The first claim is that class, sex, race, or ethnic oppression is the source of all other kinds of oppression. [10] The second claim is that the most oppressed group must develop and carry out its political action autonomously from other members of society. Separatists define the most oppressed group as the working class, women, or a racial or ethnic group, depending on whether they consider themselves to be a Marxist, feminist, or some type of nationalist. (I should note that I am using the term *separatist* in a very restricted sense and that some individuals who call themselves or are called separatists by others may not necessarily fit into this definition.) [11]

Separatists argue, in contrast to the pluralists, that there are consistent winners and losers in political contests between different social groups in the United States. They claim that the dominance of one group over another group is maintained through some combination of physical coercion, the threat of physical coercion, institutional biases, unequal resources, or ideological hegemony. In many cases the dominant group wins even when no visible contest occurs in the political realm. This is because the basic structuring of the economic and political system is biased in favor of the dominant group and also because ideological hegemony exercised by the dominant group often inhibits the subordinate group from being conscious of their oppression or from developing the confidence to fight that oppression. [12]

Separatists advocate more radical changes in the structure of society than pluralists. They argue that mere reforms or attitude changes will not bring about a more just society because oppression in the United States is institutionalized within overarching societal structures. Some separatists identify the structure as patriarchy, some as white supremacy, and others as capitalism. In any case they claim that the structure of society needs to be dismantled and rebuilt and not merely repaired. In addition, separatists often prioritize consciousness-raising activities within each of their respective political movements because they believe that ideological support for these oppressive structures has been so deeply engrained in oppressed people.

The interactive model

I propose, in contrast to the pluralist and separatist models, the interactive model, which is based on my readings of Lorde, Reagon, and Bunch.[13] I call it the interactive model because it emphasizes the interaction between various types of oppression. It selectively borrows and rejects arguments from the pluralists and separatists and so develops a more persuasive analysis of oppression. It can also generate more effective political action for long-term social change. For these two reasons I will focus on the model's analysis of the nature of oppression and its strategies for change.

An interactive analysis of oppression indicates that the structures of our society impose unfair privileges and burdens upon a number of different social groups. As Audre Lorde states:

> In a society where the good is defined in terms of profit rather than in terms of human need, there must always be some group of people who, through systematized oppression, can be made to feel surplus, to occupy the place of the dehumanized inferior. Within this society, that group is made up of Black and Third World people, working-class people, older people, and women.[14]

Lorde ties oppression to the profit motive and thus locates sources for oppression in the foundations of our economic system and not simply in the prejudicial attitudes of individuals. This clearly distinguishes her analysis from a pluralist analysis. She also suggests that many groups are primary targets of oppression, not just members of a single group—contrary to the separatist model.

The debate between advocates of the interactive model and separatists centers on the current forms that oppression takes and the means required to end oppression and not on the origins of oppression. Many advocates of an interactive approach, for example, consider themselves to be socialists, feminists, or nationalists, as do most separatists. Some within the interactive camp even claim that class, gender, or race is the original source for other forms of oppression or that it the most prominent form. They argue, however, in contrast to separatists, that (1) there are many types of oppression, (2) a single form of domination should not be considered *a priori* to be the driving force in all contexts, (3) the different types of oppression interact with each other in complex ways,[15] and (4) eliminating a single form of oppression, even if it were the primary or original source of all other oppression, would not automatically eliminate all other forms of oppression. Separatists, on the other hand, often claim that political action is a waste of resources and divisive if not directed against the specific form of oppression they consider to be primary.

The interactive model shares with cultural pluralism an emphasis on diversity. Both models present social diversity as positive and both rely on such metaphors as the crazy quilt and symphony orchestra. However, cultural pluralists perceive these metaphors as reflecting current reality, while advocates of the interactive model hold them up as symbols of an ideal to work toward. The interactive model argues that in our present society a hierarchy of values has been imposed on social differences and that this is used to justify the lower status and discriminatory treatment of particular groups. Indeed, proponents of the interactive model often view pluralists as well intentioned but naive because pluralists do not recognize that our society institutionally enforces differences in power and wealth on different social groups.

What then are the strategies for change within the interactive model? The interactive model shares with separatists their emphasis on consciousness raising. Members of the oppressed group must shed the remnants of self-hatred that they have acquired through socialization in this society. In addition, as in the separatist model, it is often important to have separate spaces available in which to go through this process. According to Reagon:

> . . . every once in awhile there is a need for people to . . . bar the doors . . . and say "Humph, inside this place the only thing we are going to deal with is X or Y or Z." And so only the X's or Y's or Z's get to come in. . . . Most of the time when people do that, they do it because of the heat of trying to live in this society where being an X or Y or Z is very difficult, to say the least. . . . It gets too hard to stay out in that society all the time. And that's when you find a place, and you try to bar the door and check all the people who come in. You come together to see what you can do about shouldering up all of your energies so that you and your kind can survive . . . that space while it lasts should be a nurturing space where you sift out what people are saying about you and decide who you really are.[16]

Advocates of the interactive model, in contrast with separatists, argue that a redefinition of one's own group and its place in society is only a first step in the transformation of one's consciousness. If we stop there, Lorde contends, we may identify the way in which we are different as the "primary cause of all oppression" and forget about other forms, "some of which we ourselves may be practicing."[17] If it is important to understand oppression in order to fight it, then ignoring oppression that does not touch us directly will reduce the effectiveness of our political action. As Reagon warns us: "At a certain stage nationalism is crucial to a people if you are going to ever impact as a group in your own interest. Nationalism at another point becomes reactionary because it is totally inadequate for surviving in a world with many peoples."[18]

The interactive model adds a third task to consciousness raising and political analysis. In addition to reclaiming the positive aspects of one's own heritage and learning about other groups' histories and current status, activists are asked to evaluate how different types of oppression interact in specific historical situations. As Bunch explains:

> Too often analysis of women's oppression isolates single factors such as class or sexual preference in a simplistic manner, trying to show the effects of each separately. But this fails to take account of their interrelatedness. . . . a feminist method suggests the necessity of looking at their interaction—at how race, class, sex, and age oppression shape each other. For example, race and class affect an older woman's problems—whether it means being abandoned in her house, trapped in an abusive nursing home, or entirely homeless. Or in looking at the exploitation of women's work, we can see the effect of factors such as race, homophobia, or physical disability, as well as class.[19]

In summary, the interactive model: (1) recognizes the existence of institutionalized subordination and domination, (2) emphasizes the numerous and complex ways in which different forms of oppression interact, and (3) identifies consciousness raising as an important method for broadening groups' understandings of their own oppression, others' oppression, and the ways in which different types of oppression interact.

I have compared and contrasted three models of social diversity and political action in order to set the stage for an argument about the necessity of political alliances in movements for social justice. In the following section I will construct this argument based on the interactive model and the concept of *standpoint* borrowed from Marx and Hartsock.

The necessity of alliances

Marx developed the concept of *standpoint* in his analysis of class, and Hartsock, among others, has integrated the concept into feminist analysis. According to Marx, the working class, through struggle, can come to a more complete understanding of the social relations of capitalist production than can their exploiters. Hartsock argues that the type of standpoint achieved by the working class through struggle is analogous to the sharper vision of gender relations that women can achieve through struggle against gender domination.[20] Taking their arguments a step further, I would contend that a number of other groups who are subordinated in society have more immediate access to a critical understanding of particular aspects of the social system than do those in more privileged positions.[21]

If we assume for a moment that the premises of the interactive model and standpoint theory developed above are valid, what might they suggest about political strategy? One strategic lesson, I contend, is that it is imperative for oppressed groups with different standpoints to form alliances in order to understand how different types of oppression interact. If different critical standpoints are more readily available to different oppressed groups through struggle, and if different types of oppression are interrelated, then it would follow that a thorough understanding of the complexity of social relations in any particular historical moment could be achieved most effectively through alliances between groups with different standpoints.

To clarify the argument raised above, it is important to remember Marx's contention that theory cannot be divorced from practical activity. He argued that workers must actively engage in class struggle in order to achieve a vision of class relations which transcends the one imposed by dominant ideologies and institutions.[22] If only one type of oppression existed, or one type caused all other types of domination, then one could gain a comprehensive understanding of societal oppression by engaging in struggle against that single or generative type. Even if there were many *unrelated* types of oppression, each oppressed group could presumably gain a comprehensive understanding of the social relations by which it was oppressed if each group struggled by itself to attain its own just treatment. If, however, there are many types of oppression which influence each other in complex ways, then cooperative struggles between a variety of social groups are needed to develop a more accurate and potentially liberating understanding of social relations.

This perspective on alliances is very different from that of separatists and pluralists. Separatists are very suspicious of alliances and enter into them only in extreme circumstances. Pluralists judge alliances on the basis of pragmatic calculations of short-term costs and benefits. Will the alliance bring in more votes, volunteers, or financial support? If the immediate benefits of an alliance outweigh its costs, then pluralists will promote it; if not, then pluralists will oppose it. Based on the premises of the interactive model and standpoint theory these pragmatic factors are also relevant. However, of equal or greater importance is the forum that alliances can provide for exploring the different standpoints that have been reached by oppressed peoples and for developing a fuller understanding of how different types of oppression interact.

Historically groups have formed alliances for a variety of reasons. In some situations the struggle on two or more fronts takes place because of a consciously determined program. For example, in 1984 gays and lesbians in London developed support groups to help out Britain's striking coal miners.[23] In other situations activists trying to limit their attention to one type of oppression are forced to recognize other types of oppression which are reproduced within their own movement. For example, the labor movement in the United States has been challenged at different times in its history to remedy its own sexist and racist institutions and practices.[24] In addition, women of color and working class women have demanded that different organizations in the women's movement confront their own and society's racism and classism.

Whether by choice or necessity, political activists who confront such diverse issues have the opportunity to see how different types of oppression interact in concrete situations. The effectiveness of their responses, though, depends not only on their willingness to devote scarce time, energy, and other resources to a variety of struggles, but also on the specific strategies and tactics which they choose.

Lorde, Reagon, and Bunch suggest using both separatist and alliance strategies. Oppressed groups need to have separate spaces in which to gain their self-respect, name themselves, and discover their own history. These same groups need to form alliances with other groups in order to compare, contrast, and identify the connections among different types of oppression. Beyond this, however, it would be difficult to prescribe a particular combination of separation and alliance which will be optimal in every historical situation. In addition, the leaders who excel in building inner group solidarity may not be effective coalition builders and vice versa. As Reagon points out, coalition work is not easy or comfortable.[25] It is hard to constantly be confronted with our own and others' bigotry. And as Bunch explains, it is "difficult to look at all the features of oppression because they are complex and demand continuous reevaluation of our assumptions."[26] For all the difficulties involved, however, I would argue that the interactive model and alliances based upon it provide us with a much greater potential to bring about fundamental social change than the pluralist or separatist models.

Notes

1. This paper is part of a larger study I am conducting on Black-Jewish relations in the United States. I wish to acknowledge the comments and suggestions given to me by Jean Anderson, Susan K. Cahn, Laura V. Castor, Jeffrey B. Edwards, Amy Fried, Greta Gaard, August H. Nimtz, Pricilla Pratt, Diana L. Swanson, Tina Birky of New Society Publishers and the editors of this volume, Lisa Albrecht and Rose M. Brewer.
2. I am not attempting to set up a dichotomy between activists and theorists. To one degree or another all feminists are both.
3. Lorde, Audre, 1984. "Age, Race, Class, and Sex: Women Redefining Difference." In *Sister Outsider*, Trumansburg, NY: The Crossing Press.
4. Reagon, Bernice Johnson, 1983. "Coalition Politics: Turning the Century," In Smith, Barbara, ed., 1983. *Home Girls: A Black Feminist Anthology*. New York: Kitchen Table: Women of Color Press.
5. Bunch, Charlotte, 1987. "Making Common Cause: Diversity and Coalitions," in this volume. Previously published in Charlotte Bunch, 1987. *Passionate Politics: Feminist Theory in Action*, New York: St. Martin's Press.
6. Hartsock, Nancy. "The Feminist Standpoint: Developing the Ground for a Specifically Feminist Historical Materialism." In Harding, Sandra, and Hintikka, Merrill B., eds., 1983. *Discovering Reality: Feminist Perspectives in Epistemology, Metaphysics, Methodology, and Philosophy of Science*. Netherlands: D. Reidel Publishing

Co., and Hartsock, Nancy, *Money, Sex, and Power: Toward a Feminist Historical Materialism*. Boston: Northeastern University Press, especially pp. 231–51.

7. Prominent works which analyze interest groups in terms of this pluralist model include A.F. Bentley, 1935, *The Process of Government*, Evanston, IL: Principia Press; D. Truman, 1951, *The Governmental Process*. New York: Alfred A. Knopf; and Robert Dahl, 1967, *Pluralist Democracy in the United States*, Chicago: Rand McNally; and Dahl, *Polyarchy*, 1971, New Haven, CT: Yale University Press.

8. Revisionist versions of pluralism include Robert Dahl and Charles Lindblom, 1976, *Politics, Economics, and Welfare*, Chicago: University of Chicago Press; Charles Lindblom, 1977, *Politics and Markets*, New York: Basic Books; and Robert Dahl, 1982, *Dilemmas of Pluralist Democracy*, New Haven, CT: Yale University Press. For an insightful critique of the original pluralist model and its revisions see John F. Manley, 1983, "Neo-pluralism: A Class Analysis of Pluralism I and Pluralism II," *American Political Science Review*, 77:368–83.

9. Much has been written about assimilationist and cultural pluralist strategies in the ethnic studies literature. For an overview see Joe R. Feagin, 1984, *Racial and Ethnic Relations*, 2d ed., Prentice-Hall, Englewood Cliffs, NJ. Another useful analysis which focuses more specifically on race is George Herman, Jr., 1984, *American Race Relations Theory: A Review of Four Models*. Lanham, MD: University Press of America.

10. The authors of *Liberating Theory* use the term *monism* to describe the notion that the source for all types of oppression can be found in a single sphere. See Michael Albert, Leslie Cagan, Noam Chomsky, Robin Hahnel, Mel King, Lydia Sargent, and Holly Sklar, 1986, *Liberating Theory*, Boston: South End Press.

11. My simplification of a separatist model does not do justice to the complexity of a number of different ideologies and separatist political movements. For instance the two major assumptions of this model need not be linked. Certainly one can believe that gender or class is the fundamental basis of oppression in our society without necessarily advocating a separatist political movement. One may also participate in separatist political activities without believing that there is one fundamental source of all types of oppression. For this reason and others a more thorough understanding of separatist movements would require more in-depth discussion. However, the simplification can be useful for comparative purposes as long as we do not forget that it is a simplification.

12. Political scientists who have studied this phenomenon include Steven Lukes, 1974, *Power: A Radical View*, London: Macmillan; John Gaventa, 1980, *Power and Powerlessness: Quiescence and Rebellion in an Appalachian Valley*, Urbana: University of Illinois Press; and Peter Bachrach and Morton S. Baratz, 1970, *Power and Poverty: Theory and Practice*, New York: Oxford University Press. The most well-known discussion of this issue in Marxist literature are works by Antonio Gramsci.

13. While I am relying on feminist authors for the outlines of this model, I do not mean to imply that feminism is the only possible source for such ideas. In their book *Hegemony and Socialist Strategy* (London: Verso, 1985), Ernesto Laclau and Chantal Mouffe make a similar disclaimer about the fact that they used Marxism as their source for a new conception of politics. Their remarks represent, in spirit, my own thoughts on the subject if you merely replace the word "Marxism" with "feminism" in the following quotation: "Political conclusions similar to those set forth in this book could have been approximated from very different discursive formations. . . . however, Marxism is *one* of the traditions through which it becomes possible to formulate this new conception of politics. For us, the validity of this point of departure is simply based on the fact that it constitutes our own past" (pp. 3–4). Works less explicitly based in feminist thought, although in most cases influenced by feminism, which have helped me think about this new model include the Laclau and Mouffe book cited above; Michael Albert and Robin Hahnel, 1981, *Marxism and Socialist Theory*, Boston: South End Press; and Arthur Brittan and Mary Maynard, 1984, *Sexism, Racism, and Oppression*, Oxford: Basil Blackwell Publishers Ltd.

14. Lorde, *Age, Race, Class, and Sex*, p. 114.
15. Bunch, *Making Common Cause*, p. 152.
16. Reagon, *Coalition Politics*, pp. 357–58.
17. Lorde, *Age, Race, Class, and Sex*, p. 116.
18. Reagon, *Coalition Politics*, p. 358.
19. Bunch, *Making Common Cause*, p. 152.
20. Hartsock, *The Feminist Standpoint*, p. 284.
21. One can formulate weak and strong versions of the standpoint argument. A strong version might argue that structural differences allow *only* the subordinated group to achieve a true understanding of social relations. A weaker version might argue that greater incentives exist for members of the subordinated group to develop a critical perspective on social relations which is opposed to, but not necessarily truer in any absolute sense, than the perspective which is dominant in society. This weaker version would also allow for the possibility that nonoppressed members of society could achieve a critical understanding of social relations.
22. Hartsock, *The Feminist Standpoint*, p. 285; and Hartsock, *Money, Sex, and Power*, p. 232.
23. Flynn, Brian, Goldsmith, Larry, and Sutcliffe, Bob. "We Danced in the Miners' Hall: An Interview with 'Lesbians and Gays Support the Miners'," *Radical America*, Vol. 19. No. 2–3.
24. Jacobson, Julius, ed., 1968. *The Negro and the American Labor Movement*, Garden City, NY: Anchor Books; and Foner, Phillip, 1981, *Organized Labor and the Black Worker*, New York: International Publishers.
25. Reagon, *Coalition Politics*, p. 359.
26. Bunch, *Making Common Cause*, p. 153.

Alliances Between Women
Overcoming Internalized Oppression and Internalized Domination

Gail Pheterson

The "Feminist Alliance Project" was organized in the Netherlands[1] in order to study and interrupt psychological processes that divide women from one another. Social divisions between women have been a primary focus of feminist scholarship, politics, and therapy for the last decade. This report does not attempt to review those developments; rather, it is a description and analysis of one project that was designed to nurture personal change, political strength, and theoretical understanding of divisions between women.[2]

Parallel groups were formed to address the racism, anti-Semitism, and heterosexism that divide women.[3] One group had seven black[4] and five white women, one had seven Jewish and five non-Jewish women, and one had seven lesbian and five heterosexual women. The balance between oppressed and dominant categories of participants was considered important to counteract the assumption of "normalcy" that white, non-Jewish, and heterosexual women were assumed to have internalized and to counteract the self-concealment and isolation that black, Jewish, and lesbian women were assumed to have internalized. An attempt was also made to balance the participants across dimensions other than the one upon which the group was focused (such as class, age, or motherhood) in order to emphasize common experiences and also to avoid perpetuating common misconceptions such as that all heterosexual women are mothers, all lesbians are nonmothers, all white women are middle-class and all black women are working class. Two women, one from each subgroup, acted as facilitators. Class differences between women were addressed within each group and also in a full-day workshop every few months in which all groups met together.

The groups were organized within one project in order to raise consciousness about the interactions between issues and to encourage sharing between groups. Each group met every two weeks for five months, at which time new groups were formed. The present report is based upon four cycles, roughly two years, of parallel groups.

Conceptual framework

The following concepts were used throughout the project to inform the analysis and structure.

Internalized oppression is the incorporation and acceptance by individuals within an oppressed group of the prejudices against them within the dominant society.[5] Internalized oppression is likely to consist of self-hatred, self-concealment, fear of violence and feelings of inferiority, resignation, isolation, powerlessness, and gratefulness for being allowed to survive. Internalized oppression is the mechanism within an oppressive system for perpetuating domination not only by external control but also by building subservience into the minds of the oppressed groups.

Internalized domination is the incorporation and acceptance by individuals within a dominant group of prejudices against others.[6] Internalized domination is likely to consist of feelings of superiority, normalcy, and self-righteousness, together with guilt, fear, projection, denial of reality, and alienation from one's body and from nature. Internalized domination perpetuates oppression of others and alienation from oneself by either denying or degrading all but a narrow range of human possibilities. One's own humanity is thus internally restricted and one's qualities of empathy, trust, love, and openness to others and to life-enhancing work become rigid and repressed.

Visibility is being oneself fully, openly, undefensively, and expressively. Visibility of the oppressed group contradicts self-concealment, isolation, subservience, and dominant denial or avoidance of oppressed persons. Visibility of the dominant group contradicts guilt, fear of exposure, projection, alienation from one's body, and detachment from others.

Pride is self-acceptance and self-respect, in particular, respect for one's identity, one's heritage, and one's right to self-determination.

Pride carries with it an indignation against the abuse of any human being, including oneself, and a vast resource for perseverance and righteous struggle. Most fundamentally, pride derives from deep love for oneself and for life. Pride contradicts both internalized oppression and internalized domination.

Solidarity is knowledge of, respect for, and unity with persons whose identities are in certain essential ways common with one's own. Constructive solidarity requires pride in oneself. Internalized oppression isolates people from one another, especially from others like themselves, and thereby prevents solidarity. Internalized domination binds people together on the basis of their power to dominate others rather than on the basis of their respect for one another. Solidarity is essential to oppressed groups for liberation and to dominant groups for collective alliance.

Alliance is knowledge of, respect for, and commitment between persons who are in essential ways different but whose interests are in essential ways akin. For dominant groups, alliance is a process of sharing power and resources with others in society in order to create structures equally responsive to the needs and interests of all people. This process requires giving up one's drive to superiority, giving up one's prejudices against others, and embracing a more flexible relation to oneself, to others, and to society as a whole. For oppressed groups, alliance is a readiness to struggle with dominant groups for one's right to an equal share of power and resources. This readiness necessitates recognition of and indignation against oppression and it generates the collective confidence and strength to bring about change. Furthermore, readiness necessitates recognition and acceptance of, never gratitude for, true alliance. Both the readiness to struggle and the sharing of power and resources are suppressed by internalized oppression and internalized domination. Pride and solidarity prepare individuals to become partners in alliance against oppression.

Group structure

A flexible structure, including the following stages, was designed across the five-month experience: (1) telling, and sometimes writing, life stories (visibility); (2) expressing feelings, both positive and negative, about oneself, one's identity, and one's history (pride); (3) exploring feelings and experiences in relation to other women who share one's group status (solidarity); and (4) exploring feelings and experiences in relation to women with different group status (alliance). Attention in the groups focused both on life experiences outside of the group and also on interactions within the group. During each meeting, subgroups would meet separately for various lengths of time; for example, black and white women would have an opportunity to discuss their feelings toward other blacks and other whites in black-only and white-only groups. The identification and interruption of internalized oppression and internalized domination was seen as a necessary condition for building effective alliances and, therefore, as a primary function of the facilitators. To help build the trust required for the task, participants were asked to meet between group meetings in changing dyads. Meetings were held at someone's home or at one of the two sponsoring institutes.

Participants read a proposal including the conceptual framework before beginning the project and they agreed upon the basic approach from self-examination to within-group examination to alliance across differences.[7] During the meetings, reference to conceptual definitions was often made in order to illuminate the political origin of internalized conflicts.

Participants

All participants were Dutch or Dutch (ex-)colonized women except the organizer and one facilitator, who were originally from the United States.[8] Each woman determined her own social status and appropriate subgroup. About eighty-five percent of the women identified as feminists; some joined to support their political work; some joined to gain skills for living or working with significant others; some joined because they felt isolated from women who shared their social position and others because they felt isolated from women with different social positions. All of the participants were strongly committed to the issues and to the project.

In the first five-month cycle of groups, the majority of participants were middle class, although about half had been raised in working-class families. In following cycles, working class women composed about a third of the participants. About one-third of the black women were born in the Netherlands; about two-thirds were born in their native (ex-)colonized lands.[9] About ninety-five percent of the Jewish women had one Jewish parent; the other five percent had two Jewish parents. About half the lesbians had active heterosexual pasts, and about half identified as lesbian since their teens. Participants ranged in ages from early twenties to late fifties; a majority were in their thirties and forties. About a third of the women were biological mothers; several co-mothered their lover's children. Over 100 women participated. The numbers are inexact because some women participated consecutively in more than one cycle, and a few women participated in more than one alliance group.

As one might expect, the groups themselves were intense and

demanding. Obviously, every participant experienced the alliance process in a uniquely personal way. The purpose here is to examine those experiences within the framework of group identity as defined by political status in society.

Each group experienced movement from defensiveness to assertion. Within each subgroup this movement was characterized by feelings that can be explained within the context of the specific oppression (i.e., racism, anti-Semitism, and heterosexism). The following discussions focus on the change itself and on the internalized resistance to change; they do not provide a literal transcription of each group process.

A common resistance

It became clear that in every group, past experiences with oppression and domination distorted the participants' perceptions of the present and blocked their identification with people in common political situations who did not share their history. Jewish women who had experienced the Nazi war trauma sometimes had difficulty identifying with those Jews who had not; black women who were born in the Netherlands sometimes had difficulty identifying with blacks who were born in an (ex-)colonized country; lesbian women who had "always" been lesbian sometimes had difficulty identifying with those who had formerly been married heterosexuals. Those who had experienced the oppression most acutely in the past were likely to feel like the true oppressed group, for example, the real lesbians or the real Jews: "You're just a nouveau lesbian" or "What do you American Jews know about being Jewish?" In other words, "You haven't suffered enough."

On the other side, those who shared the same political identity in the present but had not experienced the oppression so personally in the past were likely to reject the oppressed status for themselves: "I don't want to be one of them"; "My lesbianism is only political. Sexually I'm heterosexual"; or "My mother is Jewish, not me"; or "I've never felt black." Sometimes, however, it was exactly the person who had suffered the most who rejected the identity the strongest, and sometimes it was exactly the one who had suffered the least who embraced the identity with the least ambivalence.

Differentiations on the basis of past experiences were typical for women in dominant as well as oppressed positions: "I'm not Jewish, but I've never been Christian either"; "I'm white, but I grew up with black people"; "I'm heterosexual, but I make love with women, too." Whether in an effort to relieve guilt or to avoid exclusion, the differentiation was an expression of denial of their dominant status.

Black and white alliance

The feelings that most clearly emerged in the group of black and white women were anger from blacks and guilt from whites. Feelings of guilt were present for some of the white women from the very beginning of the group. For some women, those feelings led to paralysis in the mixed group and to anxious revelations of insecurity in the white subgroup. On the first day, in a subgroup, one white woman said, "I just sit there with the black women and feel nervous and guilty and don't know what to do." Later in the process, when a few black women expressed mistrust toward an initiative of a white woman, that woman asked repeatedly, "Why can't you trust me? I know I have integrity." Rather than call on other whites for support in the subgroup, she rejected them as less racially aware than she. Only black approval would affirm her integrity and exempt her from guilt. Those white women who acknowledged feeling guilty expressed a fear of revenge and a need for reassurance from blacks. Both the need for approval and the need for reassurance eventually outraged black women. White dependency on black women—either to affirm their integrity or relieve their fears—in effect directed the group more toward white insecurities than toward the struggle against racism that was the group's central concern.

The black women began with commitment and skepticism. The first reaction of some of the black women to the white women's guilty requests for reassurance or approval was patiently to explain why such behavior was not appropriate or helpful; other black women sat in silence; others expressed annoyance. During the first few meetings, they differed among themselves about whether and how much to meet in a separate subgroup. Only after the first emotional black-white clash did they agree unanimously on the need to meet separately. They did not want to express their differing reactions to the conflict in the presence of whites.

If guilt paralyzed the white women in the presence of blacks, anger energized the black women into insisting upon time in their subgroup and into blaming whites for being unaware and passive. As the black women met more in their separate group, they began to feel greater solidarity and their reactions and demands in the mixed group became bolder and more confronting. One black woman said, "This group is getting scary and uncomfortable for you white women. That's the way the world outside is for us," and another said, "You white women wouldn't be working on racism at all if we weren't here. If we'd never come to Holland you wouldn't work on it and if we weren't with you in a group you wouldn't be working on it!"

The black women became more expressive of their ethnic cultural differences and more committed to their racial political commonalities. They asked white women to struggle with their own insecurities, and at the same time they validated themselves as the experts on racism. The white women, having met in their subgroup each time the black women were meeting in theirs, began to need reassurance less often from blacks and to acknowledge the unawareness that racism fosters in all whites, focusing on what they could do to combat racism. They began to value the awareness they could gain from one another in their attempt to become less dependent on blacks and to feel less competitive with one another for the place of either "best ally" or "least racist." In other words, they too were moving toward greater solidarity.

All of the group's participants came to make deeper and clearer commitments to racism awareness outside of the group. The three white women in teaching positions changed their jobs to include an emphasis on antiracism work. Another white woman realized through her participation in the group how debilitating guilt was in many aspects of her life; she decided to go into individual therapy and return to the alliance project at a later time. A group of black women expanded their support networks with new initiatives specific to their needs: A black lesbian group was started, and a few women joined a black women's counseling class. A black and a white woman from the group organized seminars on racism and research on processes of change among black and white participants. Another black woman planned to organize a new alliance group like the original one after a six-month period in her black lesbian group.

Everyone in the group agreed that, although the process was difficult, their lives changed significantly. For some women it was unclear whether the changes resulted from this group or from other simultaneous activities in their lives; some felt that the changes did not occur primarily in the group but definitely *because* the group was there. One black woman said during the last meeting that she had begun to take herself more seriously as a black woman and that she had become more assertive and honest in confronting daily racism. A white woman reported the deep shock the group had given her—the shock of realizing the racial bias in every aspect of her life.

Jewish and non-Jewish alliance

In this group an underlying struggle for identity evolved that was characterized by feelings of isolation on the Jewish side and dullness on the non-Jewish side. At one meeting, when discussing the essence of being Jewish, a Jewish woman and non-Jewish woman began a critical tug of war about the cost of being special versus being ordinary.

The Jewish woman had been saying that the essence of being Jewish was being special. She was expressing both her pride and her isolation. The non-Jewish woman said, "I wish I was special. Nobody ever told me that I was special," to which the Jewish woman replied, "I wish I was ordinary," and the non-Jewish woman responded, "I've always been ordinary. I want to be special."

At another meeting, in subgroups, the non-Jews talked about their own specialness and the Jews talked about the isolation they experienced as Jews. By focusing upon their own specialness, the non-Jews confronted an internal question they often felt in their contact with Jewish women: "What about me?" One woman expressed this as follows to a Jewish woman: "I feel like I have no identity when I am with you. I don't know who I am. It would be easier if I were Jewish." The Jewish woman answered that it would not be easier for *her* if the other was also Jewish, but that she did need for the other to know *who* she was. She further admitted often feeling safest and most protected among non-Jews. Nonetheless, this woman jumped in protest when a non-Jewish woman told how she had hidden a newspaper article reporting anti-Semitic incidents from her Jewish lover to "protect her." A discussion followed wherein the Jewish women distinguished between the needs for comfort based upon internalized oppression and needs for alliance. They all saw the sharing of information as alliance.

If the Jews in the group sometimes looked to the non-Jews for protection, the non-Jews sometimes looked to the Jews for specialness by association. As one non-Jewish woman said, "I've met active, struggling women in this group and that inspires me to be like that too!" And, "As a child I always identified with Jewish history." Another woman said, "I find most of the Jewish women in my life difficult, but I do like their force and intelligence." The ambivalence of admiring qualities they associated with Jews and at the same time feeling uncomfortable with them was expressed by the non-Jews more than once: "It turned out to be the wrong group for me," said one woman, "I should have joined the black or lesbian group"; "I can get along fine with the working-class Jewish women; it's the upper-class women I can't stand."

Differences in class backgrounds caused a clash in this group. Often the lines of solidarity were drawn more on the basis of class background than on the basis of Jewish identity. The Jewish working-class women all had politically active socialist backgrounds: "If it hadn't been for our political tie to the resistance, we never would have made it. Most working class Jews didn't." Even within this small group the historical dynamic emerged of Jews pitted against one another in their search for safety; those whose backgrounds were associated closely with white gentile society were seen by everyone, Jews and non-Jews, as the oppressors.

One non-Jewish woman said, "Eight Jewish women is just too many. It's taken me all this time to get close to one!" Her reaction reflected a situation between the Jews and non-Jews that may be specific to post-World War II Europe and to other places where there are relatively few Jews. For the non-Jews (and some of the Jews) under thirty-five years old, the group afforded a first opportunity to be with many Jews at once.[10] For the Jews (and non-Jews) over thirty-five years old, the group was seen at the beginning as a place to "work on the war." The main association with Jewishness for them was Hitler. One Jewish woman said on the first evening, "I am not here to become more Jewish. I just want to work through my Jewish pain." She told about feeling uncomfortable talking about being Jewish with her children and about avoiding telling people that she had joined the alliance group. After several months, she began to reclaim parts of her Jewish heritage other than the war (such as Jewish food and culture) and began sharing that heritage with her family and friends.

The move from isolation toward contact was shared by all the Jewish women. Everyone began talking more about her Jewishness at home and at work. One woman said, "This group has been an exercise ground for how I can talk with non-Jews . . . it's safer here than in other places. Lots has changed for me." Another Jewish woman said, "I feel prouder about my Jewish identity now, so I can come out more as who I am everywhere." Another woman said, "I've decided to go after the people I want to have in my life."

The non-Jews experienced a move from inconspicuousness toward self-definition. One evening all of the non-Jews agreed that working toward alliance with Jews had challenged their most chronic feelings of insecurity: "I have to work on myself to be a good ally. I'm here for me." Another woman said, "I used to think it was complimentary to say how intelligent Jews are. Now I realize that it was a prejudice that fed my feeling dull. To be an ally I have to know that I'm smart too!" In the course of the group, the non-Jews moved toward greater acceptance of their religious backgrounds, prouder identification with their own culture, and a clearer definition and expression of their personal and political commitments. One woman wrote, "I've begun to understand how my isolation works and I realize how important it is to define myself and to find recognition and identity." And further, "One thing has become clear to me for life: my commitment against anti-Semitism, I stand for that, you can count on it."

The group was often chaotic, sometimes aggressive, and usually warm, loud, and confusing. One woman called it an "awful exhilarating experience that changed her life." Nearly everyone began to read a lot about Jews, and everyone took risks to initiate or deepen a friendship. Both Jewish and non-Jewish women reported stronger self-presentations in their personal and work lives. Alliance did not require Jews to give up or hide their identity or non-Jews to melt into the code of dominant conformity. To the contrary, the struggle against anti-Semitism demanded solid identities on both sides.

Lesbian and heterosexual alliance[11]

For the lesbian women, the alliance process was characterized by movement from defiance toward self-assertion. During the first week, everyone wrote a paragraph telling what it meant to her to be a lesbian or a heterosexual. One lesbian wrote, "I often feel illegal . . . The feeling of being different is very fundamental, it sits real deep. It also means being excluded." Another woman wrote, "I don't feel like always having to explain . . . so I don't bother much with men." And another said, "I should live as a *black* lesbian woman, but then I couldn't be lesbian anymore, or only in silence, and I don't want that!" And another, "Oi vey, what a shunde (Yiddish for shame), a Jewish girl, a lesbian?" Like every group, this group was filled with multiple interlocking identities and oppressions.

A bisexual woman who joined the group as a heterosexual because she benefits from heterosexual privileges as a married woman wrote, "I don't literally make love with a woman now, sometimes I do with a man, but I protest being called heterosexual. I feel room to move . . . where I can call myself bisexual." Another woman said, "I seldom tell anyone other than feminist friends that I sometimes make love also with women. I realize the social ease I get from a heterosexual relationship and how I rely on that for acceptance."

The ambiguity between lesbian and heterosexual identities was one recurring theme in this group. Ambiguity in group identity was also a theme for some black, white, Jewish, and non-Jewish women, but unlike women in those groups, the lesbians did not have different roots than the heterosexuals (i.e., everyone's ancestors were heterosexuals, or so they assumed), and many lesbians had heterosexual pasts.

From the beginning, group members discussed the choices and pressures that had shaped their lives. During the second meeting, the lesbian subgroup confronted the contrasting meanings lesbianism held in terms of motherhood. One woman said how pleased she was that she had become a lesbian before "making the whole mistake of motherhood and marriage." Another agreed that she was glad not to have children. A third lesbian woman sat silently for a moment and then began to tell how angry she always felt when she heard lesbians belittle motherhood and how proud she was to be the mother of seven children. Another woman explained the importance in her life of mothering her lover's two sons. When the lesbian and heterosexual subgroups joined one another, the discussion focused on motherhood as an issue for women's solidarity. Participants felt that by assuming all lesbian women are not and do not want to be mothers, and that all heterosexuals are or would like to be mothers, they had denied choice to themselves and to other women.

If the lesbians sometimes took a defiant posture to distinguish themselves from other women, the heterosexuals felt identity confusion and sometimes searched for self-definition through others. Attempts by the heterosexual women to win favor with the lesbians sometimes aroused lesbian frustration and anger: "Don't support me by telling me that you're like me. Support me by telling me that you are choosing what you want and that you're getting what you need." "Don't think you're being a buddy by complaining about men. Don't assume that I hate men and don't assume that I want you to hate men." "Every time you settle as a woman for less than you want, you insult me as well as yourself."

Movement from defiance toward self-assertion for lesbians and from confusion to choice for heterosexuals was neither easy nor consistent within the group. One woman said, "I like it more and more to be with only lesbian women." Another said, "I feel very ambivalent about being in this group. Before it started I was clear about everything and now, through this group, I see how big our differences are, also between us lesbians. I don't know anymore." One heterosexual woman said, "In the beginning I was real excited here, especially about my own background, and then I fell into a big hole of confusion." Another heterosexual woman said, "I was terribly confused at the beginning, but now it gets clearer for me. I realize that I don't suffer from lesbian oppression like you lesbians but I do suffer from it." One lesbian woman wrote in her end evaluation: "I'm more visible as a lesbian than I used to be and I have less of a chip on my shoulder. I used to feel, 'poor me or lucky me, nobody knows what it's like to be me' and now I'm better able to communicate naturally about my life and to expect respect from others. I have also begun to accept heterosexuality as a possible real choice, even for women."

As this last quote suggests, by the end of the group, both the lesbian and the heterosexual choice had gained integrity. One heterosexual woman told about objecting to a heterosexual assumption in a public lecture "without explaining that I was standing up for the rights of other women." Sexual choice had become an issue important for all women, regardless of their social status or personal life style.

Conclusion

The processes that evolved within the groups were determined by the starting point of the participants. The choice to participate in an alliance group already reflected a certain consciousness and readiness. Women joining an oppressed subgroup were assuming a politically targeted identity and acknowledging their oppression. Women joining a dominant subgroup were assuming a politically privileged identity and acknowledging their domination. Once in the project, participants were confronted with the fact that group identities are profoundly historical and symbolic. At one meeting a woman said, "I count twelve women here but I feel the presence of thousands."

This study focused its discussion of each group upon a salient dynamic that emerged from the participants' internalized conflicts. It was assumed by the project design that the issues confronted were shaped by external systems of domination and that strategies for psychological survival are necessary. Often, however, internalized oppression and internalized domination become embedded in personality at the expense of identity and freedom and without regard to external reality. Oppression seems to breed a package of psychological processes that distort reality and weaken personal strength. Angry, isolated, and defiant feelings were identified by participants in this study as reactions to oppression. Guilty, dull, and confused feelings were identified as reactions to social positions of dominance. Those feelings spiraled into blaming, needing (protection, reassurance, or approval), and excluding other women. Building alliances seemed to be an effective counterforce for those dynamics. In addition, alliance building may be transferable so that, for example, visibility as a lesbian would equip one to assert herself more powerfully as a Jew or as a white person fighting racism.

It is important to note that internalized oppression and internalized domination interact not only between different persons but also intrapsychically within one person. Oppression and domination are experienced as a mutually reinforcing web of insecurities and rigidities. Although the political consequences of oppression are opposite to those of domination (e.g., powerlessness vs. power), the psychological consequences are surprisingly alike. The fear of violence one feels as a victim of oppression reinforces the fear of revenge she feels as an agent of oppression. The isolation resulting from feelings of inferiority reinforces the isolation resulting from feelings of superiority. The guilt felt for dominating others likewise reinforces the guilt felt for one's own victimization. Since maintaining a posture of dominance is often tenuously balanced upon denying inferior status, the individual suppresses and conceals characteristics which reveal social powerlessness: "I can make it as a professional if they just never discover that I'm a lesbian"; or "As a white person I can become a member of any club, if I don't let on that I'm Jewish."; or "I can't hide being a woman but I can pretend to be one of the boys." The method of domination becomes collusion with oppressive forces, and the cost becomes rigidity and fear of personal growth. The more guilty the white woman feels about her racism, the less adequate she is likely to feel about effecting change and the more dependent she will be on black women to do the work of changing racist attitudes. The more the non-Jew resists recognition of her own social identity, the more she will resent Jewish identity. The more dependent a heterosexual woman is upon male approval, the more threatened she will be by lesbian autonomy. Every human difference thus becomes a confrontation with self.

The organizational and conceptual framework of this project did provide the confrontations for which it was intended. By focusing upon the norms of dominant status and oppressed status, those norms gained political significance and at the same time, lost personal significance. Variations in sexual preference, appearance, and religion all became more apparent and more accepted once the illusion that there were only two politicized poles dissolved. White, straight, and ordinary images of humanity were transformed into more realistic perceptions of human diversity. The recognition and interruption of internalized forms of domination and oppression supported that transformation and supported movement from antagonism toward alliance between women. I want to thank the group organizers and facilitators with whom I worked: Nurith de Vries, Lex Jacott, Eloise Sewell, Flora Kleynjan, Lya Djadoenath, Julia de Lima, Joke Hermsen, Anja Meulenbelt, Anneke van Wijk, Christien Quispel, Tineke Sjenitzer, Bernie de Bie, and Ellen van Aggelen. I am grateful to both the women's team of IVABO and the women's project of the Institute of Clinical Psychology, University of Utrecht, for integrating this project in their study programs. I am also grateful to Bertha van Amstel for her consultations during the first year of the project and to Gosina Mandersloot for her constant emotional and intellectual support. Most essentially, I give credit for what I have learned about alliance to the group participants; it was their openness and earnestness and their solidarity as women that made this project possible.

Notes

1. The project was sponsored by the Institute of Clinical Psychology at the University of Utrecht and the Institute of Advanced Social Studies (called IVABO) in Amsterdam, the Netherlands.

2. The project framework was influenced by Paulo Freire, Pedagogy of the Oppressed (New York: Continuum, 1970); Erving Goffman, Stigma, Notes on the Management of Spoiled Identity (New York: Prentice-Hall, Inc., 1963); Albert Memmi, The Colonizer and the Colonized (Boston: Beacon Press, 1965); Gail Pheterson, "Love in Freedom," Journal of Humanistic Psychology 23, no. 3 (Summer 1981):35-50. Hogie Wyckoff, Solving Problems Together (New York: Grove Press, 1980). Parallel work of particular relevance includes Elly Bulkin, Minnie Bruce Pratt, and Barbara Smith, Yours in Struggle (Brooklyn, N.Y.: Long Haul Press, 1985); Louise Derman-Sparks and Carol Brunson Phillips, The Teaching/Learning Dimension of Anti-Racism

Education (Pasadena, Calif.: Pacific Oakes College, 1985; Rickey Sherover-Marcuse,"Toward a Perspective on Unlearning Racism: Twelve Working Assumptions," Issues in Cooperation and Power, no. 7 (Fall 1981), 14-15.

3. An initial report including an elaboration of group methods is published in Dutch: Gail Pheterson, "Bondgenootschap tussen vrouwen: Een theretisese en empiriese analyse van onderdrukking en beurijding," Psychologie en maatschappij, no 20 (September 1982), 399-424. The present report is based on two years of continuous simultaneous participation in (and facilitation/organization of) black and white, Jewish and non-Jewish, and lesbian and heterosexual groups. As of 1984, groups have also been run to explore divisions between disabled and able-bodied women, between women in the presence of men, and between prostitute, exprostitute, and nonprostitute women.

4. After much discussion, the women whose personal or ancestral origins were in (formerly) colonized nations decided to identify themselves uniformly as black—rather than specifically by nationality or culture and rather than Third World, colored, or non-white. The cultural heritages represented were Surinamese, Antillian, Molluccan, and Indonesian. The decision to unite under one strong color identification was an act of solidarity for the purpose of exposing and resisting common racist oppression.

5. See Freire; Suzanne Lipsky, "Internalized Oppression," Black Re-Emergence, no. 2 (Winter 1977), 5-10; Albert Memmi, Portrait of a Jew (New York: Viking Press, 1971); Richard Sennett and Jonathan Cobb, The Hidden Injuries of Class (New York: Vintage Books, 1972).

6. Although the author coined the expression "internalized domination," the basic concept can be found in Alice Miller, For Your Own Good: Hidden Cruelty in Child-Rearing and the Roots of Violence, trans. Hildegard Hannum and Hunter Hannum (New York: Farrar, Straus, & Giroux, 1983); William Ryan, Blaming the Victim (New York: Random House, 1971); Jean-Paul Sartre, Anti-Semite and Jew (New York: Schocken Books, 1965); Ricky Sherover-Marcuse, Emancipation and Consciousness: Dogmatic and Dialectical Perspectives in Early Marx (Oxford: Basil Blackwell, 1986); Lillian Smith, Killers of the Dream (New York: W. W. Norton & Co., 1949).

7. See Gail Pheterson, Liberation and Alliance: A Proposal for Work Groups to Study and Counteract Racism, Anti-Semitism, and Heterosexism between Women (Amsterdam: Institute of Advanced Social Studies, 1979).

8. The Netherlands has a long colonial history in South Africa, Indonesia, Surinam, and the Antilles. Only the Antilles are not now independent, but the Dutch influence remains strong in all its ex-colonies. Although each country has a very different relation to the Netherlands, the Dutch colonialists occupied the highest positions, the Dutch language became the official language, and white skin became the sign of higher status in each country. That power relation carried over into relations within the Netherlands after waves of immigration. Great numbers of Indoeuropeans (people of mixed Indonesian and Dutch heritage) and Moluccans (people from one set of islands who served in the Dutch army) were shipped to Holland in 1949 when Indonesia gained independence. The Surinamese (especially middle-class men) immigrated in small numbers before independence in 1975 and in great numbers as whole families after independence. For a study of immigrants and their descendants from the colonies to the Netherlands, see Jan Lucassen and Rinus Pennix, Nieuwkomers immigranten en hun nakomelingen in Nederland, 1550-1985 (Amsterdam: Meulenhoff, 1985); and Rinus Pennix, "Research and Policy with Regard to Ethnic Minorities in the Netherlands: A Historical Outline and the State of Affairs," International Migration 22, no. 4 (1984): 345-66.

9. See n. 4 above.

10. Eighty-five percent of the 140,000 Jews living in the Netherlands before the Second World War were killed in Nazi concentration camps. Undoubtedly, the devastation of that loss is the primary association to anti-Semitism in Dutch society today. As an occupied country during the war, the Dutch were forced into positions

of either active resistance against Nazism, passivity, or active collaboration with Nazism. That history left behind an enormity of grief and guilt, both of which are sometimes triggered by the mention or presence of Jews. See J. Presser, *Ashes in the Wind: The Destruction of Dutch Jewry* (London: Souvenir Press, 1968).

11. The Netherlands is one of the least heterosexist countries in the world by law. A provisional antidiscrimination law including homosexuals is taken seriously by the Dutch. For example, a foreign homosexual can acquire Dutch residency and work rights on the basis of a stable relationship with a Dutch citizen. Such legal justice flows from the Dutch movement for homosexual rights that began with individual activism at the beginning of the twentieth century. The movement took the form of a private club before the Second World War and organized into a formal association of homosexuals (called COC) in 1946. Lesbians are granted legal rights equal to those of homosexual men, although their position in COC is clearly a subordinate one. During the last fifteen years, a distinct lesbian movement has become politically and culturally visible. Within that movement lesbians of color have begun to organize separately both in response to racism and in order to rediscover and develop a distinct black lesbian culture. Jewish lesbians have also begun to organize on a very small scale. Sexual diversity among lesbians, including S-M, has recently emerged as a topic of discussion. Several lesbian magazines are published with specific focus, such as black lesbians, sexuality, and literature. See Rob Tielman, *Homoeseksualiteit in Nederland* (Amsterdam: Boom Meppel, 1982). For a comparison of lesbian oppression in the Netherlands and the United States, see Gail Pheterson and Leny Jansen, "Lesbian Struggle against a Pillow or a Wall: A Dutch-American Dialogue," Journal of Homosexuality, nos. 3/4 (1986), in press; also see "Special Issues: Research on Homosexuality in the Netherlands." Journal of Homosexuality, nos. 3/4 (1986), in press.

Making Common Cause
Diversity and Coalitions *

Charlotte Bunch

I want to begin by questioning the title of this panel, "Common Causes: Uncommon Coalitions—Sex, Race, Class, and Age." In my twenty years of political organizing, I have been part of numerous coalitions. Some were successful, others disastrous, and most fell somewhere in between. I am not sure that any were really uncommon. For coalitions are one of the most common strategies for creating social change, and the problems that accompany them are recurring themes in all movements. Discourse about when, where, and how to build coalitions is particularly important when we seek to make change that is inclusive of diverse perspectives. For feminists, the ability to create a movement that includes and responds to the diversity of women's lives is crucial.

What feminists need to explore is why coalition efforts have not been more common in our movement, and what is required to build effective coalitions? We must ask why, instead of coalescing more,

---

* This speech was originally presented at the National Women's Studies Association Annual Conference in Seattle, WA, in June, 1985. It was first published in *IKON* No. 7 (Fall, 1986) and reprinted in *Passionate Politics,* by Charlotte Bunch, St. Martin's Press, 1987.

women have to continually separate into distinct groups in order to be heard? Whether on the basis of race, class, age, ethnic identity, sexual preference, or physical abilities, each group has had to find a separate space and identity in order to create conditions where their perspectives would be seen by others. Why do we have such difficulty responding to diversity, and how can we move beyond the necessity of separatism to building inclusive coalitions? In short, I want to talk about how to make coalitions more common, less frightening, more comprehensive, and more successful.

I assume that if coalitions are to work, there must be a common cause. The reason to go through the process, which is often painful and difficult, is because we have some shared goal, broadly or narrowly defined, that motivates us to work across diverse lines. As diverse groups unite around some common goal, there is a greater possibility of learning about and incorporating diversity at a deeper level. The particulars of each coalition vary, of course. But assuming that one goal of feminism is struggling against domination in all its forms, then a critical issue for all our coalitions is how to approach diversity and domination.

Diversity and domination

Patriarchy has systematically utilized diversity as a tool of domination in which groups are taught that certain powers and privileges are the natural prerogatives of some people. We learn in childhood that such things as sex and race bring differences in power and privilege, and that these are acceptable. This idea that difference justifies domination is deeply embedded in society and defended as natural. Take, for example, the refrain: "there will always be poor people" used to perpetuate class privileges. But as women who have challenged the so-called naturalness of male supremacy, feminists must also question it in other areas of domination.

When power hierarchies are accepted as inevitable, people can be manipulated to fear that those who are different are a threat to their position and perhaps even to their survival. We are taught to be afraid—that "they" *will* hurt us—either because they are more powerful or because they want our privileges. While that fear takes multiple forms, depending on where we fit in the various scales of domination, all of us are taught to distrust those who are different. Some aspects of this fear may be necessary to survival—whites *do* lynch blacks, men *will* rape women—and we must watch out for dangers. But fear and distrust of differences are most often used to keep us in line. When we challenge the idea that differences must be threatening, we are also challenging the patriarchal assignment of power and privilege as birthrights.

Opposing the ways that differences are used to dominate does not mean that we seek to end diversity. Feminist visions are not about creating homogenized people who all look like a bland middle-class television ad. Many aspects of diversity can be celebrated as variety, creativity, and options in life-styles and world views. We must distinguish between creative differences that are not intrinsically tied to domination and the assignment of power and privilege based on the distinctive characteristics of some. Diversity, when separated from power to control others, provides valuable opportunities for learning and living that can be missed if one is embedded in an ethnocentric way of seeing reality.

Diversity among feminists today can be a resource for gaining a broader understanding of the world. We see more clearly and our ability to create effective strategies is enhanced if we move beyond the boundaries of our assigned patriarchal slot. Quite specifically, in 1985, white women can look to the growing women of color movement in the West and to feminism in the Third World as sources of both insight and information. But too often, we fail to respond to each other's potential for enriching our lives and the movement because of unconscious fears of race, class, of national differences. It is not just a matter of learning about race and class—although that is important—but also of understanding women's lives and the world as viewed by others.

Learning from a wider diversity of women and making coalitions does not mean watering down feminist politics, as some fear. Rather, it requires engaging in a wider debate about those politics and shaping their expressions to respond to more women's realities. I see this process as reclaiming the radical spirit of feminism that calls for going to the roots of oppression. In the United States, for example, this wave of feminism began in the 1960s in close connection to the black civil rights movement and its demand for recognition of the rights of radically diverse groups. Yet racism is all too often reflected in the lack of acknowledgment of those origins and the invisibility of women of color who were a part of feminism's resurgence. As Gloria T. Hull and Barbara Smith note in *But Some of Us Are Brave* (Old Westbury, N.Y.: The Feminist Press, 1982, p. xx): "Black women were a part of that early women's movement as were working-class women of all races." This included famous speakers such as Florence Kennedy as well as women like the welfare rights mothers that worked in the late 1960s in coalition with Washington, D.C. Women's Liberation to achieve improvements in the city's health services for women. In the 1970s, efforts to develop diverse coalitions and a broader-based agenda were often eclipsed by many factors including intense movement controversies and the media's emphasis on the pursuit of equality within the system. By focusing again on the diversity and depth of women's perspectives and needs in the 1980s, I see feminists reasserting the radical impulse for justice for all and thus strengthening the movement as a force for fundamental change.

There is commonality in the fact that all women are subordinated, but when we examine our diversity, we see that the forms that takes are shaped by many factors. Female oppression is not one universal block experienced the same way by all women, to which other forms of exploitation are then added as separate pieces. Rather, various oppressions interact to shape the particulars of each woman's life. For example, an aging black lesbian who is poor does not experience oppression as separate packages—one sexism, one poverty, one homophobia, one racism, and one ageism. She experiences these as interacting and shaping each other. Seeing this interaction is vital for coalitions around issues.

Too often analysis of women's oppression isolates single factors such as class or sexual preference in a simplistic manner, trying to show the effects of each separately. But this fails to take account of the interrelatedness. Further, it often winds up in battles over a hierarchy of seriousness of forms of oppression or over how one really is the cause of the other. For example, race and class affect an older woman's problems—whether it means being abandoned in her house, trapped in an abusive nursing home, or entirely homeless. Or looking at the exploitation of women's work, we can see the effect of factors such as race, homophobia, or physical disability, as well as class.

Strategies that fail to examine how female exploitation is shaped in different forms often set some women up against others. The interactive approach—taking into account female diversity—is thus essential for effective coalitions. However, it is often difficult to look at all the features of oppression because they are complex and demand continuous reevaluation of our assumptions. Further, attitudes and emotions around diversity are deeply rooted and often volatile. Systems such as racism, anti-Semitism, classism, nationalism, and homophobia are so much a part of the culture that surrounds us from birth that we often have biases and blind spots that affect our attitudes, behavior, strategies, and values in ways that we do not perceive until challenged by others.

Many problems that arise in coalitions stem from resistance to being challenged about oppressive attitudes and reactions. These need to be approached matter-of-factly, not as moral judgments on one's personhood, but as negative results of growing up in patriarchal culture. We must change such attitudes and behavior because they oppress others and interfere with our own humanity as well as impede the process of creating feminist strategies and coalitions. For example, white middle-class North Americans are often unaware that the perspectives of that culture—which usually coincide with the media's portrayal of reality—are not the only of seeing the world. Since these ethnocentric biases are reinforced constantly, we must make an extra effort to see other points of view. This does not mean that nothing of this culture is of value. It simply means that we must go beyond its limits to see what can be taken as useful and not oppressive, and what must be challenged.

In looking at diversity among women, we see one of the weaknesses of the feminist concept that the personal is political. It is valid that each woman begins from her personal experiences, and it is important to see how these are political. But we must also recognize that our personal experiences are shaped by the culture with its prejudices—against people of color, lesbians and gay men, the aged, and so on. We cannot, therefore, depend on our perceptions alone as the basis for political analysis and action—much less for coalition. Feminists must stretch beyond, challenging the limits of our own personal experiences by learning from the diversity of women's lives.

Divisive reactions to diversity

In the 1980s, various groups, such as the women of color movement, are expanding the definitions of, and possibilities for, feminism. But many women's reactions to diversity interfere with learning from others and making successful cross-cultural, multiracial coalitions. I call these divisive reactions because bringing up racism or class or homophobia is not itself divisive to the movement. Rather, what is divisive is ignoring such issues or being unable to respond to them constructively. I want to outline some reactions that I have seen interfere with efforts at coalition building and suggest ways of getting beyond them.

The most obviously divisive reaction is *becoming defensive* when challenged around an issue of diversity. If one is busy making explanations about how some action or comment was not really what you meant, it is hard to listen and understand criticism and why it is being made. This does not mean passively accepting every critical comment—for in dealing with such emotional topics, there will be exaggerations, inaccuracies, or injustices that must be worked out. But these problems do not excuse anyone from struggling with the issues. If one remains open, while retaining a sense of one's own authenticity, it is usually possible to deal with these by listening and responding constructively. If a critique does not make sense to you, ask about it, or try to figure out what led to it—even if it seems unfair. It is not always easy to listen to criticism first and then sort through what that means, but it is the job of feminists to do just that. To listen carefully, to consider what other views mean for our work, and to respond through incorporating new understanding where appropriate—this is a feminist necessity if we are to make coalitions among diverse women.

Often defensiveness is related to another unhelpful reaction—guilt. It may be appropriate to experience shame over the actions of one's ancestors or at how one has participated in another's oppression. But personal guilt is usually immobilizing, particularly if one sits with it for long. Successful coalitions are not built on feeling sorry for others or being apologetic about one's existence. Coalitions are built around shared outrage over injustice and common visions of how society can be changed. Few of us had control over our origins, and the point is to not feel guilt about the attitudes or privileges that we inherited. The question is what are we going to do about them now—how are we going to change ourselves and work to end domination in the world? For example, white women feeling sorry about something like racism is not as useful to women of color as working to eliminate it in society as well as in one's personal life.

Often women are sidetracked by *overpersonalization* when dealing with diversity. The issues raised are personal and do require individual change, but it is important not to get stuck there. Sometimes feminists become so involved in trying to be pure and personally free of any oppressive behavior that they become paralyzed and fear taking any political action because it might not be correct. Yet it is through concrete efforts to challenge domination—no matter how small—that we learn and can become more effective and more inclusive in our political work. For example, if a man tells me that he is becoming totally antisexist but is not in some way challenging the structures of patriarchal power that continue to oppress women, then his personal changes—if I believe him at all—are of minimal value to me. The same is true for women of color who see some whites talking about racism but not taking action against it in the world.

Another aspect of overpersonalization is *withdrawal*. Sometimes feminists have become so personally hurt by criticism or feel so left out when a group is creating its own space that they withdraw from political engagement. For example, some heterosexuals during the height of lesbian feminist challenges in the 1970s withdrew into their feelings of being attacked or left out rather than working on how they could fight homophobia while still being with men personally. This only reinforced the separation between us. I see similar behavior among some white women today. The hurt is often understandable because there is pain in confrontations around difficult issues, and feminists sometimes spend more energy criticizing women's oppressive behavior than taking on the systems of oppression. Still, reacting to this by withdrawing prevents learning from what has happened. This is sometimes like children who want to be the center stage and pout when not in the forefront. Instead, we need to see that at any given moment one group may be the creative edge of the movement, but that their work will enrich all of us in the long run.

One of the more infuriating reactions is acting *weary and resentful* when someone brings up "that issue" again. No one is more tired of homophobia and having to bring it up again than a lesbian like myself. Probably women of color feel the same way about racism, Jewish women about anti-Semitism, the elderly about ageism, and so on. But the problems still exist and someone must address them. Until feminists learn to include the concerns and perspectives of those women whose oppression we do not directly experience, then the "others" will have to keep bringing up those issues. We must strive to become "one-woman coalitions"—capable of understanding and raising all issues of oppression and seeing our relationship to them: whites speaking about racism, heterosexuals about homophobia, the able-bodied about disabilities, and so on. Only as we do this will we be able to build lasting coalitions.

The last divisive reaction that I want to include here is *limiting outspoken "minority women" to "their issues."* When someone speaks out strongly about her group's specific oppression, she often becomes a token whose leadership in other areas is restricted. For example, I have felt pressure either to work only on lesbian issues or to downplay them if I am involved in other areas of feminist activity. Yet while I am out of the closet and concerned about homophobia, there are many other topics that I want to address besides lesbianism, just as women of color have much to say about many issues in addition to racism. To counter this tendency, I decided in the late 1970s that I would not write any more only about lesbianism, but instead I would address other subjects and incorporate my lesbian feminist analysis within them. Women of all races, classes, ages, and nations have much to say on a whole variety of topics from their particular perspectives. If we limit each to one identity and approach feminism as a string of separate unrelated issues, we narrow the possibilities for insight, growth, and leadership throughout the movement.

Our chances of building successful coalitions are great if we can avoid divisive reactions such as these and see diversity as a strength. As we struggle to learn from our differences rather than to fear or deny them, we can find our common ground. In this process, we also build the atmosphere of good faith and respect necessary for strong coalitions. For while we do not need to love one another or agree on everything, we do need to be able to challenge each other from the assumption that change is possible. Another requirement when diverse groups coalesce is that each be clear about its bottom line. We must know what we need in order to survive in a coalition and how to communicate that to others.

Coalitions that are successful must also be aimed at taking meaningful action in the world. Coalition is not abstract. It functions when groups or individuals are working together around something that each cares about and sees as advancing its goals or vision, or at least protecting the space necessary to develop that. When a coalition has some effect, then it is worth going through the trouble and strife of making it work. It is in the process itself that we often discover the common causes that make it possible to create common coalitions of women in all our diversity working toward both common and varied feminist visions.

II
WOMEN'S LEADERSHIP & POWER

Introduction

Lisa Albrecht and Rose M. Brewer

What we want to underscore in this section of the book is the necessity of feminist theories and practices that not only reflect the diversity of our leadership models but offer us an understanding of how we can be women leaders who create social change. In building successful coalitions, this means we need to respect how we lead differently and assess leadership within the context of a diverse body of feminist theory that helps us attribute differences positively. Nora Hall, in her essay in this collection, quotes Johnetta Cole on leadership: "leadership, at its very base, is about service. It is not about what one accumulates for oneself; it is about what one is able to do in the interest of others." This has certainly been the crux of leadership in the African-American community. This message resonates with both Beth Brant's and Rayna Green's definitions of leadership as well. We find this model of leadership powerful and useful for revisioning women's alliance. It seems to us that members of dominant communities could learn much from these examples of leadership.

The notion of women believing we can be leaders is heretical. Patriarchy has conditioned us to look to men as leaders; when women have risen as leaders, we often get characterized as pushy, aggressive, and bitchy. Everything negative is assigned to female leadership. Clearly women are leaders on multiple fronts, but we have come to believe leadership in the family/private domain is less valuable than

58

leadership in the public domain. Reinforcing that is a history that has looked at male-centered, public acts of leadership as the only kind of leadership worth recording (Kelly, 1984).

As an alternative, Ella Baker practiced a model of leadership worth examining. In Carson's study of the Student Nonviolent Coordinating Committee (SNCC) (cited in Payne, 1989), he articulated Baker's leadership as group-centered. It opposed hierarchy of authority and emphasized the role of ordinary people in the movement. This notion of leadership is an inversion of the traditional thinking we have about leaders; Baker's message is that leaders must constantly engage in self-examination. Leaders need to put their egos and need for recognition second to their work. The seductiveness of media recognition makes this even more dificult. Baker believes that leaders who become media stars lose some of their political effectiveness. "There is also the danger in our culture that, because a person is called upon to give public statements and is acclaimed by the establishment, such a person gets to the point of believing that he [sic] *is* the movement. Such people get so involved with playing the game of being important that they exhaust themselves and their time and they don't do the work of actually organizing people" (Baker, 1972).

It seems to us that Ella Baker's kind of leadership is central to the formation of multicultural alliances. All the pieces in this section of the book represent Baker's vision of "the extraordinary potential of ordinary [women]"(Payne, 1989:885). The women leaders here all believe in themselves, even when going against tremendous odds. They also have a sense of humility that allows them to constantly reflect upon their place in the movement for social change. Rayna Green is quick to remind us that geting her words into print is important but that it means little if she hasn't served her Indian community. Nora Hall's work with Leadership for Black Women reflects a similar commitment. Going hand in hand with belief in self and humility is a constant sense of taking risks. Women leaders, like the women of the International Sweethearts of Rhythm, live at risk, as do the Palestinian women in the intifada. Parkerson's black women filmmakers also live at risk, given their economic marginalization and their marginalization by the film industry. Beth Brant, as a lesbian and an Indian, is always at risk, juggling either homophobic reactions among Indians or racist marginalizations from white feminists. Judith McDaniel, as a white, middle-class woman, urges white women to take risks, and by doing so, reminds us that women with privilege need to break from dominant patterns of comfort.

In understanding leadership and power today, we must constantly reflect on our lives and the material conditions that shape our existence.

In doing so, the women's lives on the forthcoming pages help us to determine the paths of our own lives.

References

Baker, Ella. 1972. "Developing Community Leadership." In Lerner, Gerda, ed. *Black Women in White America: A Documentary History*. New York: Random House.
Kelly, Joan. 1984. "Did Women Have a Renaissance?" In Kelly, Joan, ed. *Women, History and Theory: The Essays of Joan Kelly*. Chicago: University of Chicago Press.
Payne, Charles. 1989. "Ella Baker and Models of Social Change." *Signs* 14:4, 885–99.

American Indian Women
Diverse Leadership for Social Change

Rayna Green

I can't see you out there, because of the stage lights, and I like to see who I'm talking to, so I beg your pardon if I can't look right in the eyes of people I know out there. I know there are people out there that I've known and loved and enjoyed a friendship with in this life, and there are many people here in Minneapolis who have welcomed me into their hearts time and again, and I want to say thank you for that, because I feel like I belong here and am at home. Always, in the Indian world, I am home; there is a kind of kinship, and I want to talk about the importance of kinship in terms of leadership. That kinship comes down close to the real and personal level, and I wish I could see the faces of people that I know and am in that relationship with by the extension of our work together over the years. I especially want to thank all of you of the American Indian Women's Advisory Committee.[1]

But I want to try and bring this issue of leadership home. Because home, community, and family are what Native people are about anywhere, all over the world, and as Laura Waterman Wittstock said, that essential connection to other indigenous people occurs across the world.[2] That is who we are, and it is where we belong. Deprived of our homes, deprived of our communities, we are not able to exercise any of the models that I believe are essential for a survival into a new

61

world that I know all of you believe in. And that is the model that we must continue to strive for. Somehow, deprived of home, to return to it, to restore home never had, to repatriate, essentially, the roles that we all have in our communities. That is the task I want to talk about today.

I want to tell you a story, and some of you may be part of this story, that happened out in Montana a number of years ago. I know there are some people out in the audience from Montana. And I think this story illustrates a little bit of what we're talking about when we talk about leadership roles and when we talk about change. And change is a part of the process that we must factor into leadership.

Everybody usually wants Indian women to talk about tradition instead of change. And so I'm also going to talk about tradition today. I said I would absolutely mention Grandmother Spider at least once in my talk; I'll mention the word "circle" four times. I will refer back to some of those old stories that all of you want to hear real bad. I know you do, I know you do. I know you're out there; and I'll try to do my best.

But I want to talk about change, and really in many ways I want to talk about revolution. Some of you heard me say this before; that in Indian country, maybe the most radical revolution we will ever have is a return to tradition. That paradox is part of what we live with. So I want to tell you this story about a meeting in Montana years ago that was a meeting on energy development in the high plains, a really critical issue there.[3] Now with the bottom out of the coal and oil market, it's not so much of an issue. But then, in 1977, it was a hot one. And in a hotel in Billings, Montana, in the "Custer Room" of the motel, where old battles got replayed every ten seconds—Crow, Cheyenne, Sioux, Gros Ventre, Assiniboine, Flathead, Kootenai, people from oil development firms—and we were having a hot meeting. One gentleman stood up, an Indian gentleman, who in many ways had been very much prodevelopment, very much involved in development—stood up in the middle of the meetings, in a rather strange speech, and said one of the difficulties we were having out in Indian country, and one of the reasons development was such a threat, was that it had destroyed our traditional communities. One of the ways in which those communities had been destroyed, he said, symbolically, was that our women had changed out in Indian country and, oh, they have. There were women in that room, who were sitting at that table, negotiating, discussing. There were women presiding, and it upset him because they weren't back home with their families the way he thought they ought to be and the way he had been taught by missionaries that they ought to be. We all knew that, and he made a very passionate speech about the breakdown of moral order in Indian country as exemplified by the change in these women who were really behaving rather badly. A young woman stood up and tried to make a passionate speech against that opinion, and she didn't get very far until an older lady stood up, and that older lady happens to be from Laura Wittstock's country. Iroquois country, and they have some extraordinary role models out there for Indian women, let me tell you, and she stood up and said, "You know, I'm very interested in your speech about the old days—your old days must have been really different than our old days, because in our old days, women were at the seat of power; women were, with men, equal sharers of whatever we now call power; women and men had mutual responsibilities, mutual dependencies, mutual roles, in carrying out the business of survival for our people. In our old days, women were at the center of knowledge and understanding about leadership, about distribution of power, about the distribution of goods and about the allotments of roles and power. Because they of all people, are the mothers. They raised up the chiefs to power for life, essentially, unless they betrayed the trust of the people, which was unlikely; when they put those chiefs in power, they did so because they of all people, who had raised all of the children, knew who would best carry out the responsibilities of the people. A long time ago in Iroquois country, when the Peacemaker came to Jigonsanhsanh,[4] a woman at a place called Gadondagon many years ago, she believed his message of peace; she believed in the great law of peace; and she was the first Seneca person to believe that message, Jigonsanhsanh was—in Cherokee we call her *Ghigau*—was the first clan mother, the first Beloved Woman, in essence.[5] Because she believed in that message of peace, a special role for women in our world was created. And that special role really meant that women were at the center of leadership. Let's talk about the old days; I say, 'Bring on the old days.' "

And she brought down the house. And I say in some ways, bring on the old days, but of course the old days are here with us always. The old days are always with native people, because our historical memory exists into the present, and we act on historical memory; history is for us the living present. Sometimes it chokes us, sometimes it breaks our hearts again. But I believe we are here to fulfill the promise of our history. We of all people in America are here to fulfill American history's purpose. And in a way, our leadership can help take American history back from the dark swamp into which it has fallen. In many respects, our notions of leadership could help in taking our own history back if in fact our traditions for leadership were acknowledged, understood, and appreciated, in their differences, in the conventional role models for leadership that we have now.

I want to talk about some of these conventions for leadership in our communities, for women and for men. I want to talk about how they've changed and how they move, and how we can reinterpret them. I want to talk about the expectations for leadership, the styles of leadership, and the models for leadership we have. I think there will be some surprises in those. But I also want to talk about what types of leadership we are *not* about, and I want to talk about *who* and *what* leadership is for. I hope that we can come to redeem the notions of what leadership is for in our own communities, as well as set our own examples for our own communities for the future. If those examples have any relevance for other folks, so be it; we're not in the business of peddling our culture in order to have it expropriated. Nor need we be in the business of peddling our culture as morally right when others are morally wrong, any more than we are in the business as women of peddling a vision of humankind where there is absolute moral right and moral wrong. We all bear the burden of our own failures and must, as we bear the burden of change for the future.

Let me talk about some of those kinds of leadership. There are our traditional models of leadership—and here we get to the stories that everybody likes, and I like them too. There are many traditional models for leadership. But I don't want to talk about them in the way that people often talk about them, as generic Indian categories, because there ain't no such thing. There is no such thing as "Indians," of course. That is an invention of anthropologists, and I'm trying to liberate us from some of those categories. There are many, many native people of this world, and each of them has leadership models that apply to the roles of women.

If Paula Gunn Allen were here, she would talk about Grandmother Spider, I think. She would talk about the weaving, and she would talk about the web that is woven by Grandmother Spider, who is one of our mothers in particular parts of Indian country.[6] Sue Williams, if she were here, and flo wiger,[7] who is here, could talk about other kinds of grandmothers; they would talk about White Buffalo Calf Woman. Many of you, I think, know some of those stories; and they would talk about that model for leadership. It's a very different model from Grandmother Spider in many ways; yet some of the roles are the same. From my own Southeastern people I would talk about Selu, Corn Mother, or the Beloved Woman, who are our mothers, too. All of these promote different models, not necessarily because of the actions required from them, but the different domains in which they govern our lives. Those models are with us all the time; there are hundreds of those models, hundreds of them; some people would call it mythological characters, I simply call it history.

We all have to pay attention to those traditional models, those historic models, those artistic models, when we look at our roles in

Indian country. Some of us were born to weave the web of life. Paula Gunn Allen was born to do that, Laura Waterman Wittstock, flo wiger, those of us who are writers in many ways, and artists, have that responsibility upon us. To weave the web of life, to keep it together, to tat up the web, to keep the threads together, to keep the warp weft together, this is what we were born to do. For others of us, we were born, metaphorically, to till the soil, perhaps, but I think more importantly, to feed the people, to be the staff of life, to be the grain, to be the bread for the people, and that is another model.

For others of us, we were born, like White Buffalo Calf Woman, to bring truth, like Jigonsanhsanh, to bring the word of peace. Bringing the pipe, White Buffalo Calf Woman brought truth and the ability to tell the truth. Perhaps, in our time, she would have been called a politician. But how perverted that notion has become, how perverted the notion of a diplomat has become, if we do not follow the real model of the peacemaker, of Jigonsanhsanh, the woman of peace, who was a real historical character, or White Buffalo Calf Woman, who is the aesthetic character, the mythological character who gives us the character for our behavior in some parts of Indian country. Those perverted models for behavior are many. But they exist alongside models that are just as important and that women have been deprived of. I'm talking about other possibilities for traditional behavior, like Coyote, Rabbit, and Spider.[8] Those have traditionally been thought by literary people and anthropologists to be male figures. And I say to you here, women are tricksters, too. We like a joke as well as anybody, and we can turn the tables. Like all of those characters, even White Buffalo Calf Woman, there is a sexual element to that world; Indian women who have been deprived of that remarkable energy that comes from a reclamation of their own sexuality can claim Coyote, Rabbit, Spider and many other characters as their own as well. We are not simply pristine chapels of blonde holiness, with a guru-like wisdom; we too can fail, and we play tricks, and we have fun. And if we do not remember those models, we will have lost our own souls. So, I think, we have to reclaim those models. We will not be denied creative craziness; we need all our artistic roles, not just a small sampling of them.

But there are other models that are just as significant, and I want to talk about those traditional models because they belong to everyone. We understand them differently from community to community, but I'm talking here about models of kinship: mother, sister, grandmother, aunt. And it is those models that universally are used by Indian women to measure their capacity for leadership and to measure the success of their leadership. I want to talk about that in contrast with achievement models, which in fact are somewhat uncomfortable for us. Because those roles of grandmother, aunt, sister, and mother belong to all of us, just as uncle, father, grandfather, and brother belong to men. We each have our domain, and the domains each mean different things to different people. But all of us in Indian country have to achieve in those domains. Please, don't hear me say that all of us have to be each one of those literally. Because a bunch of us would flop if we had to be one of those literally. I am more of a biological mother to my dog, as my friends know. He bonded to me instantly. Several of my friends accuse me, with my computer and my dog, of dating out of my species. So women like me are going to blow it in the role of mother if left to the narrow, biological role. But in Indian country, that role was never understood necessarily only as a biological role; grandma was never understood as a biological role; sister, and aunt were never understood in the narrow confines of genetic kinship. How liberating that can be, if we believe that the community of humankind is our community and our family, how liberating it can be, and yet how burdensome to realize that we can fulfill all of those roles to our fellow human beings—our sister human beings—because that complexity is our life, our continuity, our family, our clan, our children, our nephews, our nieces, our brothers, our sisters, our dear children, our grandchildren. Whether or not we fill the biological roles in the Indian community, they are there for us.

To be an Indian grandma is probably the nicest thing that could ever happen to anybody, and Laura Wittstock talked just a little bit about that joy to know an Indian grandma. I wish everybody had one. But we're not going to issue you one at the back door. Maybe for a small amount, we can work it out. To get me as a grandma could cost you, but I'm not signing up for that. Still, to be an Indian grandma is an extraordinary role. There's a wonderful film made by a Canadian Indian artist named Alanis Obomsawin called *Mothers of Many Children,* and in the native community, the primary roles of leadership are the roles with those kinship names. They are not the role of doctor, lawyer, you know what. They are not the role of Princess Summerfallwinterspring, or whatever her name is. They are not the role of Miss Mazola. My people do call it maize, but . . . we don't sell it on television. This gift of the female spirit is not a commodity to be sold, or bought, or acquired. It is simply a presence to be experienced. And the burdens placed upon those roles of auntie, grandma, and sister are extraordinary in Indian country. At the Smithsonian, the standing joke is that I'm Auntie Rayna, because I get these Indian kids from all over the country to come and be my interns. A lot of my friends send their kids; I've currently got two young men who are the children of one of my best friends. She calls Auntie Rayna once every week to test my temperature and see how

I'm holding up. At the Smithsonian, that role is called an internship sponsor or a mentor; but the real truth is, that the way it translates out, in Indian country, is that I'm fulfilling my leadership in Indian country by being an aunt. You can call it anything else you want. Yes, I'm an academic sponsor. Yes, I monitor their academic progress. Yes, I give them scholarly assignments, research, and so forth. But that's not what it's about. And the burden on me to do that does not come from my annual evaluation of my personnel file and credit gained in civil service heaven. The burden on me to do that does not come from anything the Smithsonian Institution—Mother Museum, I call it—asks me to do. In fact, I invented that category there, because I was born to be an auntie.

The Indian community expects that of me. Because the role is one of care taking, it's a surrogate role—we invented surrogate parenting, by the way—I want to tell you, it's an old story with us. An old man in the Indian child welfare hearings a few years ago was asked, or the question was posed to him by social workers, about the huge number of "illegitimate children" on Indian reservations (this used as a justification for taking them away from their natural biological families, which means mommy and daddy). And this dilemma was posed to him, that there are so many illegitimate children on Indian reservations. "What are you going to do about that?" they asked him. And he said, "Oh, but we love all our children, we love all our children."

In the Indian community, the act of loving all our children is precisely the role that we must all play, whether or not it has a biological underpinning. All of those roles give us enormous opportunity and flexibility, because we can mutate, we can move, we can be mother, sister, grandmother, and aunt at the same time. And those roles have different burdens upon them. The role of grandma to teach, to be wise, and bring that wisdom to bear upon the teaching of young people is enormous. I'm reminded of a wonderful story that was told by a friend of mine about inviting a distinguished speaker to a university one time, and the distinguished speaker arrived in a condition that was somewhat disgraceful. He was not able to speak. They propped him up with some food and coffee, and he finally got on the stage, and he started to tell about what happened when he got his doctoral degree. He'd been away from home a long time. He started to speak, and said, "I've been away from home, I've been away from my grandma." And in Indian country, just the word "grandma" means "sit up, take notice—she's the one." "And so," he continued, "when I finished my doctorate, I'd been away from my people for so long, and I wanted to go and see my grandma. So I went back home, and I rented a pick-up truck, and I drove far out in the desert (this was in the Southwest) to see my grandma. And I got there, and she gave

me some hot coffee, and some food, and I sat down in her home, and
I said, 'Grandma, teach me the old ways.' And you know, the old
bitch never told me a damn thing."

Contrary to the implied stereotype of the old lady who teaches old
ways, she didn't tell him a damn thing because he wasn't worth telling
anything. But she had fulfilled her role, because Indian grandmas teach
the willing and they teach the able. And to know who is willing and
able is part of grandmahood, out there in Indian country. I can't be
a grandma yet because I'm still making some inept distinctions; I'm
not yet able to do it. But those roles are critical. And they are at the
heart of what we talk about when we talk about leadership, because
leadership is bonded and defined in community. Leadership for us is
not achievement, in the normative mainstream sense. That I have a
doctorate makes not a damn bit of difference in Indian country. That
I ever write a line makes no difference. That I ever give a speech like
this makes no difference. What makes a difference for me, and for all
the other native women, who are shaped and formed in the cradle, the
cradle-board, I should say, of Indian leadership, is what we give to
our communities. If I never do a thing that counts in this forum—and
I honor this forum, I assure you, I honor it, I've learned to, and I
appreciate it, and I enjoy this forum, for another reason which I'll talk
about—if I never do these things again, it won't matter to me or to
my community, if I have not done what is demanded and expected of
a person with real leadership ability in my community, which is to
give to it. The richest person in the Indian community is the person
who gives the most away. Indian people will know that. We can't stay
rich long. Even if the outside world validates our parking ticket of
life by adding a check to it, that check will get chopped up and
redistributed if we are, in fact, the leaders we say we are or that our
community believes us to be. In fact, our communities don't talk about
leadership in those terms at all, because leadership is validated and
uniformly informed, in our communities, by the invisibility of things
that are called leadership in the mainstream communities. Degrees,
lists of achievements, lists of high-powered jobs, the wearing of power
suits—I look ridiculous in one—are nothing. What counts is how
much we give. And how much we are a part of the community. I was
telling Margaret Raymond last Friday night as I was flipping
hamburgers for thirty kids who were at the Smithsonian this summer
as interns, I thought to myself, why am I here? What am I doing
here—it was 104 degrees, I'm turning hamburgers on a grill, I've got
thirty hungry kids out there—and here I am, you know, I don't have
to do this. Well, I do have to do it. I have to do it because it feels
good. The reason that it feels good is because I'm doing what I was
made to do. Now don't hear that another way: I was not, in the sense

of an Indian country and western song written by a friend of mine called, "Mama Was Born to Chew Hides." That's about all I would have been good for, by the way, in the old days—I have so few traditional skills that in the old days they would have put me out to die. Don't hear that as a speech that says, women should go back to the home and hearth. That's not what I'm saying. I'm saying, home and hearth is a kind of fulfillment that is legitimate and real. And it can be paralleled with other roles; it always has been. You could call it clan mother, you could call it grandmother, you could call it aunt, you could call it tribal chairman—it does not matter. You could call it doctor, lawyer, you know what. The point is that none of those exist alone. In Indian country, there never was a choice for leadership between doing just one thing and doing everything else. It is the everything else that is expected. We have our specialties, and there are kinds of leadership we acknowledge that are extraordinary. And I believe in the context of the women's movement and of Indian self-determination, that we can come back to acknowledge those roles after neglecting them for a long time.

Another role of leadership that we could always fulfill in our communities was an aesthetic role—the role of artist, however artist is defined. That aesthetic role is essential to our identity; it is not apart from it. It is an aesthetic role that demands beauty, however beauty is defined by tribal people. It demands that we participate in it, by creating it, by loving it, by understanding it, and by interpreting it throughout the centuries for our people. That artistic role is not alien. It's not separate from our role as leader, in whatever forms we choose to exercise that leadership. We are healers, and those roles are valued. We are the people who give to our communities and operate in that context. That creates difficulties for us in the mainstream world. Because very often our notions of leadership and our notions of credibility and our notions of how we will be evaluated and judged in that world don't match with the other world. We are the mothers of many children.

People talk about the stress experienced by people of color living in the majority world. Well some of that stress is caused, not by the conflict of living between two worlds—I'm half German/Jewish and half Indian, with a bagel in one hand, a peace of frybread in the other. It's not like that; that's not the kind of stress I'm talking about, although it gets kind of interesting. Do you put cream cheese on your frybread, or dip your bagel in sassafras tea? What I'm talking about is our confusion when a role of leadership that's valid in one context is not valid in the other. Or when those roles of leadership are complete opposites. It's hard for me to get my ticket punched in the mainstream world for being an auntie. You have to be called something else. And perhaps one of the roles of leadership that we can exercise is enabling people to translate what we are into what they think we are, but in many ways I don't want to be responsible for that translation. I would like it if I could fulfill both of those roles and have them called the same thing. But that's not possible perhaps. The conflicts in those roles are difficult, and they do cause stress, and they make it impossible for native women *and* native men to live in the world that expects different things of them and that values different things. Our achievements on paper, our jobs, our awards, our grades—however these things are valued—our civil service ratings, our chairmanships, and so forth, are roles of leadership that can count for nothing in our communities if they do not translate back to good health and survival for Indian communities, and so that makes for a difficulty.

With someone like me, I write, and I write for myself, primarily. But when I write and publish, if that publication has no use in Indian communities or in the communities to which the publication is directed—and they often have been directed to other communities, to mathematicians, to groups of women, to a wide range of people—I feel a failure. And yet in the scholarly world, such a utility is the last thing that is valued. So I'm stuck, I have to have things be useful. Service—service publications, service jobs, you know, all those of you in academia, you understand this—are not valued, but in our communities, they are deeply valued. What I do with my scholarship has got to work for people—to make change, to create dynamic change, or for me, it doesn't work, it's no good, it's not beautiful. A poem must work, as well as mean, as well as be.

Who my leadership is for matters to me. My leadership, as well as the leadership of other native women, measured by the values in our communities, has relevance for whom it works. And what I do cannot be for someone who is my "supervisor." It cannot be for someone who is my boss. It has to be for other people, or it does not work for me. It has to work for Indian people and it has to work in those communities. So words like community and concepts like "kinship," "grandma" and "aunt" are not antithetical to the words "leadership" and "power." In fact in our communities, I believe these words are the equivalent of it. Power is given to those who give. Power belongs to those who give it away. Or as an old hippie professor of mine used to say, "You know you can get a lot of work done if you don't care whose name is on it."

The credit counts, the names count. I love seeing my name in print—we all do. It's a big thrill; every time I get something published I think it's wonderful. I get such a charge out of it, if I like it. Sometimes after I've written it I don't like it at all, but ultimately the name doesn't matter. It is "anon," who is of course a woman. But it's more important than anonymous. It is in fact the message and not the author which is validated in the Indian community; it matters that they take pride in the message *and* the authorship, I believe fully. I don't always act on it, but I do believe it—that such notions are what leadership and power are about in our communities.

Let me speak just a couple of minutes on something leadership and power are not about. Our leadership in native communities has got to be primarily for, by, about, and with Indian people. That may seem exclusive, it may seem narrow, it may seem profoundly parochial. But that is its necessary direction. If we choose to take some of those roles to a national forum, a regional forum, outside of our own communities, that is because there is a certain personal satisfaction in this and because Indian people need something from that venue. I don't want you to think for one minute that any satisfaction that comes to any Indian woman or any Indian man in this world comes only from giving up everything to the community. We are not thoughtless communitarians. We are individuals. We do take personal pride and personal pleasure in things. And that is important, it's significant. I don't want to diminish that aspect. But it is evaluated and understood in the context of our community. Our power and our leadership has to be for those communities, because they need us for their survival. If it has relevance outside, it's because it has relevance outside and can be used and can be understood, can be appreciated. And so our turning inward is for survival, and our leadership must be understood in those contexts.

Another thing that leadership is *not* about, though—I think this is really critical—it worries me deeply that many people look toward Indians to fulfill this need for leadership. Healing is an important category in our own communities, but I do not believe that non-Indians should look to us for healing. We know in Indian country never to speak for anybody else, but I think I'll go out on this limb and speak for many who feel as I do. We are not your gurus, we are not your healers, and we cannot fulfill that role for you. Non-Indians want us to be their spiritual leaders, to be their gurus. To take our roles of leadership as understood internally in our own communities and to turn them outward to heal America of its ills. And we cannot do that. There has been so much abuse of this role that it's frightening. I'm not diminishing the need. I'm not diminishing our actual power in those realms—*all*—indigenous peoples have that power, because we speak from the earth. That's a cliche, and yet it stands, I think. But we cannot heal you; only you can heal yourselves. That's a cliche, yet it holds truth. If we have any model to give, it is an aesthetic model, a cultural model, that works for us. And we must continue to work for *us*. And it must continue to work primarily in our own communities, because we have ills too, just like you, and we need to heal ourselves as well. We need all of our spiritual leaders right now in our communities. We were never intended to move outside of those; we don't proselytize; we're not selling a religious commodity. That is a type of leadership I don't believe many of us want to exercise. It cannot be sold or bought. It stands for itself alone. That it is attractive to people is understandable; that it is important and that it survives against the onslaughts and the assaults that the American government and missionaries and the whole range of people who tried and now try to assault it is what counts.

That it needs to survive is perhaps an area of responsibility that falls on non-Indians, on you. But to teach you to take it and be a part of it is not the kind of leadership we are about. We are not about exercising a kind of leadership that is morally defunct; we are not about exercising a kind of leadership that will fail us all. We have our own failures to account for, and in our own communities we know those as well.

What native people are about is survival—the survival of those types of leadership that we've talked about today. And if you have any role in those, if you do not belong to a Native community, it is the role of your friendship. It is the role of your support. It is the obligation role of your care taking of American life and culture, and we are squarely in the mainstream of that culture. We are not apart from it. We are, in fact, essential to it. If we have any leadership role to project at all, that is critical for the survival of our own people and for the survival of all the people of the earth, it is that role as the definer and heartbeat of American culture, of American history. To take that back means that we will all survive in the future. That is the role of leadership and power that we can exercise even outside our own mortality. What other gift could you give, what better gift could you give to the future, than that role, and that is the role I hope we can play for all of you, certainly for all of us.

Notes

1. The American Indian Women's Advisory Committee came together to work with other Minnesota women in planning the NWSA 1988 conference. This committee was responsible for the large presence of American Indian women at the conference and their participation at all levels of the event. The committee members were Sharon Day, flo wiger, Rose Robinson, Margaret P. Raymond, Elaine Salinas, Mona Smith, and Wanda Weyaus.
2. Laura Waterman Wittstock (Seneca), an activist and journalist from New York, is Director of Migizi Communications in Minneapolis. Migizi publishes a newsletter and produces a regular public radio program on Indian affairs. She was also a speaker at the 1988 NWSA conference.
3. For a superb resource on Indian energy and minerals resource development and protection, see Marjane Ambler, *Breaking the Bonds: American Indian Minerals Development*, University of Kansas Press, Lawrence, KS, 1990.

4. The Peacemaker, in Iroquois Tradition, is the person who brought "The Great Law of Peace" to the Iroquois peoples. This law sets down the sacred and secular rules by which the six tribes of Iroquois banded together and by which they must live.

5. *Ghigau* is the word that refers to the Beloved Woman of Cherokee tradition. She would have been the senior clan mother or person who was the most acknowledged wise female person of her time; she directed the Women's Council and led the people in various forms of decision making.

6. For an explanation of traditional mythological figures such as Grandmother Spider, Selu, White Buffalo Calf Woman in feminist and literary terms, see Paula Gunn Allen. *The Sacred Hoop: Recovering the Feminine in American Indian Traditions.* Beacon Press, Boston, 1986. Paula Gunn Allen (Laguna/Sioux/Lebanese) is a literary critic and writer who teaches at University of California Berkeley, in Native American Studies.

7. Susan Williams (Sioux) is a noted lawyer from Albuquerque; flo wiger (Sioux) is an academic activist from St. Cloud State University, St. Cloud, MN.

8. See Allen, *Sacred Hood,* for references to traditional trickster/transformer figures.

African-American Women Leaders and the Politics of Alliance Work

Nora Hall

Questions regarding the social status of African-American women have been raised by many notable scholars over the past decade, but very little critical attention has been given to studying our leadership roles. There is much to learn from African-American women as a group since we have exercised influence in American workplaces since the seventeenth century. Even though the boundaries of our "workplace positions" have been severely limited by our social status, we have managed to build strong political alliances[1] intraculturally[2] and cross-culturally.[3] Such alliances have been formed within African-American communities and with other communities, as well as across gender, class, racial, ideological, and philosophical lines.

Despite our apparent influence, as Patricia Bell Scott found in her 1982 study, our "leadership potential is not being realized and contributions of contemporary African-American women leaders are largely unrecognized."[4]

We should, therefore, give significant attention to exploring African-American women's leadership with a strategic focus on leadership as it pertains to working across party lines. While African-American women have had success in building alliances across political lines, the barriers that we have faced have been tremendous.

The purpose of this chapter is to begin that inquiry by concentrating on a theoretical exploration of the contemporary African-American woman's skills in alliance building. Building stronger alliances is a major challenge for all leaders in the future as we move toward greater acknowledgment of pluralism. Without ongoing attention to skill building for stronger alliances, even African-American women who already know a great deal about building political relationships will not be able to clearly articulate the Black woman's agenda in the highly competitive, limited-resource society that we are fast becoming. It is already clear to me that future alliance building will prove to be far more demanding than building political relationships today.[5]

Extensive attention to the details of competing parties and limited resources will force alliances in many areas. If we do not hone in on the skills that African-American women have practiced for centuries, we will find ourselves involved in conflicts beyond our imagination and miss opportunities for social change.

This chapter will use a case study from my research and secondary sources to demonstrate how African-American women have used mediation and negotiation skills in their alliance work. It will link the existence of such skills to leaders in alliance work and outline the value of leadership training that assists individuals in skill building.

The specific questions posed in this discussion are: (1) What are the varying social contexts in which African-American women leaders operate in their efforts to build alliances? (2) What are the sources and limits of African-American women leaders' power when attempting to build alliances?[6] (3) What are the connections between personal growth/development and social change?

Race/gender leadership and alliance building

An important aspect of the African-American woman's skills in alliance building has been shaped by her social status: She is both African-American and female. Gender and race affiliations have made it necessary for African-American women to develop political relationships across cultural lines as a matter of survival. One might argue that coalition workers of any race give close attention to factors such as race, gender, class, religion, or political ideology. However, leaders have been significantly lacking in their mediation and negotiation skills; thus many collaborations have failed at the onset.

Establishing strong, sustainable alliances requires much greater attention to such factors than leaders today realize. Likewise, the multiple definitions of factors such as race, religion, class—when operable within particular groups and individuals—calls for strong mediation skills among alliance leaders. It is important for leaders to have the ability to use the nuances of the group while moving toward action and vision.

As early as 1944 Gunnar Myrdal recognized the value of studying race and leadership. His book *An American Dilemma* included a chapter on "Negro Leadership."[7] John Higham is also among the scholars who have explored race and leadership. His book *Ethnic Leadership in America* was published in 1978 following a symposium at Johns Hopkins University.[8] Higham's work discusses Jews, Japanese, Germans, Native Americans, eastern and southern Europeans, Irish and African-Americans. Higham explained the complexity of political relations, especially when a group is led by a nongroup member. One example of such a relationship is the slave as follower and master as leader.[9]

Of the few scholars who have researched leadership from the perspective of race, the contributions of John Hope Franklin and August Meier are of particular interest. While connections between race, gender, and leadership are more difficult to find in existing literature, it is increasingly evident to politicians and other leaders that they must personally build and designate staff time to political group relationships across gender and racial lines. As an example, Donna Brazile, who worked closely with Michael Dukakis during his 1988 presidential campaign, was reported to be Dukakis' "in-house expert on black politics."[10] Likewise the abortion issue will continue to force political leaders in the 1990s to be more sensitive to women.

While attention to the politics of race, gender, and leadership may be new to many, African-American women have worked with the salient factors of race, class, and gender all our lives. Our socially ascribed statuses have made us sensitive to the politics of being women and African-Americans. As such, many of us have learned to bridge cultural gaps and juggle the political realities of having distinct and often conflicting political allies. No doubt, many individuals have profited from our long histories as cultural mediators without even being conscious of the skills exhibited. Consider, for example, the African woman's role during slavery. She was often forced to maintain one relationship with the mistress, another with the master, and had yet other relationships with her family and her community.

In 1982, when Scott introduced research on African-American women leaders, she called for greater public recognition of African-American women and the development of programs that trained women leaders.[11] Scott understood what African-American women could teach others as well as a need for more information-sharing among African-American women as a group.

Contexts for alliance and coalition work

> Without a doubt, Black women were and still are the "builders" in
> these United States of America. They stand as survivors at the socio-
> political, educational, cultural, economic, and religious crossroads of
> the American scene.[12]

As Marianna Davis points out in her research, which chronicles 200
years of African-American women's contributions in the fields of
politics, government, media, business, commerce, law, medicine,
science, civil rights, sports, art, and education, we have and continue
to exhibit leadership in nearly every conceivable field even when
obstacles to our success seem insurmountable. A few notable
accomplishments by contemporary African-American women include
the election of Crystal Bird Fauset to the Pennsylvania State Assembly
in 1938—marking the first election of an African-American woman
to a major U.S. public office. In 1968, Shirley Chisholm became the
first Black woman in the U.S. to be elected to the House of
Representatives. Rebecca Lee, a graduate of the New England Female
Medical College, became the first African-American woman doctor in
the U.S. in 1864. Lee established a successful practice in Richmond,
Virginia, following the Civil War. Jewel Plummer Cobb, a scientist,
has received international attention for her research on cancer, which
began in 1955.[13] The first African-American woman war correspondent
to cover the Vietnam War was Ethel L. Payne. Maggie Lena Draper
Walker, the daughter of a slave, became the first woman bank president
in America and the first African-American female to hold such a
position. Payne formed the St. Luke's Penny Savings Bank of
Richmond, Virginia, around 1886. The bank was later renamed the
Saint Luke's Bank and Trust Company.[14] Despite these firsts, it has
not been possible for mass numbers of African women to enter
professional fields. Jacqueline Jones explained in her study about the
work and family life of Black women from 1830 to 1980:

> Because of their doubly disadvantaged status, black women were
> confined to two types of work that seemed ironically contradictory—
> the first was domestic and institutional service, . . . the other was
> manual labor . . . The vast majority of black female wage earners
> were barred from peacetime factory labor and from the traditional
> (white) female occupations of the 1960s.[15]

The field of work, however, has never been the defining characteristic
of the African-American woman's power. We have been required to

"politic" whether or not our sphere of influence was in the corporate board room, the cotton field, or the family. Our social status has clearly made us aware of the alliances that were and are necessary for protection. Consequently, Black women have taken responsibility for building alliances in five major areas: (1) organizations/institutions serving a broad public interest both profit and nonprofit, including government agencies, religious institutions, political appointments; (2) community and grassroots organizing; (3) special interest groups, such as organizations serving African American communities and specialized service areas; (4) corporate enterprises, including small business ownership and agriculture/farming; and (5) fighting for children's rights.

Sources and limits of power: the paradox in alliance work

My research with more than 400 African-American women in Minnesota suggests that we often define our power as "personal rather than institutional." That definition prevents us from limiting ourselves to the boundaries of our often narrowly defined roles within organizations. African-American women from all walks of life report that they are very comfortable "being in charge." We share collective memories of parents, especially mothers, who taught us to be resourceful and independent. In that context we see our personal power bases as limitless.[16]

Often, however, we are not as successful as we want to be in our use of personal power to attain goals. For example, today many African-American women who have obtained positions in the corporate world feel like outsiders, "unable to fit into the predominantly white, male corporate culture."[17] Though we have the skills to understand and connect cross-culturally—skills acquired and polished as a result of our social status—the value of these abilities often is not recognized by colleagues, even though such individuals benefit from the way we mediate and negotiate cross-cultural interactions. As one African-American woman reported:

> I have good relationships with whites, but I recognize that yes, I'm the one who makes the effort. Ever since I can remember, that's been my job, to be the integrationist; I don't even resent it any more. Maybe I've been doing it so long that I'm not really even aware of it.[18]

Being handed the integrationist responsibility becomes a challenge for African-American women, even though we relish the role as an extension of our talents. Since so few leaders practice and/or acknowledge the value of negotiation and mediation skills—the skills required for effective cross-cultural interactions—it becomes difficult for such leaders to fully utilize the contributions of African-American women as well as make use of many other forms of diversity among team members. Poor cross-cultural skills result in conflicted and nonsupportive working relationships. This same scenario can play itself out when community organizers attempt to build alliances.

In alliance work, many African-American women attribute lack of success to nonsupportive political factions: individuals and groups that benefit from our skills yet attach no concrete authority to our roles. Such dominant American processes and structures, with established patterns of exclusion that benefit from but do not acknowledge diversity, construct many barriers for us. Patterns derived from case studies of African-American women, be they political group leaders, nonprofit directors, special interest group leaders, government appointees, academic administrators, child care workers, clergy, and/or homemakers, suggest that the American public needs enormous help in framing social and political issues so that policies, procedures, and structures are more inclusive of racial, ethnic, cultural, gender, and class concerns—to name a few. Yet we continue to place very little value on the skills and expertise of those we can learn from.

African-American women leaders will argue that our "personal" power is derived from family and friendship connections and our political supporters are the source of public power. Most of us will admit that we allow two narrowly defined political groups to become the focus of our attention. Those groups are the dominant American culture (i.e., white) and African-American communities. Recently, some of us have started to acknowledge Asian, Hispanic, American Indian, and other political groups as potential allies. Within all of these groups are many political factions that we must appeal to. An African-American woman, working in a corporate environment, points out the realities of a diverse society:

> working in a white environment, sooner or later you're forced to acknowledge your Blackness. Even if you come from a background where you're just one of the kids—white, Asian, brown, whatever—someday there's going to be something, and either you're going to have that inner strength to fall back on, or it's going to throw you. [19]

How does an African-American woman respond cross-culturally in today's complex world, which places no value on the politics of difference? The point is easily demonstrated by District Judge Pamela Alexander commenting during a conference held for Black women leaders in 1988. Judge Alexander acknowledged that racism continues to exist and leaders must use their skills to respond to such situations when they occur in the context of their work environment:

> White defendants have called me nigger. But I was lucky enough to
> be able to say "Contempt 90 days!" There are always adjustments that
> people are going to have to make anytime we get into positions of
> authority.[20]

No matter what type of position an African-American woman holds,
incidents such as this one are likely to occur at significant points in
her career. The future is apt to hold far more complexity around these
issues. Thus if African-American women and other leaders do not
continue to build cross-cultural skills in the wake of an ever-changing
society, our efforts to build strong alliances will not succeed.

We recognize that it is important to create new strategies in response
to these challenges. They require that we fine tune our cross-cultural
skills and acquire more information about how to deal with varying
political factions. For many of us these barriers seem impenetrable.
Thus, it becomes vital for African-American women to build alliances
in response to such injustices. Political relationships that are racially
and gender-biased pose the greatest threats and challenges for African-
American women, yet we cannot avoid responding to them whether
we are building alliances at the grassroots or legislative level.

As an example, the African-American woman's relationship with an
African-American male corporate colleague is sometimes shrouded
when she meets that same male in the African-American community
because her power is likely to be diminished. African-American
communities reflect dominant culture in the way they defines women's
roles. African-American communities have not done a very good job
of responding to sexual oppression; thus in many cases African-
American women leaders are not viewed as seriously as males in
leadership roles. In such cases we must use different strategies to acquire
support when interacting with African-American males in contrast to
skills used for interactions with dominant or other culture males.
African-American women and men have tangled histories, particularly
when it comes to workplace politics. The way an issue is framed in
the African-American community, whether or not it is factually
inaccurate, can create obstacles for women attempting to build alliances.
As Gloria Joseph and Jill Lewis point out: "The Black movement scorns
feminism partially on the basis of misinformation, and partially due
to valid perception of the White middle-class nature of the
movement."[21] That framework, for example, creates distrust among
some African-American males toward corporate women, women who
call themselves independent, feminist, womanist, or any label that
suggests equality with African-American males. For those who do not
understand African-American culture, such factors can severely limit
cross-cultural interactions.

Another source of conflict is the notion in African-American communities that males are not given the same economic and educational opportunities as women. The politics of that situation places enormous strain on both family and colleagial relationships. This has been a historical issue for African-American women. To be sure, it creates tensions within community settings and when African-American males and females work colleagially.

These distinct perspectives as viewed by dominant culture and African-American culture are in no way simplistic. In many cases both perspectives are both true and false. For example, of the groups in the U.S. labor force, African-American women remain the lowest paid as a group. They are often the last hired and first fired in some job categories. African-American males, on the other hand, often reach higher levels within the corporate structure than do women. Males are still the highest paid Black professionals. Yet unemployment among African-American males is the highest in the nation.[22] The contradictory elements create great dilemmas when building political relationships. It is not unusual, then, for African-American women to report shock when they experience sexism from Black males because we share the burden of racism. A similar blow is felt when we encounter racist white feminists.

The degree of the African-American woman's success in building alliances is strongly linked to her cross-cultural skills and the cross-cultural skills of the key players in political groups. When political group members do not have good cross-cultural skills, it limits our success.

Generally, African-American women leaders find that they must develop cross-class skills no matter what socioeconomic level they reach. Class issues raise major concerns for Black women when dealing with African-American and white political groups.

Issues of class within the African-American community, like sexism, have not been properly addressed. In some circles, for example, one has to be from a middle- to upper-income bracket to be considered for certain positions. Similarly, individuals perceived to be from the "Black bourgeoisie" may not be welcomed at the grassroots level.

Of all political relationships, perhaps the greatest challenge that we as African-American women face today is building strong alliances among ourselves. In the past, we did a commendable job collaborating with one another. Josephine St. Pierre Ruffin is perhaps most notable for her early work in this area.

In 1895 she convened the First National Conference of Colored Women in Boston. During that meeting the women agreed to form a national organization. Thus the National Federation of Afro-American Women (NFAW) was founded that same year with Margaret Murray

Washington as president. The NFAW united thirty-six women's clubs in twelve states. In 1896 the National Association of Colored Women (NACW) was formed, bringing together the National League of Colored Women, the National Federation of Afro-American Women, and more than 100 local women's organizations. Gerda Lerner reports that "it became a unifying force, an authoritative voice in defense of Black womanhood." At its ninth biennial meeting in 1914 it represented more than 50,000 Black women in twenty-eight state federations and over one thousand clubs.[23]

Our history demonstrates the power of organizing. Recalling it provides us with data to support our current efforts. Our sisters undoubtedly recognized that the African- American woman's agenda is best represented when she can be called upon in mass to respond. There is a lesson in that for contemporary African American women. First, African-American women today should draw upon their histories for resilience and support. Second, we must use our cross-cultural skills to better discover, clearly define, and build upon ourselves.

For generations we have concentrated on the political factions at work within the African-American community as a whole. This meant that we dealt with the African-American male's agenda and did not consider building and fostering leadership among African-American women. We have also spent a great deal of energy focusing on dominant culture only to realize that neither feminists nor white males had our best interests at heart. Many of us are now discovering that we must work together with other African-American women to create effective strategies to further our success in our various leadership roles. This does not mean that we will not join together with feminists, African-American males, and other political groups in alliances we can benefit from. Rather, we acknowledge a need to comfortably participate in many different cultural contexts, and we recognize that our overall effectiveness as African-American women is greatly enhanced if we share existing information and build new strategies to increase our power base as women.

Envisioning leadership for Black women

My vision to create a place where African-American women could come together to share ideas, disappointments, successes, and develop a better political understanding of the situations that governed our lives prompted the founding of Leadership for Black Women in 1987. Its purpose was also to highlight the importance of formulating new strategies to address racist and sexist behaviors that hindered our leadership work, as well as explore the dilemmas and contradictions posed by the interlocking factors of race, gender, culture, class, and leadership.

The program grew out of my own isolation and need for networking within a university community that is predominantly and historically white and male. It was developed to assist African-American women in developing skills that will enhance success and increase power, influence, and authority. This meant that we had to look at the nature of political relationships among African-American women and other groups, as well as focus on institutional racism and sexism.

While the program, offered through the Reflective Leadership Center of the Hubert H. Humphrey Institute at the University of Minnesota in Minneapolis, was established to explore the dynamics of leadership as it pertains to African-American women, LBW is a case for leadership study. Details regarding the program's development are offered here as a case study on African-American women's leadership in action. The details provided here are intended to be instructional and are offered as a means to better understanding. The role and perspective of the higher education community in the education of and research on African-American women is key to this analysis. To offer insight into our skills at alliance building within predominantly white communities is crucial to this discussion.

Founding Leadership for Black Women

One of the goals of Leadership for Black Women from its beginning was to create an environment that fostered working together across ideological lines such as class, appearance, skin color, age, sexuality, political party and community affiliations—issues that have tended to divide Black women. LBW was designed to explore and document the leadership work of African-American women. Women who participated in a needs assessment before LBW was founded specifically requested a program that would assist them in planning for successful and/or more gainful leadership work. LBW was founded with this hope of addressing both the "how-tos" of strategy and the issue of limited 'practical' literature. Its primary goals are to assist all African-American women in developing strategies for individual and collective empowerment and to assist in alliance building and teamwork within African-American communities, across cultural, racial, gender, and class lines.

LBW's definition of leadership is the empowerment of individuals to effect valuable change in their personal, organizational, and community life. LBW acts as a catalyst by developing and implementing programs and providing resources for African-American women that support their individual and collective leadership work.

Competition among members of a group is one factor that inhibits alliance building. When certain forms of competition exist within a group it often leads to conflict. African-American women have often allowed such competition to prevent us from working together. In thinking about such issues, we have attempted to utilize varying ideological perspectives in building programs. Program developers have been encouraged to build on a variety of perspectives, often as far apart as can be managed, in an effort to dispel the myth of a monolithic African-American community. Moreover, we believe that we have a better chance to build more equitable communities and better understand the strains and dimensions of such communities if a variety of perspectives exist in the same environment.

When conflict arises as a result of, for example, competing philosophies, processes, or goals, as it often does in LBW advisory board meetings, those situations are used as learning opportunities. We often ask a board member to facilitate a discussion of the situation that will allow time for each person to discuss her perspective. Those opportunities have worked in allowing us to modify programming or processes to keep LBW on track or acknowledge that "we don't all agree," yet are committed to moving the organization's agenda forward based on our best solution to the situation at the time.

As an example, LBW asked professional fund-raisers to assist us in the 1990 fund-raising effort. Many board members were opposed to the fund-raiser's recommendations. One such suggestion called for the recruitment of more corporate women for the board. The basic point of disagreement with the fund-raiser's recommendations was "it goes against LBW's mission to treat certain women as if they are 'more important than others.' " We asked ourselves: What will happen if we concede to the recommendation and recruit others given the fact that our existing advisory board is prestigious in its own right? The outcome of that disagreement, following many hours of debate and discussion, was to find a way to use the talents of the advisory board in fund-raising and ask certain corporate women to assist our effort without joining the board.

The varying social contexts in which LBW exists pose particular challenges for us in our efforts to build alliances among African-American women. The program's two part-time staff (a director and research assistant) and a twenty-eight-member advisory board work with the demands of two distinct and broad-based political groups, whose demands and expectations are often mutually reinforcing and antagonistic.

One group, the University of Minnesota, is a large, predominantly white, midwestern land grant institution. Like other higher education institutions, the University of Minnesota, through its structure, academic culture and traditions, perpetuates values that are reflective of the overall society. Thus, whether intentional or not, the University supports programs, research, teaching, and service activities that serve a predominantly white population. What that means for a Black woman's program is there is little leverage with which to manipulate the political actions of the University. It is difficult to find administrators, faculty, or others who recognize our value.

Historically, disproportionately fewer resources have been available to programs in higher education that serve specialized populations.[24] The twin barriers of limited economic resources and academic tradition have plagued the program since its inception. Even though LBW's value has been substantiated by the participation of more than 400 women in its programs and activities over the past three years and the University has stated that diversity has a high priority within the University system, finding permanent funding for the program, and acceptance of the program as a vital aspect of a higher education community, continues to be one of our challenges.

University faculty, staff, and administrators have difficulty understanding the need for the LBW program despite its response to two tenets of the University's mission—those of research and service. Most University employees look perplexed when they hear about Leadership for Black Women. The inevitable comments are: "I can understand a program for all minority women, but a program just for African-American women seems incomplete, limited, too narrowly focused." One faculty member pointed out that a program for African-American and Hispanic women would be more appropriate, especially since "so little has been done for Hispanic women." Others believe that a broader-based, coeducational program, linking all people of color, would be far more appropriate. The fact that programmatic explanations are constantly necessary point out the difficulty we have in appealing to the varying political factions within the University. Furthermore, the fact that faculty, administrators, and staff find it so easy to dismiss the value of LBW suggest an arrogance that can only be linked to severely entrenched institutional racism. No matter how detailed our explanations, negative attitudes about the program's value within a higher-education institution persist. Some of the louder forms of resistance have come from women administrators and feminist scholars who do not support the existence of a "specialized service program" at the University of Minnesota.

We give enormous political attention to the complexity of relationships within the University. Rarely are situations clear cut. When negative attitudes exist, I generally hear about them in the form of penalties or indirect comments or questions. As an example, faculty members have asked "Why isn't this program, that serves no direct recruiting function, nor offers University course credit, in the Black community?" Translated, that usually means the program does not belong at the University. LBW also struggles to sustain an academic home within the University. Even though it was founded in the Reflective Leadership Center, its permanent location was long debated. In its first year, LBW was viewed as a program of the "whole University," meaning no department, unit, or college wanted economic responsibility for such a program. Clarity about our mission and perseverance despite the barriers have paid off for the program in terms of its location in the University. Alternative sources of funding outside of the University have been sought and obtained in small amounts. LBW staff continues to seek economic support from a variety of sources, such as corporate foundations, foundations that target organizations for women and people of color, African-American organizations, and the University of Minnesota.

The African-American community in all of its complexity is the second major political group that the LBW staff and advisory board must rely on for support. An immediate reaction in most African-American communities when predominantly white universities are mentioned is distrust. One reason is that for many years our communities as well as other communities of color have withstood the indignities of research conducted by scholars at predominantly white colleges and universities. Still others distrust predominantly white universities and colleges because of the negative experiences of sons, daughters, friends, and others as workers and students. Given the general attitude within the African-American community, it is understandable that an immediate problem for LBW was its credibility. A test of credibility within African-American communities is a long, arduous task. The measure of success can only be demonstrated over enormous periods of time. We have made some progress toward gaining acceptance from African-American communities because we have involved community leaders in our programs. Word of mouth from satisfied participants has done a great deal to improve our image. We believe that our scholarship program that is open to low-income participants who wish to apply has done a great deal to promote LBW as a credible organization.

Many African-Americans who work in predominantly white academic communities become isolated from the community. The same is true for African-Americans who work in corporate or other predominantly white situations. Such isolation is apparent in the form of speech patterns, both in diction and choice of words, mannerisms, interests, and style of dress. All of these assist people in belonging to particular communities and are often viewed by the African-American community as more structured for white approval than community connectedness. Institutional pressures, particularly the tenure system and other rules of tradition in organizations, feed this process of isolation.

Obtaining and maintaining the support of African-American communities is not something we can ever take for granted. Our histories of exploitation as African-Americans provide good reasons for suspicion. We at LBW expect that we must constantly work to earn the support of African-American people. This ongoing process is an excellent evaluative tool for us.

One of the primary goals of LBW is to work with individuals across these varying ideologies. One way LBW has addressed this issue is to comprise a large advisory board with a representative group of women from a variety of socioeconomic, education, field, age, and employment position levels. The advisory board operates without a board of officers. Generally meetings are chaired by me, the LBW director. From time to time leadership for meetings is rotated among board members. Having a mixture of board members has greatly assisted LBW in connecting with various aspects of the Black community.

An important aspect of LBW support must come from African American males. Too often Black males have viewed programs aimed at women as hostile to males. This belief follows a long-held perception that women's organizations deflect from the overall movement for equality and justice among African-Americans. Another aspect of the argument is that African-American males fear that Black women will be co-opted by white feminists who do not hold African-American community interests as a priority. That is an ongoing concern for us. All LBW programs are open to males who wish to attend, and one LBW program has been devoted to relationships between African-American men and women. As a matter of mission, however, LBW programs always place women at the center no matter what the subject matter. That is a necessary approach if women are to understand their lives in relation to others.

LBW has attempted to explain its purpose to males who have in some instances protested the existence of a woman-only leadership program. In particular, we have pointed out that men have had more opportunities to practice leadership in African-American organizations. Examples include Black churches, colleges, universities, and community organizations. Some of the most powerful and stable institutions within African-American communities have traditionally excluded women's participation in visible and/or high level decision making roles. Still males remain a political group to reckon with. It is important for us to choose our course carefully, so as not to be more injurious to African-American males, who can also benefit from further attention to their roles as leaders and emerging leaders. LBW's success is largely dependent upon our ability to maintain alliances among African-American women, with and within African-American communities. Alliances within the University and the larger community are also necessary.

Sources and limits of power

From the beginning we were aware of our collective power and drew a great deal of strength from that in the early stages of the program, when it appeared that no University administrator was willing to champion the program. We knew, for example, that even though African-American women faculty, staff, students and administrators at the University were fewer than one percent of the University population, African-American women represented a larger percentage of the University employees and student body than did Black men and other "special" populations the University served. We also reminded ourselves that more than 15,000 African-American women live in Minnesota and that there are over eleven-million African-American women nationwide.[25] Those data gave us a great deal of confidence in presenting a case for a leadership program. It has also been useful for us to remind one another that the University is a publicly supported institution and that African-American people, especially women, support the U.S. tax structure and thus the University.

It was also important for the advisory board and staff to pool personal financial resources and barter services to conduct the first program in December 1987. Our group, like many African-Americans who have internalized racism, viewed itself as helpless and unable to host a program without University financial support—despite the fact that the opposite was occurring. We were amazed by our own resourcefulness and did not believe that we were successful even when there was clear evidence of success.

Periodically, it is still necessary for LBW staff and advisory board to remind each other of our humble beginning as we undertake a major fund-raising campaign for the 1990s. LBW has not sponsored any events solely for the purpose of fund-raising. Our operating income has come from four small grants from two foundations and two University departments. Economics and organized people are the source of power in a capitalist nation; therefore, it is easy for us, given our limited financial resources and our role as novice organizers, to feel victimized. As a means of sustaining our collective power, it has been important for us to claim dignity for ourselves at every stage of the program's development. Often that meant reviewing our history and circumstances.

Despite our occasional lapse into victim roles, we recognize that a major source of power for LBW has been the skills that its leaders have in building relationships across cultural lines. The board has been able to interact from a place of strength and influence with University administrators. The degree of unity that exists among board members, given their varying backgrounds, has provided LBW with a wider frame of reference for explaining the value of a program for African-American women.

In a rather odd contrast, the sources of power for us have also been limits to power. For example, we recognize that our strength is often defined by difference and our ability to effectively communicate across difference makes us extremely valuable in a multicultural society. On the contrary, University administrators tend to value sameness or traditional academic approaches. Many administrators are confused about difference because they think African-Americans and other people of color are suppose to assimilate not "separate." Therefore, administrators are unwilling to prioritize and fund programs that are not viewed as in the best interest of the university.

We realize that our ascribed social status as African-Americans and women make us less likely to be in positions to provide economic support to organizations that we believe in. African-Americans have not traditionally been hired in the foundation world. Thus, it is likely that LBW and similar programs will have to make a case for themselves with foundation representatives that do not understand the history, culture, and necessity of such programing. Further, there are not enough African-Americans in middle and upper class income levels to provide sustaining financial support to an LBW program. Economic development in African-American communities is an extremely important area. It is harshly underscored when women and African-Americans seek political office or found programs that require an economic base to operate.

Cooperation, competition, and conflict

LBW is fully committed to the elimination of the barriers such as appearance, skin color, party affiliations, class, age, and sexuality that have prevented African-American women from working together. To the extent that such competition and resulting conflict is allowed to exist, African-American women diminish their collective power to bring about social change. Such uses of group time and energy can never benefit leaders; however, political foes who would like to keep women divided have much to gain from such divisiveness.

We know, however, that barriers must be fully addressed before they can be eliminated. It is not enough to merely expect to get on with other things. At every stage of LBW's development it has been important to give serious attention to the processes that govern the intragroup relations as well as those that govern the politics of the University and African-American community.

Personal growth/development and social change

A major aspect of personal growth lies in learning about one's self within a group context. Indeed, it is difficult for leaders to be effective if they are not clear about how personal dynamics transfer to group dynamics, which then affect social change. In LBW seminars participants discover how personal and group dynamics interact in the organization of people. This is done by discussing how our personal passions (i.e., the things we believe and stand for, our personal histories and struggles) translate into our power in groups. Such passions often generate support and momentum within groups and thus generate actions that can lead to organizing for social change. Often these personal passions grow out of the different ways that African-American women have experienced racism and sexism in America. As an example, I discovered how my personal frustrations of isolation as an African-American woman administrator were similar to those experienced by other women when I discussed my experience within a group. My personal energy, frustration, and determination to assist other women in similar positions fueled the structure of Leadership for Black Women.

We believe that African-American women are in a better position to provide service if they know and have clarity about who they are. LBW is designed to assist African-American women in personal discovery while at the same time working in service to others. In LBW programs, participants discuss how individual people feel about one another and how such feelings translate into social systems.

> . . . folks today have gotten a little confused about what leadership is. There's this misunderstanding that leadership is about individual accumulation, individual wealth, individual status. But I think leadership, at its very base, is about service. It is not about what one accumulates for oneself; it is about what one is able to do in the interest of others.[26]

In responding to Spelman College's mission to "educate black women leaders," President Johnnetta Cole defined the role of leaders. Cole's emphasis on service over individual status is a primary goal of LBW. Developing programming around central issues affecting African-American women such as long-term poverty, economic exploitation, institutional racism and sexism, the changing structure of African-American families—and how African-American women can organize around those issues—is a central program objective. LBW programs are geared toward identifying issues and acting on them.

Job promotion and advancement is a key area of concern for many

African-American women. How the U.S. power structure operates in relation to African-Americans and women has created caste systems in organizations. Attitudes, values, and beliefs that promote stereotypes such as: "They aren't the best qualified"; "There aren't any out there"; "They'll want astronomical salaries"; and "They wouldn't want to live here"[27] have prevented many a job search from hiring qualified people of color.

For several decades now, researchers have been linking personal growth within organizations to system changes, finding that the more individuals learn about themselves and how they function in relationship to teams, the more successful the team relationship. Without opportunities to define, discuss, and create strategies to address such situations, African-American women will not be able to create system changes in areas that directly affect them nor will they be able to exercise the power of their positions to create broad changes within society.

Over the years, many researchers have attempted to measure to what degree African-American women suffer from racial, gender, and/or class oppression. Such findings have been mixed.[28] LBW leaders feel that it is critically important to develop strategies that address gender, class, race, and culture, as it is the interaction of those factors that often stifles African-American women's personal as well as collective growth and development.

We feel it is necessary to create workshop experiences designed to assist African-American women in identifying their personal qualities and determining how aspects of their self-esteem and/or self-confidence are affected positively or negatively by the heinous stereotypes of race, class, gender, and culture.

In its effort to distinguish among women's experiences, LBW's design teams have made programming decisions while recognizing that not all women encounter the same degree of "isms" injury. That is, African-American women have experienced oppression to greater and lesser degrees. Therefore, LBW programs reflect a diversity of experience on any given topic.

The central guideline for LBW programming has been a belief that most African-American women experience some form of degradation in leadership roles no matter what position they hold. Sociologist Cheryl Bernadette Leggon's work has been of vital importance to LBW staff in formulating program objectives. Writing in 1980, Leggon, whose research emphasis is the professional African-American woman and organizational dynamics, theorized about the improbability of any African-American professional woman escaping racism/sexism in society:

> . . . there is a status hierarchy in which ascribed status supersedes
> achieved status; . . . within the ascribed status hierarchy, the status
> of race supersedes that of sex . . . although it is often difficult to
> distinguish between the two. . . . [29]

Leggon's findings and those of other researchers suggest that the leadership roles of African-American women are indeed unique. LBW's founders knew that it was essential to investigate such roles and provide forums for strengthening and developing leadership skills.

Implications for alliance work

There is much for all of us to learn from the past work and current practices of African-American women. It used to be that people thought there was one way to practice leadership and build alliances: the white male way. The white male model is still widely applied within our society from the grassroots level to the political arena. Women's organizations still for the most part use and share power in the traditional ways that white males have taught us. As we move into a future, however, that will grow more and more complicated as the intricacies of pluralism openly manifest themselves within American society, we will need to examine new ways of governing ourselves. Many will be met with resistance. Others will seem too closely akin to fields of psychology than business. An example of such processes are focus group interviews and quality circles. I believe that traditional models of leadership are making way for and may eventually give way to new forms. In particular, the leader as mediator, negotiator and visionary, a role often modeled by African-American women.

Since we have been among the initiators of these styles, it seems appropriate for African-American women to further develop them through alliance work and programs that challenge us to merge and stretch our ideas into new forms that will assist us and the rest of humanity. African-American women, interested in building strong alliances, must commit to a process of candid dialogue. A dialogue that is not a "homogenized unit" rather a commitment to examining side by side the differences and conflicting visions that keep groups separated.[30] This attention to the details of others' visions will greatly assist us in our effort to negotiate difficult situations; mediate conflicts when they arise; and demonstrate a greater sense of equity in groups— all of which are vital to successful alliances.

Perhaps the greatest challenge for us is creating a sense of equity among individuals and within institutions. I believe that leaders can be more effective by trying new skills that attempt to integrate respect, equity, understanding and an affirmation of human difference. This attention to the details of human difference requires a great deal of time. It is not unusual for leaders to resist it because they feel it gets in the way of "products" and "real action." The fact is, attention to human difference within political factions is always in process. It is a question of when and how it is done. It would be rare, for example, for any individual to talk with another perceived to have "greater power and authority" and or "some influence which equals authority of a sort" without considering the politics of the situation: "What do I have to lose? If I respond in this way, this might happen, etc." In building alliances with African-American women at any level it is important to consider them with the same respect that is bestowed on other stakeholders. Too often we miss opportunities to learn from one another because we discount human value and attach more clout to positional roles in organizations (e.g., president, chair of the board) rather than building on difference.

Notes

1. Political alliances are used throughout this paper to designate the many relationships that African-American women maintain within African-American communities, among women, and across other cultural lines. These relationships are political because they arise from partisan factors and have enormous influence on the African-American woman's social status, thus must be taken into account in her decision making.

2. For the purpose of this discussion, *intracultural* is defined as within African-American culture.

3. Cross-cultural refers to any groups other than Black/African-American.

4. Scott, Patricia Bell. "Some Thoughts on Black Women's Leadership Training," Working Paper No. 90. Wellesley, MA: Wellesley College, Center for Research on Women.

5. Americans face far more complexities that affect public policy formation than ever acknowledged before. Consider, for example, how the legal system has responded to domestic partnership cases in California and New York. Such cases have challenged all of us to publicly redefine definitions of family that go beyond American traditions. This is a single example that forces us to focus in on what it might be like to think about forming an alliance around family issues with gay men and lesbians, single parents, low-income people, African-American, Hispanic, American Indian, Asian, and others. Today many of us would not consider broadening our alliances to include all of the above groups.

6. The questions that appear here are a modification of questions raised for future researchers in the work of John Hope Franklin and August Meier, *Black Leaders of the Twentieth Century*, Urbana, IL: University of Illinois Press, 1982, pp. x-xi.

7. Myrdal, Gunnar, 1944. *An American Dilemma: The Negro Problem and Modern Democracy*. New York: Harper and Brothers. (Includes a chapter on "Negro Leadership.")

8. Higham, John, 1978. *Ethnic Leadership in America*. Baltimore, MD: Johns Hopkins University Press.

9. Ibid, pp. 2-3.

10. Brazil's role (as explained in an article by George E. Curry. "A Season in Hell," *MS*, Oct. 1989, p. 60) so clearly articulates the race and gender politics of our time: "She was finding it increasingly difficult to reconcile the candidate's failure to court the black vote with his going all out to win 'Reagan Democrats'. And it always became

her responsibility . . . to reassure skeptics in the Black community that Dukakis had their best interests at heart."

Speaking about her role as an African-American woman working with a Black male, Brazil reflected on her work with Jessie Jackson during his first bid for president of the United States. Her experience also points out how internalized oppression affects African-Americans. In this case the Jackson staff perpetuates the oppression that Brazil experiences: "One week I'd be mobilization director, but when they found a white person to be mobilization director, they would move me. . . . Then I'd be Rainbow Coalition Director for a week and then they'd find a white person and move me."

11. Scott, Patricia Bell. "Some Thoughts on Black Women's Leadership Training," Working Paper No. 90. Wellesley, MA: Wellesley College, Center for Research on Women.

12. Davis, Marianna W., 1982. *Contributions of Black Women to America*. Vol. II, Columbia, SC: Kenday Press, Inc., p. vii.

13. Ibid., pp. 181, 234, 377, 426–7.

14. Davis, Marianna W., 1982. *Contributions of Black Women To America*. Vol. I, Columbia, SC: Kenday Press, Inc., pp. 278–80; 357–8.

15. Jones, Jacqueline, 1985. *Labor of Love, Labor of Sorrow*. New York: Basic Books, pp. 3–4.

16. "Courage to Lead: Major Challenges Facing Black Women Today." 1988. Published proceedings from a conference held at the Hubert H. Humphrey Institute of Public Affairs, University of Minnesota. St. Paul, MN: GrayHall, p. 6.

17. Porter, Evette. "Breaking Ranks." *Essence,* Sept. 1989, p. 87.

18. Ibid., p. 88.

19. Ibid.

20. "Courage to Lead: Major Challenges Facing Black Women Today." 1988. Published proceedings from a conference held at the Hubert H. Humphrey Institute of Public Affairs, University of Minnesota. St. Paul, MN: GrayHall, p. 6.

21. Joseph, Gloria I., and Lewis, Jill, 1981. *Common Differences: Conflicts in Black and White Feminist Perspectives*. Boston: South End Press, p. 6.

22. Brewer, Rose M., 1988. "Black Families, Minority Families, and Public Policy." Minneapolis, MN: Center for Urban and Regional Affairs Focus Paper, November 1988. Contains data on economic equity and Black families.

23. Lerner, Gerda, 1972. *Black Women in White America*. New York: Vintage Books, pp. 435–47.

24. For a provocative discussion on elitism in higher education read Pearson, Carol S., Shavlik, Donna L., and Touchton, Judith G., 1989. *Educating the Majority: Women Challenge Tradition in Higher Education*. New York: Collier Macmillan Publishers. See also Hull, Gloria T., Scott, Patricia Bell, and Smith, Barbara (eds.), 1982. *All the Women Are White, All the Blacks Are Men, But Some of Us Are Brave: Black Women's Studies*. New York: The Feminist Press.

25. Statistical data on Black women compiled by the 1980 census.

26. Cole, Johnnetta. Quoted in Edwards, Audrey, June 1989. "The Inspiring Leader of Scholars [and Dollars]." *Working Woman*, p. 72.

27. For an excellent discussion of the myth and realities of the job search process in higher education institutions read *Achieving Faculty Diversity: A Sourcebook of Ideas and Success Stories*, 1988. Madison, WI: University of Wisconsin System.

28. See, for example, Epstein, C.F., Jan. 1973. "Positive Effects of the Multiple Negative: Explaining the Success of Black Professional Women." *American Journal of Sociology,* pp. 913–35; and Dumas, Rhetaugh Graves, 1980. "Dilemmas of Black Females in Leadership." In Rodgers-Rose, La Frances, 1980. *The Black Woman,* Newbury Park, CA: Sage Publications, pp. 203–15.

29. Leggon, Cheryl Bernadette, 1980. "Black Female Professionals: Dilemmas and Contradictions of Status." In Rodgers-Rose, La Frances, ed., 1980. *The Black Woman*. Newbury Park, CA: Sage Publications, p. 195.

30. This term from the work of Joseph, Gloria I., and Lewis, Jill, 1981 (*Common Differences: Conflicts in Black and White Feminist Perspectives,* Boston: South End Press), means dialogue with the goal of creating sameness rather than an appreciation of difference.

All-Women's Musical Communities
Fostering Creativity and Leadership

J. Michele Edwards

All-women's musical communities have played a formative role in supporting women's creativity. Historically, they have offered arenas less burdened by tradition where women can shape their own world and—as a result—effect changes in the dominant society. The examination of these communities moves toward what Carroll Smith-Rosenberg called "one of the principal goals of women's history": "to so redefine the canons of traditional history that the events and processes central to women's experience assume historical centrality, and women are recognized as active agents of social change."[1]

In this article I will look at two women's music communities: the International Sweethearts of Rhythm, a racially and ethnically mixed jazz band, and the Bay Area Women's Philharmonic with JoAnn Falletta, music director. I will explore briefly the varied circumstances under which these women chose separatism. Additionally, I will show the impact and products of these exceptional communities, including the development of leadership and expertise which give women's creative work greater visibility. Despite diversity of race, ethnicity, and class-plus temporal and stylistic differences, both of these women's communities give voice to women through supportive environments, through opportunities to advance skills, and as alternatives to the expectations of the dominant culture.[2]

International Sweethearts of Rhythm

The International Sweethearts of Rhythm was organized in 1937 as a fundraising effort by the Piney Woods Country Life School in Mississippi—a coeducational school founded early in the century primarily to teach poor and orphaned African-Americans a trade.[3] Students participated in work-study programs to help cover the cost of their education. The school also had an extensive music program with many single-sex ensembles which made extensive tours to raise money for the school.

From its conception, the International Sweethearts of Rhythm combined Black and white experience. Laurence Jones, the school's founder and president, envisioned the all-girl jazz group after he heard Ina Ray Hutton and Her Melodears. Hutton launched the Melodears, an all-white women's band, in 1934, and they had several successful years of touring and recording. In organizing the Sweethearts, Jones merged his new awareness of a white women's swing band with the African-American tradition of the touring Fisk Jubilee Singers. The Jubilee Singers, still part of the university's program today, began fund-raising tours in 1871 with nine singers—young women and men who were former slaves. They raised money to purchase land for Fisk University and continued as an important source of revenue during Fisk's early decades.[4]

The Sweethearts had the longest history among women's swing bands and were generally recognized as the "hottest" women's jazz band of the 1940s.[5] From a modest beginning, the Sweethearts passed through several career phases during their twelve-year history (1937–48): a local beginning with regional fund-raising tours; the addition of a few professional players early in 1940;[6] the split from Piney Woods School in 1941; an increase in the number of seasoned professional players, including some key soloists; experience playing in the big time, including a 1945 USO tour in Germany and France; and the postwar letdown leading to the group's disbanding in 1948.

Their steady development of musical expertise is evident from the venues where they performed and from the audience response noted in the Black press. Their appearance at Washington's celebrated Howard Theater in 1940 was a sensation, and by 1941 they were a top box office draw at many major Black theaters and clubs across the country.[7] Vi Burnside (tenor sax) and Tiny Davis (trumpet), both seasoned pros, became two of the Sweethearts' featured soloists and lifted the playing of the entire band.[8] The International Sweethearts was at its peak from 1945–46, especially during its European tour.[9] Evelyn McGee, the original vocalist with the Sweethearts, recalled her experience: "It was hectic, really—but who cared. I mean, for me it was an escape; I was just delighted. . . . and not being able to get off the stage because the people are applauding you. I can still hear the applause ringing in my ears!"[10]

Several women provided guidance for the International Sweethearts, especially in the early days, and many gained valuable leadership experience. Consuella Carter, a graduate of Piney Woods, taught syncopation and swing to the original Sweethearts. She drew some of her first pupils from the marching band but recruited others for their first musical training.[11] After leaving Piney Woods, she completed bachelor's and master's degrees in music and went on to lead outstanding school bands in Mississippi during most of her forty five-year teaching career.[12] Edna Williams, the "female Satchmo," was hired as the Sweethearts' first musical director. She remained with the Sweethearts for five years and then resumed her career as freelance performer. In 1945, in the spirit of the Sweethearts, she formed her own racially integrated all-women's sextet.[13] Star trumpet player Tiny Davis was among the performers who later led her own ensemble. During its six-year span her sextet, The Hell Divers, frequently toured as the warm up band for Louis Armstrong. In the 1970s she organized a trio in which her own daughter performed.[14]

In reading the biographies of many of the women who played with the International Sweethearts, I discovered the richness and diversity of their musical lives after they left the Sweethearts.[15] Some of the women formed their own all-women's jazz groups; others pursued careers in concert music or as educators; still others fought racial and sexual discrimination against musicians.

The community forged by these young women was built out of necessity. Doubly displaced by gender and race, they created their own supportive environment—first at Piney Woods, then on the road, and finally as an independent, creative unit touring extensively. According to jazz pianist Marian McPartland, "the earlier camaraderie had grown into a bond of friendship that had been strengthened by the many experiences, good and bad, that the girls had shared."[16]

Evidence of professional networks and alliances formed during tenure with the Sweethearts is seen in the frequency that alumnae worked together after leaving this band. For example, Pauline Braddy, the original drummer who played with the group throughout its history, later played with a trio including two other alumnae: Edna Smith (bass) and Ray Carline (piano). Both Edna Smith and Pauline Braddy also worked with Vi Burnside, another former member of the Sweethearts.

The International Sweethearts of Rhythm was the first racially integrated women's band. From the beginning the band reflected the multiracial makeup of the school, including women from Chinese, Mexican, Native American and Hawaiian backgrounds among the preponderance of African-American performers.[17] Since a multiracial group could not get hotel accommodations nor restaurant service, the school bus became the students' world. They ate and slept there, practiced their instruments and did school work. Even later when the group broke away from Piney Woods, they continued communal living. Rae Lee Jones, originally hired as a chaperon for their tour, purchased a ten-room house in Arlington, Virginia, which was home base for all the Sweethearts.[18]

In 1943, after more than five years of playing together, the band chose to integrate several white women into this already ethnically diverse group. In an interview, Roz Cron, the second white woman to play with the Sweethearts, spoke about the need for whites to pass for Black in southern towns.[19] Across the United States, the band played primarily for Black audiences and in Black theaters.

The racial-ethnic alliances visible in the Sweethearts spilled over into audience response. Thomas Jefferson Anderson, now Fletcher Professor of Music at Tufts University, recalled his experience on hearing and seeing the International Sweethearts as a teenager in 1940:

> It was their physical beauty that attracted my eye—a group of women the color of the rainbow. Here I sat in a segregated audience and was witnessing a performance by women who looked like they were from all over the world. This was my first visual experience with integration—my glance into what the civil rights movement would be about approximately two decades later. This advanced visual image of what the United Nations would become was indeed impressive and these women working together to make music only further served to emphasize what could happen in other areas in the future.[20]

The very existence of the International Sweethearts of Rhythm cut against the grain of America's Black and white cultures. They turned upside down and inside out many of the normative gender, race, and class relationships of their world. Although the racial-ethnic mix of the group may be the most obvious challenge, other taboos were also defied.[21] Jazz was not an accepted art form; therefore, its affiliation with an educational institution was unusual. Jazz was also viewed in opposition to religion and a wholesome life; thus its sponsorship by a Christian school was even more surprising. The growing Black middle class rejected jazz because it was linked with dives and slums. As a schoolgirl band, the Sweethearts' youth and clean-cut appearance stood in contrast to the image of many well known blues singers. Further, the independence and professional orientation of the girls at Piney Woods, and certainly the women in the later years of the Sweethearts, moved outside socially acceptable roles for women. The story of the

International Sweethearts of Rhythm exemplifies the intersection of gender, race, class, and other forms of oppression. Yet the positive part of this story is their success and the ways in which their alliance forged new possibilities for the future.

Bay Area Women's Philharmonic

Alongside the tradition of all-women's jazz bands is a parallel stream of all-women's symphony orchestras. Since the orchestra and orchestral music appear high on the patriarchal pyramid of western concert music, it is particularly difficult for women to gain access to this musical institution either as performers or composers.[22] The Bay Area Women's Philharmonic responds to the needs of today by providing opportunities for women musicians and new experiences for audiences.

In the first half of the twentieth century, especially during the 1930s and early 1940s, all-women's symphony orchestras in the United States emerged to offer women players and conductors experience and employment.[23] Women created their own opportunities because they could not get positions in all-male (so-called "standard") orchestras. Although an occasional white woman player was hired by a major orchestra in the mid 1920s, many major symphonies hired no full-time women players until quite recently: Boston Symphony in 1945; New York Philharmonic in 1966;[24] and the Berlin Philharmonic hired no women except a second harpist until 1983.[25] Not until 1964 was the first Black woman under contract with a major U.S. orchestra: pianist Patricia Jennings with the Pittsburgh Symphony.[26] By the 1960s women players had made much progress in gaining access to professional symphony positions; however, women conductors remain a rarity today and little music by women composers is programmed by professional orchestras (see Table 1).

Only two women have held conducting positions with major symphonies in the United States.[28] Catherine Comet, associate conductor of the Baltimore Symphony from 1984 until 1986, was the first. A year later JoAnn Falletta became the second when she was appointed associate conductor with the Milwaukee Symphony. Falletta resigned that post at the end of the 1988 summer season, leaving no woman holding a conducting position with a major symphony.

To give some idea of the infrequency of women's compositions on programs by professional orchestras, I examined the programming of the two large-budget, professional orchestras in the Twin Cities for the seasons from 1986–87 through 1989–90. The results are not encouraging and are especially grim for the Minnesota Orchestra (see Table 2).

Table 1: Women Employed in American Orchestras 1943 to 1988[27]

	Major Orchestras*			Metropolitan Orchestras*	
	Number of orchestras	Number of women	Percent of women	Number of women	Percent of women
1943	(16)	140	*ca.* 2%		
1947	31	150	*ca.* 8%		
1953–4	31	199	18.4%		
1964–5	18		18.3%		36.5%
1972	5**	38	7.2%		
1974–5	31		21.8%		39.7%
1975	31		24.9%		40.6%
1977	5**	51	9.7%		
1982	30		26.3%		*ca.* 48%
1983	30	760	27.8%	1520	48.4%
1985–6	40	996			
1986–7	40	1072	30.8%		
1988	5**	100	19.4%		

* Categories are based on budget size as defined by the American Symphony Orchestra League.
** Statistics for the "Big Five" orchestras only: Boston, Chicago, Cleveland, New York and Philadelphia. Note that these five orchestras lag significantly behind major orchestras as a group in terms of the percentage of women performers.

Table 2: Women Composers Represented on Subscription Series Concerts

	Minnesota Orchestra	Saint Paul Chamber Orchestra		
	Subscription Series	Subscription Series	Sunday MN Series	New Music Series
1986–7	Vivian Fine Libby Larsen	Germaine Taileferre	Janika Vandervelde	none
1987–8	none	Ellen Taaffe Zwilich	Mary Ellen Childs	Libby Larsen
1988–9	none	Joan Tower Marianne Martinez	**	none
1989–90	*	none	**	none

* Not yet available
** Not applicable

Because women cannot get orchestral compositions performed, they have often avoided writing them.[29] The experience of composer Ruth Crawford Seeger illustrates the breadth of the negative impact of women's exclusion from the orchestral scene. Although she had sketched two orchestral pieces in Paris, neither these, nor any other compositions for full orchestra, were completed. Apparently, this was at least in part the reason Crawford's request for a year's extension of her Guggenheim Fellowship was denied.[30] Even her husband, ethnomusicologist Charles Seeger, articulated an orchestral, male bias:

> The next few years will decide whether this most promising young woman will rest content in the rather narrow, but recherche, field in which she has hitherto moved and had her being, or whether, following her bid for orchestral laurels, she will enter into the already brisk competition among men in the larger fields.[31]

The motivation for forming alternative musical institutions changed over the decades of this century. No longer do women orchestral players require a separate women's orchestra if they are to play at all. The all-women's symphonies founded in the 1970s and 1980s have had a different impetus and mission than earlier ones, that is, to foster women conductors and to provide a forum for performance of compositions by women composers. However, the importance of all-women's orchestras has not diminished, and they remain essential for emerging leadership and creativity among women.[32]

We can trace this transformation of function and at the same time see how already in a few short decades, the links and networks among women are developing. Antonia Brico, a frustrated conductor from the 1930s until her death in August 1989, founded the New York Women's Symphony Orchestra in 1934, when she and other women musicians could not find performance opportunities. Composer-conductor Kay Gardner described the founding of the New England Women's Symphony in Boston, which she cofounded in 1978.

> Brico was the inspiration for the New England Women's Symphony . . . . The point she needed to prove was that women can play any orchestral instrument. . . . We didn't need to make that point; everyone knows that now. What we needed to prove was that women can conduct and that there are fine women composers.[33]

Flutist Nan Washburn gained experience working with and doing research for the New England Women's Symphony. In 1981 she joined with two other women to found the Bay Area Women's Philharmonic, which is currently led by Washburn as artistic director, music director JoAnn Falletta, and executive director Miriam Abrams. This musical network stretches from New York to San Francisco and from the 1930s to the present.

For the Bay Area Women's Philharmonic the music itself was the primary starting point and clearly remains the focus.[34] This means recovery of music by women composers from the past, commissioning new works by women, and promoting performances of these repertories. According to Miriam Abrams, "what we're really trying to do is change the repertoire." Eighty percent of the music on their programs is by women composers. To further their goals and in response to a growing number of inquiries from orchestras across the country about works to program, the Bay Area Women's Philharmonic has created an adjunct organization: the National Women Composers Resource Center. Nan Washburn, in charge of this service, hopes it can become a widely used agency for orchestral programming.

The Women's Philharmonic is involved in circulating compositions by women in other ways. Prior to conducting the Bay Area Women's Philharmonic, JoAnn Falletta had never conducted a work by a woman composer. Now Falletta, whose conducting career looks very promising, is learning this repertory for San Francisco and then programming it in other locations.[35] For example, Falletta first performed Sinfonia in C by Marianne Martines (a singer, pianist, composer, teacher, and artistic stimulus in late eighteenth-century Vienna) with the Women's Philharmonic. During the 1988–89 season, she conducted this composition in a guest appearance with the Saint Paul Chamber Orchestra. Falletta and the Bay Area Women's Philharmonic recorded the work during spring 1989, and it is slated for release in 1990 as a compact disc by Newport Classics. Falletta also transported a symphony by Amy Beach to Colorado where she conducts the Denver Chamber Orchestra.

When premiering commissioned works or performing other compositions by living composers, the Women's Philharmonic often brings the composer to San Francisco. As a result some of her other compositions get distributed among the players and subsequently performed. Twin Cities composer Libby Larsen made her first San Francisco appearance with the Bay Area Women's Philharmonic and as a consequence has made a return visit and has had several other performances of her works in that city.

In addition to support given women composers, the Bay Area Women's Philharmonic also fosters women as guest artists. When I interviewed Washburn and Abrams in January 1988, Jorja Fleezanis, associate concertmaster of the San Francisco Symphony, had just received rave reviews for her performance of a violin concerto with the San Francisco Symphony.[36] Washburn described how the Women's Philharmonic had played a role in this significant performance.

> The fact is that Jorja Fleezanis last night played an incredible performance, and she hasn't played that many concertos. We had her

play the Barber [Violin Concerto with the Women's Philharmonic last year]; that was a big deal for her . . . . All the people from the [San Francisco] Symphony came to watch and hear her, and it gave her an opportunity to solo when she's primarily an orchestra player . . . . everyone got their socks knocked off. . . . So in a way I feel like we were part of that performance last night because we had her solo [with us].

During 1988–89 Fleezanis assumed an even larger leadership role as she traveled periodically to Minneapolis to serve as acting concertmaster with the Minnesota Orchestra, where she has since accepted that position on a permanent basis.[37]

Washburn believes that music can transform people. Perhaps this link between art and life is partially responsible for some of the ways the Women's Philharmonic is different from many other professional symphonies and has served as a role model for other organizations. They have shown a real consciousness for people, both the performers and the audience members. For example, child care is provided for the players. In discussing organizational style, Abrams stated:

> We wanted the orchestra to be as egalitarian as possible. We didn't want to see . . . lots of competition between players for the principal seat, for moving up. . . . We just wanted a different kind of group spirit, enthusiasm, commitment; and we do what we can to encourage that.
>
> One way in which they have worked to avoid the boredom often experienced by orchestral players is by focusing on less familiar repertory by both women and men.

Many in their audience are not regular concertgoers. Abrams senses that some people are intimidated by the formality of traditional concerts. She said, "[we] try to create an atmosphere at the Women's Philharmonic both in the way people perceive us when they walk into the concert hall that feels warm and friendly and easy to get into right away, and challenging at the same time." Affordable ticket prices and preconcert talks, often with a featured composer, have also been part of their audience development strategy.

Despite the long history of all-women's musical organizations, the Bay Area Women's Philharmonic is still a pioneer. This community of women is working to change the attitudes of conductors, players, audiences, and critics about women making music together and about women as composers. They are helping critics get past the "novelty" element in their treatment of women creating and performing music. They are supporting women performers in an atmosphere which is different from other ensembles. They are disseminating music by women so that it will become a part of our heritage.

Valuing separatism

In an article entitled "Separatism as Strategy," Estelle Freedman encourages us to avoid entrenching inequality through female institutions but at the same time suggests that

> we must not be self-hating of that which is female as we enter a world dominated by men. . . . [W]e should not forsake, but rather we should cherish both the values and institutions that were once [and I would add, sometimes still are] women's only resources.[38]

Separate women's musical communities have generally grown out of discrimination and the oppression of women, yet women making music together manifest dynamic and empowering realities. The impact of their ideas and values on the dominant musical community is strengthened by the separatist nature of their organizations. Through these coalitions women have found—and are finding—support, encouragement, and opportunities to effect social change.

Part of the significance of doing women's history is the realization that we are not alone. As voiced by musicologist Jeannie Pool:

> Knowledge of this history gives women a new base of confidence from which to work out their lives. . . . Women, without this history, are fragile, tentative pioneers, groping in the dark, striking out in seemingly new territory because we do not know the stories of those women who accomplished those goals before us.[39]

Leadership in creative musical areas seems more possible when we can hear the voices of our foresisters and foremothers. In communities of women, today and in the past, these voices resound.

Notes

1. Dubois, Ellen, Buhle, Mari Jo, Kaplan, Temma, Lerner, Gerda, and Smith-Rosenberg, Carroll. 1988. "Politics and Culture in Women's History: A Symposium," *Feminist Studies* 6:1 (Spring): 56–7.
2. For some interesting ideas on women's communities in literature, see Nina Auerbach, *Communities of Women: An Idea in Fiction* (Cambridge: Harvard University Press, 1978), esp. 3–19.
3. For information about the International Sweethearts of Rhythm, see especially D. Antoinette Handy, *The International Sweethearts of Rhythm* (Metuchen, NJ: Scarecrow Press, 1983); idem, *Black Women in American Bands and Orchestras* (Metuchen, NJ: Scarecrow Press, 1981), esp. 45–52, 59–60, 69, 89–94, 130–1, 138–9, 150, 200–201; Rosetta Reitz, "Sweethearts on Parade," *Helicon Nine* No. 17 and 18 (Spring 1987): 135–44; Sally Placksin, *American Women in Jazz: 1990 to the Present* (n.p.: Wideview Books, 1982), 90-N 3, 131–48, 161–7, 175–8, 187–92; Marian McPartland, *All in Good Time* (New York: Oxford University Press, 1987), 137–59; Linda Dahl, *Stormy Weather: The Music and Lives of a Century of Jazzwomen* (New York: Pantheon Books, 1984), esp. 53–6.

4. *New Grove Dictionary of American Music*, s.v. "Jubilee Singers" by Geneva H. Southall.

5. See, for example, Reitz, "Sweethearts on Parade," 135; Handy, *Black Women*, 46; Placksin, *American Women in Jazz*, 131, 134; Dahl, *Stormy Weather*, 53.

6. According to Reitz, "Jean Starr, a hot Harlem trumpet player and veteran of male bands, joined the Sweethearts in December 1940. Her experience sparked the band. . . . Her entry marked the beginning of the Sweethearts' move into another realm" ("Sweethearts on Parade," 139).

7. Handy, *International Sweethearts of Rhythm*, xi, 135, 163; Placksin, *American Women in Jazz*, 132.

8. See *Tiny and Ruby: Hell Divin' Women* (1988) for profiles of Tiny Davis and her lover Ruby Lucas; 16 mm film/video, 30 min, color; produced by Jezebel Productions and Rosetta Records; directed by Greta Schiller and Andrea Weiss; available from The Cinema Guild, 1697 Broadway, New York 10019.

9. Recordings of performances from 1945–46 are available on *International Sweethearts of Rhythm*, Women's Heritage Series, Rosetta Records, RR1312. Some of these cuts are also available on *Women in Jazz: All Women Groups*, Stash Records, ST-111; *Jazz Women: A Feminist Retrospective*, 2 vols. in 1, Stash Records, ST-109; and a recording insert in *Helicon Nine* Nos. 17 and 18 (1987).

10. From an interview included in "The Sweethearts of Rhythm," a National Public Radio "Horizon Series" program; produced, written and narrated by Sally Placksin, 1986; cassette order No. HO-861105. 01/01-C.

11. Dahl, *Story Weather*, 53, quoting from a 1980 interview Leonard Feather conducted with Sweethearts personnel.

12. Handy, *International Sweethearts of Rhythm*, 120–1.

13. Handy, *Black Women*, 47; idem, *International Sweethearts of Rhythm*, 198.

14. Hardy, *Black Women*, 131.

15. Profiles of many of the International Sweethearts are given in Handy, *Black Women*, see esp. 51–2, 69, 89–94, 130–1, 150. Also see profiles on the musical activities of some members in Handy, *International Sweethearts of Rhythm*, 190–8.

16. McPartland, *All in Good Time*, 151; see also p. 150.

17. Reitz, "Sweethearts on Parade," 138, 143.

18. McPartland, *All in Good Time*, 145–7.

19. *The International Sweethearts of Rhythm* (1986), 16 mm film/video, 30 min. color; produced by Jezebel productions and Rosetta Records; directed by Greta Schiller and Andrea Weiss; available from The Cinema Guild, 1697 Broadway, New York 10019.

20. Handy, *International Sweethearts of Rhythm*, 200, reprints his letter written in July 1982.

21. See Handy, *International Sweethearts of Rhythm*, 142; Dolores Janiewski, "Seeking 'a New Day and a New Way': Black Women and Union in the Southern Tobacco Industry," in *To Toil the Livelong Day! American Women at Work, 1780–1980*, ed. Carol Groneman and Mary Beth Norton (Ithaca: Cornell University Press, 1987), 167, on the relationship of gender with sacred and secular music.

22. On gender associations with specific musical genres, see Judith Tick, "Passed Away Is the Piano Girl: Changes in American Musical Life, 1870–1900," in *Women Making Music*, esp. 336–8.

23. See Carol Neuls-Bates, "Women's Orchestras in the United States, 1925–45," in *Women Making Music*, 349–69; idem, *Women in Music*, 247–64; Christine Ammer, *Unsung: A History of Women in American Music* (Westport, CT: Greenwood Press, 1980), 99–115 (on all-women's orchestras), 200–23 (on recent developments for women in professional orchestras).

24. Christine Amer, *Unsung*, 200–201.

25. Eva Rieger, " 'Dolce semplice'? On the Changing Role of Women in Music," in *Feminist Aesthetics*, ed. Gisela Ecker (Boston: Beacon Press, 1986; 1st pub. by The Women's Press Limited, 1985), 135–6; plus information from Kathy Saltzman Romey, telephone interview, 28 July 1988. Rieger reported that in 1979 Conductor Herbert

von Karajan was asked at a press conference why no women performed with the Berlin Philharmonic and he responded, "a woman's place is in the kitchen and not in the symphony orchestra." Four years later von Karajan's position had apparently shifted. Although a woman clarinetist continued to win the blind auditions in 1983, members of the orchestra did not want to hire her. Von Karajan threatened that if she were not hired, he would restrict his activities with the orchestra to those covered by his contract. He would no longer conduct the Berlin Philharmonic on recordings nor at the Salzburg Festival. The orchestra finally relented.

26. Handy, *Black Women,* 193–5.

27. Neuls-Bates, "Women's Orchestras in the United States, 1925–45, 363, 368 n. 35; Judith Tick, unpublished table for "Implications of Women's Studies for the Arts Curricula," a workshop sponsored by Great Lakes Colleges Association, Denison University, Granville, OH, 6–7 November 1987; Adrienne Fried Block and Carol Neuls-Bates, *Women in American Music: A Bibliography of Music and Literature* (Westport, CT: Greenwood Press, 1979), xxvi; "Status Report. Women of Note," *Ms.,* March 1989, 82; American Symphony Orchestra League statistics.

28. Using information covering appointments held between 1983 and 1986, Judith Zaimont identifies forty-one women who are orchestra conductors in the U.S., plus sixteen more as conductors of youth orchestras. This tabulation encompasses a wide range of orchestras, including professional orchestras, community symphonies, chamber orchestras, opera companies and college/university ensembles (*The Musical Woman: An International Perspective,* vol. II, 1984–1985 [New York: Greenwood Press, 1987], 52–4).

29. In commenting on Symphony No. 3 (1849), a "rediscovered" work by Jean Louise Dumont Farrenc, Karen Liberatore claimed: "Most surprising is that Farrenc's work is a symphony, a rarity for a woman composer" ("Women's Orchestra. A Sound Adventure," *San Francisco Chronicle,* Nov. 8, 1987). Liberatore's article continues, quoting Nan Washburn: "A composer isn't going to write something that won't get performed—which often has been the case with women—especially a symphony."

30. Ruth Crawford, letter to Nicholas Slonimsky, 20 January 1933, as quoted by Carol Neuls-Bates, *Women in Music,* 307; Matilda Gaume, "Ruth Crawford Seeger," in *Women Making Music,* 383–4.

31. Charles Seeger, "Ruth Crawford," in *American Composers on American Music. A Symposium,* ed. Henry Cowell (New York: Frederick Ungar Publishing, 1962, 1st ed. 1933), 118.

32. Institutions working toward social change are often themselves transformed during the process. For example, consider the evolution from the first Montgomery Bus Boycott—originally begun by women in an effort to dignify segregation—into the Civil Rights Movement, whose agenda was quite different. Similarly, women's orchestras, as an institution, have changed their focus of activity to remain vital and relevant. I am grateful to discussion in a Macalester College Mellon faculty workshop, "Women, Race and Class" (June 1988), and especially to Kimberly Phillips, for prompting this comparison.

33. "Female Composition" [an interview with Kay Gardner], in *Women's Culture: The Women's Renaissance of the 70s,* ed. Gayle Kimball (Metuchen, NJ: Scarecrow Press, 1981), 169.

34. Unless otherwise indicated, information on the Bay Area Women's Philharmonic and all quotations from Miriam Abrams and Nan Washburn are from an interview conducted by the author in San Francisco, January 15, 1988. Although the management of the Women's Philharmonic indicated that they have shifted away from feminist politics to hone in on the music, I would like to suggest an alternative reading. They may no longer talk much about feminism, but their actions speak and confirm the special place of feminism and gender issues in their enterprise.

35. In 1985, Falletta was first prize winner of the Leopold Stokowski Conducting Competition and winner of the Toscanini Conductors Award. In addition to her

conducting positions with the Bay Area Women's Philharmonic and Milwaukee Symphony (1985–88), she is conductor of the Denver Chamber Orchestra (1983–) and music director for the Queens (NY) Philharmonic (1979–). Judith Lang Zaimont, ed., *The Musical Woman. An International Perspective,* vol. II (1984–85) (New York: Greenwood Press, 1987), 52; articles in *Milwaukee Sentinel* and *Milwaukee Journal,* September 25, 1987. Thanks to Lia Gima (Macalester College, class of '90) for research assistance at the Milwaukee Public Library on Falletta. Falletta's conducting is exciting, effective, and impressive in *A Woman Is a Risky Bet. aka Six Orchestra Conductors,* film, 80 min, color; directed by Christina Olofson; produced by Inger Antonsson; Hagafilm and the Swedish Film Institute, 1987.

36. *San Francisco Examiner,* January 15, 1988, pp. F1, 16; *San Francisco Chronicle,* January 16, 1988, p. C1. Is it reasonable to speculate that even in some intangible way Fleezanis' leadership was strengthened and nurtured by her experience with the Bay Area Women's Philharmonic?

37. Michael Anthony, "Classical Music," *Star Tribune* (Twin Cities), July 22, 1988, p. 6E; *Star Tribune,* November 18, 1988, p. 4E. Anthony was correct in his speculation that Fleezanis would assume the position on a permanent basis.

38. "Separatism as Strategy: Female Institution Building and American Feminism, 1870–1930," *Feminist Studies* 5:3 (Fall 1979): 526. For comments on the negative images projected by mythologies dealing with women and music see Batya Weinbaum, "Music, Dance, and Song. Women's Cultural Resistance in Making Their Own Music," *Heresies* 6:1, issue 22 (1987): 18–21. These images need to be replaced with positive life experiences of women making music.

39. Jeannie G. Pool, "A Critical Approach to the History of Women in Music," *Heresies* 3:2, issue 10 (1980): 4. Thanks to Kim Nielsen Tuff (Macalester College, class of 1988) for bringing this passage to my attention.

Did You Say the Mirror Talks?*

Michelle Parkerson

> If there is a single distinguishing feature of the literature of black
> women—and this accounts for their lack of recognition—it is this:
> their literature is about black women; it takes the trouble to record
> the thoughts, experiences, words, feelings, and deeds of black women.

Introducing the anthology, *Invented Lives,* editor Mary Helen
Washington's assessment of the aesthetics and dilemma of the literature
of Black women parallels the circumstances of Black women
filmmakers.

Our films document the same survival, utilizing the power of images
just as writers employ the precision of words. We both seek to humanize
and to broaden a medium of expression steeped in the iconography
and oppression of male, Eurocentric definitions of art.

Black women writers and filmmakers share common ground. We
equip literature and cinema with cultural directives for social change.
Social change is a founding tenent in the alliances formed by African-
American women. Out of service to one's race and sex have come such
traditional Black women's organizations as The National Council of

---

* With generous excerpts from a previously published article, "No More Mammy
Stories", by Michelle Parkerson, in *Hurricane Alice: A Feminist Quarterly,* Vol. 4, No.
2, 1987.

Negro Women, the Delta Sigma Theta and Alpha Kappa Alpha sororities, The National Association of Colored Women's Clubs, The Links, and the Eastern Star chapters of the Prince Hall Freemasons. In other alliances forged in response to racism, economic oppression, and sexism, Black women have also organized political groups, quilting clubs, domestic workers' exchanges, church auxiliaries, educational groups, professional societies, and literary clubs.

These associations were, in one sense, "extended families" of women who constructed their own arenas for networking, training, and development outside the barriers of a Black woman's prescribed place. Although contemporary Black women writers and filmmakers are in the forefront of redefining our history and broadening the social/political context of our future, neither group has catalyzed formally into a national organization. Indeed, among African-American women filmmakers, it is an informal sisterhood—a support system of other filmmakers who, because of race, gender, age, and years in the media, have experienced many of the same things, professionally and personally. Networking may consist of cutting a public television deal utilizing a team approach to producing or simply calling a sister filmmaker to see how she's coping.

There are many correlations in the literary and cinematic traditions of Black women. As Mary Helen Washington points out, "the thoughts, experiences, words, feelings and deeds" of Black women are central to our work. To mirror and document ourselves are sources of personal power, of renewal, of validation, and of visibility.

Another intersection between the literature and films of women of the Black Diaspora is our approach to audience. We engage the reader/ viewer's emotions, intellect, and imagination to interact in the equation of creativity. No detached comfort zone marked "spectator" exists for those who open themselves to the literature and films of Black women. As Audre Lorde has noted, "the personal is political"—for both the creators and consumers of black women's visions. Where before there was no documentation of our lives, work, and worth, Black women have reshaped literature and film to fill the void.

Just as there are parallels in the motivations of Black women writers and filmmakers, there is also a point at which the disciplines converge— an alliance of crafts.

Writing is the heart of media production. The script or the detailed treatment guides all the technical, aesthetic, financial, and marketing considerations of a film or video. Further, "novelizations" (screen adaptations of literary works) have historically been a mainstay of Hollywood entertainment. The adage goes that the good novel will inevitably make a good movie. The formula is frequently espoused, but the product is rarely attained.

Through decades of racism, sexism, and homophobia, the contributions of traditional Black women writers—from Harriet Jacobs to Zora Neale Hurston and Gwendolyn Brooks—have been marginalized. The film industry is, of course, an accomplice to the silence—prioritizing any Pee Wee Herman spinoff over the literary classics of African-American women.

In the early days of Hollywood, white women were often scenarists, developing the story concepts upon which movies were made. In 1988, African-American women still remain, to a large extent, segregated out of screenwriting and other opportunities in the film industry.

When Lorraine Hansberry translated her award-winning play, "A Raisin in the Sun," to the screen in 1961, she broke new ground for Black writers entering Hollywood. Then in the midst of the turbulent 1960s and an industry-wide financial disaster, Hollywood discovered that "Black themes" could make money and mass-produced the formula throughout the "blaxploitation" phase of the 1970s. Few Black women reaped the benefits of Hollywood's brief consciousness, but Maya Angelou prevailed to see her first screenplay, "Georgia, Georgia" (starring Diana Sands), reach first-run exhibition.

Twenty-five years after Hansberry, Pamela Douglas is one of a few Black women in the Writer's Guild of America, the trade union of network and Hollywood writers (whose membership is less than ten percent Black). Contemporary Black women writers like Toni Morrison, Alice Walker, Gloria Naylor, and Virginia Hamilton have at least breached the first light of script development deals with the television networks and Hollywood. But the success of a few does not validate the exclusion of many. Nor do these overtures signal substantive change in the image of Black women in media. I dream a world where films based on the novels of Bessie Head, Audre Lorde, and the science fiction of Octavia Butler play at multiplex theatres nationwide.

In the production and promotion of Alice Walker's "The Color Purple," Hollywood's exploitative approach to the literary work of a Black woman was to make it "mass appeal," stripping it of all anger, rebellion, complexity, and color. Once the option has been negotiated, creative control is removed from the domain of the writer and the work becomes a property at the behest of the latest white male corporate executive at the studio.

But there is a steadfast, little recognized phenomenon afoot. Black women are also making movies. Our presence behind the camera as directors, producers, writers, editors, and technicians reverses a cinematic legacy of long-suffering mammies, sepia exotics, and tortured mulattoes. By controlling content and production, Black women filmmakers are countering the limited roles of Blacks in films, particularly Black women in films, as simply entertaining grist for the

Hollywood mill. We are also redefining the telling of our experiences and our history, using the same technology that has stereotyped us since the infancy of moving pictures. Today, we are image makers, not just shadows distorted on the silver screen.

White women, by virtue of racial privilege, have a legacy in filmmaking dating back to the Silent Era, when Lois Weber, Alice Guy-Blache, and later Dorothy Arzner were among the leading Hollywood directors. African-American women have a more recent history in film.

Twenty years ago, Madeline Anderson was one of a handful of women of color employed as a film editor and, later, as a director. In addition to her own films, she directed several episodes of "Sesame Street" and "The Electric Company." She was the first Black woman producer at National Educational Television (the pre-PBS public television system) as part of the "Black Journal" documentary team in the late 1960s. Her film on a Black hospital workers' strike entitled, "I Am Somebody," was an award-winning prototype for labor-organizing media.

In the early 1970s, Monica Freeman's documentaries heralded a new generation of Black women producing independent films about Black women. During this decade, more women of color undertook media careers as a result of affirmative action initiatives within the industry. Many of us received technical training in university film schools or "outreach" programs.

Approaching the 1990s, there are roughly twenty African-American women in the U.S. who work professionally as film/video directors or producers. On the east coast are Kathleen Collins, Ayoka Chenzira, Fronza Woods, Linda Gibson, Ellen Sumter, Muriel Jackson, Cheryl Chisholm, Kathe Sandler, Alile Sharon Larkin, Jackie Schearer, Joy Shannon, Carroll Blue, and Julie Dash. In the west are Barbara McCullough, Carol Munday Lawrence, and Debra Robinson. And our numbers are growing.

In the Diaspora, the feature films of Mozambiquan Sarah Maldoror illuminate the experiences of Blacks in Francophone Africa. And Maureen Blackwood, Martina Attile, and Nadine Marsh-Edwards of Britain's Sankofa Collective exemplify the wellspring of activity among Afro-European women.

In contrast, Black women have been *on film* since Thomas Edison's experiments with the kinetoscope at the turn of the century. The raw naiveté of a Black mother and child in "The Morning Bath" (1895) was the opening scene in a systematic rape of Black women's images. Over the next ninety years, the movies became the studios, the studios became the film industry, and the film industry is currently clustered into media conglomerates. With each decade, Hollywood developed new stereotypes which strip Black women of humanity and intricacy.

And Black women writers (who could have revolutionized our images on screen) were, of course, locked out of that system.

Fifty years ago, the roles of Louise Beavers, Hattie McDaniel, and Butterfly McQueen typified maids and mammies. Fredi Washington, in "Imitation of Life," immortalized the tragic mulatto. Nina Mae McKinney and Dorothy Dandridge, though consummate performers, were relegated to the tan sex siren/sepia exotic category. And Lena Horne was always Lena Horne.

The civil rights movement ushered in social consciousness to Hollywood films and the African-American experience on film was, for the first time, portrayed with some semblance of realism in the 1960's. Abbey Lincoln's role in "Nothing But a Man" indicated a new depth in Black women's characters. In the 1970s, "blaxploitation" movies increased the quantity of Black women appearing in film, but the quality of Black women's images were more variations of previous stereotypes. Cicely Tyson in "Sounder" and Tamara Dobson in "Cleopatra Jones" embodied the range (or lack of it) of Black women's roles during this period. But in this decade, significant numbers of Black people gained entrance into the film industry as technicians as well as performers.

Today, Whoopi Goldberg and Oprah Winfrey work with characters that flounder amid feminism, nostalgia, and mainstream acceptance. The 1980s finds Black women on film pigeonholed between invisibility and pseudo-liberation. Nola Darling in "She's Gotta Have It" characterizes the void. The Black sex object now speaks for herself, while the box-office beat goes on . . .

Films made by African-American women span a variety of genres: from animation to documentary, experimental to dramatic features. The subject matter is diverse: a profile of a domestic worker (Fronza Woods' "Fannie's Film"); an animated short on the Black hair/identity crisis (Ayoka Chenzira's "Hairpiece: A Film for Nappy-Headed People"); a 1940s vignette on a Black woman "passing" her way through the Hollywood studio system (Julie Dash's "Illusions"); a documentary on Black comediennes (Debra Robinson's "I Be Done Been Was Is"); and video art (Barbara McCullough's "Water Ritual No. 1" and Annette Lawrence's "Beyond Carte Blanche").

Essentially, the works of Black women filmmakers preserve, affirm, and explore Black culture through women's eyes. Productions by Black women are sporadically seen on public television or at international film festivals. But community groups, women's organizations, and educational services remain our primary markets for rentals and sales. The dramatic feature "Sugar Cane Alley," by Martinican filmmaker Euzhan Palcy, was a recent exception. Her 1983 feature film received an extensive theatrical release. Though it was an overwhelming critical and artistic success, "Sugar Cane Alley" garnered only a fraction of the box-office generated by Spike Lee's "She's Gotta Have It" and Robert Townsend's "Hollywood Shuffle." This disparity not only underscores the importance of distribution factoring in the films of Black women, but it also confirms the notion that the mainstream market will welcome the occasional Black film—as long as it is a comedy or musical.

Being a Black woman filmmaker requires your best womanish and womanist[2] (i.e., courageous, willful) behavior. To keep producing is a constant test of your artistic and political commitment given the realities of job discrimination in Hollywood, sexism and homophobia within the Black independent film community, and racism and class oppression in the feminist film community. Further, the economic drought imposed by the Reagan (and now Bush) administrations on social and cultural services has impacted most drastically on films by women of color, because local and federal grants are the major funding source for these productions.

Filmmaking, albeit show business, *is* business. It is the costliest art form to produce. No matter how revolutionary, philanthropic, politically correct, or worthy of support the film may be, money stands between it being just another creative concept and audiences actually being moved by it. Today, "broadcast quality" independent films and videos average $2,000 per minute. Funding is a crucial issue for Black women filmmakers and the independent community-at-large. We are utilizing strategies such as foreign coproduction deals, limited partnerships, and crew collectives to confront the ongoing financial oppression plaguing our productions.

Some of us teach film theory and production at the university level. Others work in the industry as well as independently. Carol Munday Lawrence assisted Francis Ford Coppola during the filming of "The Cotton Club." Fronza Woods was on the film crew of John Sayles' "The Brother from Another Planet." Carroll Blue worked as a production assistant on the film "On Golden Pond." Mary Neema Barnette, currently one of four African-American women in the Directors Guild of America, made the transition from independent production to directing episodes of "Frank's Place" and feature projects at Columbia Pictures. She is currently directing "Zora Is My Name" (starring Ruby Dee) for PBS American Playhouse.

TV director Debbie Allen, who starred in "Fame," the TV series, began her directing career on this popular NBC show. She is credited with the facelift of the No. 2 rated sitcom, "A Different World" and directed Disney's TV movie remake of "Pollyanna." Elaine Head has directed several episodes of ABC's new season hit "Snoops," which was filmed on location here in Washington, D.C. Black women filmmakers are the heirs to generations of Black women who did what they had to do to make it possible for us to do what we do best.

In the Silent Era, small, all-Black film companies flourished during the segregated 1920s. The forerunners of this movement were Black men like Oscar Micheaux and George and Noble Johnson. They were challenged to create popular entertainment for Black audiences against the odds.

The only woman noted in this era of early Black film is Eloyce Gist. An evangelist traveling the rural South during the Depression, she scripted, produced, and exhibited her self-styled revivalist films to stir the faithful. And in 1943, Frances Williams was the first Black woman to attend the University of Southern California film school. In the 1930s, she was inspired by Soviet filmmaker Sergei Eisenstein while touring the U.S.S.R.

Against the backdrop of the feminist movement, the groundbreaking efforts of women like Madeline Anderson and Monica Freeman helped establish the new presence of Black women behind the camera in the 1970s and 1980s. The expanding body of works by Black women filmmakers is the residual—the harvest of their determination. A new trend is also developing. Several dramatic feature films directed by Black women will reach the screen over the next year. Euzhan Palcy has recently completed her long-awaited second feature, "A Dry White Season"; Joy Shannon's first feature, "From Rags to Reality," is in distribution; and Julie Dash's "Daughters of the Dust" (with partial funding from PBS American Playhouse) will be completed in 1990. This movement toward longer, more expensive, serious dramatic films follows a precedent established by the late Kathleen Collins. Kathleen Collins' films, "The Cruz Brothers and Miss Malloy" (1980) and "Losing Ground" (1982), signaled a new day for Black women entering the inner sanctum of independent feature film production.

That Black women filmmakers exist, survive, and multiply in this precarious, underfunded business of independent production is nothing short of divine—Black, womanish, and divine. For those Black women independents persevering into the 1990s, the media offer challenges of content and technology. The new faces of racism, the issue of "color-casting"—the internalized oppression between light and darker-skinned Black people—and our global connections with other people of color will be explored. And for the first time, the history and experiences of Black lesbians and gays will be documented.

The 1990s promise a new visibility to themes of sexuality, "otherness," and alliances in the independent films and videos of Black women. Media with a mission to examine the systematic and imperceptible lines we draw across racial, sexual and cultural identities.

But unless and until we address the conditions of the 1980s, the 1990s will find us with more convoluted images and no recognition of Black women's achievements in the craft of independent film.

From Phyllis Wheatly to contemporary African-American women writers, a continuum exists. Those ties also bind Black women filmmakers, from Eloyce Gist to Neema Barnette. The health and connection of our creative communities are summarized in this memoir by filmmaker Carroll Blue:

July 1985

I am invited to meet Euzhan Palcy at Daphne Muse's in Oakland. I look with admiration at this beautiful, strong young Black woman filmmaker who could well be my daughter. Is it her confidence that creates her beauty? She tells us Robert Redford cried upon seeing her "Sugar Cane Alley" at Sundance. Invisible to this group, I turn and in my mind's eye, I see Frances Willams standing behind us . . . She was a strong force in finishing "Salt of the Earth" in 1952. She now appears on "Franks's Place" and television commercials to make a living. When Frances sees us, her eyes sparkle, jumping out of her old and crippled body. She greets all of us with her "Hello there, my little babies." I meet the courageous eyes of Euzhan and realize now that Frances greets herself in meeting all our eyes. Our heritage makes us a real family.

Notes

1. The title is taken from a poem by Essex Hemphill.
2. *Womanist*: See Alice Walker's essay, "In Search of Our Mothers' Gardens." In *In Search of Our Mothers' Gardens: Womanist Prose*. 1983. San Diego, CA: Harcourt Brace Jovanovich.
3. Blue, Carroll Parrott. 1987. "Sometimes a Poem is Twenty Years of Memory," *Sage: A Scholarly Journal on Black Women*, vol. IV, no. 1, Spring.

Filmography

Collins, Kathleen. 1980. "The Cruz Brothers and Mrs. Malloy" (16 mm, 60 min). Distributor: (8).
Collins, Kathleen. 1982. "Losing Ground" (16 mm, 86 min). Distributor: (8).
Chenzira, Ayoka. 1979. "Syvilla: They Dance to Her Drum" (16 mm, 25 min). Distributor: (3).
Chenzira, Ayoka. 1982. "Flamboyant Ladies Speak Out" (3/4" video, 30 min). Distributor: (3).
Chenzira, Ayoka. 1985. "Secret Sounds Screaming: The Sexual Abuse of Children" (3/4" video, 30 min). Distributor: (3).
Chenzira, Ayoka. "Poets on the Dance Floor" (work in progress).
Woods, Fronza. 1978. "Killing Time" (16 mm, 8 1/2 min). Distributor: (2).
Woods, Fronza. 1980. "Fannie's Film" (16 mm, 15 min). Distributor: (2).
Gibson, Linda. 1978–80. "Dance Videos" (3/4" video). Inquiries: (1).
Gibson, Linda. 1985. "Flag" (3/4" video). Inquiries: (1).
Sumter, Ellen. 1988. "Rags and Old Love" (16 mm,. 30 min). Contact filmmaker: (404) 237-7964.

Jackson, Muriel. 1985. "The Maids!" (3/4" and 1/2" VHS, 28 min). Distributor: (1).
Chisholm, Cheryl. 1987. "On Becoming a Woman" (90 min, 16 mm; video). Distributor: (1).
Sandler, Kathe. 1981. "Remembering Thelma" (16 mm; video, 15 min). Distributor: (1) (2).
Sandler, Kathe. "A Question of Color" (work in progress).
Larkin, Alile Sharon. 1979. "Your Children Come Back to You" (16 mm, 27 min). Distributor: (2) (4).
Larkin, Alile Sharon. 1981. "A Different Image" (16 mm, 51 min). Distributor: (2).
Shearer, Jackie, 1977. "A Minor Altercation" (16 mm; video, 30 min). Distributor: (1) (2).
Shannon, Joy. 1981. "Echo" (16 mm, 30 min). Distributor: (2).
Shannon, Joy. 1986. "Until the Last Stroke" (3/4" video, 30 min). Distributor: (2).
Blue, Carroll Parrott. 1979. "Varnette's World: A Study of a Young Artist" (16 mm, 26 min). Distributor: (2).
Blue, Carroll Parrott. 1984. "Conversations with Roy DeCarva" (16 mm, 60 min). Distributor: (5).
Dash, Julie. 1978. "Four Women" (16mm, 7 min). Distributor: (2).
Dash, Julie. 1982. "Illusions" (16 mm, 34 min). Distributor: (1) (2).
Dash, Julie. "Daughters of the Dust" (feature film in progress).
McCullough, Barbara. 1980. "Water Ritual No. 2" (3/4" video, 30 min). Contact: 1832-1834 W. 24th St., Los Angeles, CA 90018.
McCullough, Barbara. 1981. "The World Saxophone Quartet" (3/4" video, 30 min segments).
Lawrence, Carol Munday. 1980. "Were You There?" (3/4" video, 30 min segments). Distributor: (7).
Lawrence, Carol Munday. "The Nicholas Brothers" (work in progress).
Robinson, Debra. 1984. "I Be Done Been Was Is" (16 mm, 58 min). Distributor: (2).
Freeman, Monica. 1975. "Valerie, a Woman, an Artist, a Philosophy of Life" (16 mm, 15 min). Distributor (2).
Freeman, Monica. 1977. "A Sense of Pride: Hamilton Heights" (16 mm, 15 min). Distributor: (2).
Freeman, Monica. 1979. "Children's Art Carnival—Learning Through the Arts" (16 mm, 17 min). Distributor: (2).
Parkerson, Michelle. 1980. "But then, She's Betty Carter" 16 mm, 53 min). Distributor: (1) (2) (4).
Parkerson, Michelle. 1983. "Gotta Make This Journey: Sweet Honey in the Rock" (3/4" video, 58 min). Distributor: (2) (4) (6).
Parkerson, Michelle. 1987. "Storme: The Lady of the Jewel Box" (16 mm; video, 21 min). Distributor: (1) (4).
Parkerson, Michelle. 1987. "I Remember BETTY" (16 mm; video, 10 min). Distributor: Eye of the Storm Productions, P.O. Box 21568, Washington, D.C. 20009; (202) 332-7977.

Distributors (request catalog)

1. Women Make Movies, Inc., 225 Lafayette St., Suite 212, New York, NY 10012; (212) 925-0606.
2. Black Filmmaker Foundation, 80 8th Ave., Suite 1704, New York, NY 10011; (212) 924-1198.
3. National Black Programming Consortium, 929 Harrison Ave., Columbus, OH 43215; (614) 299-5355.
4. First Run/Icarius Films, 144 Bleecker St., New York, NY 10012; (212) 674-3375.
5. Museum of Modern Art, Circulating Film/Video Library, 11 W. 53rd St., New York, NY 10019; (212) 708-9530.

6. Nguzo Saba Films, 2482 Sutter St., San Francisco, CA 94115; (415) 921-1507.
7. Mypheduh Films, 48 Q St. N.E., Washington, DC 20001; (202) 529-0220.
8. Third World Newsreel, 335 W. 38th St, 5th floor, New York, NY 10018; (212)947-9277.

References

Blue, Carroll Parrott. 1987. "Sometimes a Poem is Twenty Years of Memory." *Sage: A Scholarly Journal on Black Women,* Vol. IV, No. 1, Spring: 37–38.

Boseman, Keith. 1986. "Ayoka Chenzira: Starving the Empowerment of Women." *Black Film Review* 2, Summer: 18–19, 25.

Campbell, Loretta. 1983. "Reinventing Our Own Image: 11 Black Women Filmmakers." *Heresies* 16, Fall: 58–62.

Gossage, Leslie. 1987. "Black Women Independent Filmmakers: Changing Images of Black Women." *Iris: A Journal About Women,* Spring/Summer, 4-11. Women's Studies, University of Virginia, Charlottesville, VA.

Harris, Kwasi. 1986. "New Images: An Interview with Julie Dash and Alile Sharon Larkin." *The Independent,* December, 16–20.

Hooks, Bell. 1986. "Black Women Filmmakers Break the Silence." *Black Film Review* 2, Summer: 14–15.

Kafi-Akua, Afua. 1987. "Ayoka Chenzira, Filmmaker." *Sage: A Scholarly Journal on Black Women,* Vol. IV, No. 1, Spring: 69–72.

Oliver, Denise Roberts. 1983. "What's She Doing Behind the Camera?" Black American Film Program, Black Filmmaker Foundation, 7–8.

Parkerson, Michelle. 1987. "Answering the Void." *The Independent,* April, 12–13.

Wali, Monona. 1986. "L.A. Black Filmmakers Thrive Despite Hollywood's Monopoly." *Black Film Review,* 2 Summer: 10, 27.

Washington, Mary Helen. 1987. "Introduction." In *Invented Lives: Narratives of Black Women, 1860–1960.* Garden City, NY: Doubleday.

Recovery and Transformation
The Blue Heron

Beth Brant

Last weekend in Minneapolis was the first gathering of gay and lesbian Indians—The Basket and the Bow.[1] This gathering was a joyful reunion, much like a powwow, where we go to see old friends, share stories, catch up on tribal happenings, take care of Indian business—the difference being that this reunion was between people who had never met.

As I talked with my sisters and brothers and listened, listened to the voices telling their stories, two words kept insisting their message onto my brain.

Recovery. Transformation.

Recovery. Transformation.

Recovery is the act of taking control over the forces that would destroy us. Recovery from alcohol and drug use—most definitely. But another kind of recovery is taking place in my Indian family. Recovery from the disease of homophobia. This disease has devastated my Indian family as surely as alcohol, smallpox, and tuberculosis has devastated our Indian communities. Recovery is not an act that ignores the disease. Recovery is becoming stronger than the disease. The evidence was there before my eyes. For two days I heard the people assure me that we won't self-destruct anymore, we won't be shamed anymore, *we won't go away*.

118

There is a coming-clean that takes place before the transformative work begins. We cleanse ourselves according to our world view. Albert told a story of how he wanted to participate in the Sun Dance but was fearful of homophobic reaction. He went to the Medicine Woman, who told him, "You will present yourself to the Creator, not the people." Albert took the message to heart. A Sun Dance can last a number of hours or even days, until a communion with the Creator is made. Albert made this communion and presented himself with a full knowledge of who he is in his own mind, as well as the knowledge of who he is to the community. I like that phrase, *present yourself.* It seems to fit us so much better than *coming out.* We are a complicated people, my family. We are not simple nature-worshipping people, as I heard some woman describe us at this conference. We do not worship nature. We are a part of it.

Presenting ourselves to the Creator means realigning ourselves within our communities and within ourselves to create a balance that will keep us whole. To be an Indian lesbian and gay man at this time means to be on a path that won't be blocked by anyone or anything. To be an Indian lesbian and gay man at this time means that a woman like me won't have to search for the Barbara Camerons to keep me sane.[2] The Barbara Camerons of the future are here in the printed word, on the tapes, on film, on this stage, in this audience. There will be no coverup in this recovery—by white imperialism or by my own people. There are too many of us now. We are too savvy, too knowledgeable of the colonialist's mind, too well-versed in our politics to allow the obvious to be hidden again under the layers of anthropological bullshit, denial, or the looks of anger that come from our heterosexual brothers' and sisters' eyes.

If our existence can be denied, then so can the existence of racism be denied. So can the existence of infant mortality or uranium in our drinking water and the chipping away of our lands, stone by stone. If you believe in the existence of a Blue Heron, wild rice, the moon—then you have to believe in me.

Recovery means that we transform ourselves. Presenting ourselves means that we transform the world. This was made even more clear last weekend. Albert has started a gay Native organization on his reservation. Beverly and Charlene have started their own spiritual retreat for women, for lesbians of all colors to come and be renewed for the political acts that *must* follow the presenting of ourselves. So many of my family are substance abuse counselors, lawyers skilled in tribal sovereignty issues. My family are health care workers, teachers, midwives, artists, writers. Our political acts—and our very survival *is* a political act—are transforming the face of Indian Country and making inroads into the heart of the country.

There is a personal recovery taking place in me. For the last two years I have been on a journey of physical illness, culminating in a small stroke and a ten-hour surgery to bypass a blocked artery that had almost stopped the flow of blood to my legs. This journey took many turnings I would not have chosen for myself—the incredible pain each day as I walked from room to room. This journey caused me to distrust people who loved me. Made me be unkind to those who would have helped me. Made me give up the thing that kept me sane—writing. Made me welcome my oldest friend, self-hatred.

As the stroke was beginning in my arm, traveling to my right leg, then moving up to my face, I shouted "NO!" The echoes of that *no* bounced around in my ears. Terrified and almost incapable of thought or action, the words *not yet, not yet, not yet,* were sounding like a drum with each of my heart's beat. Later in the hospital I thought about the arrogance of those words, *not yet, not yet.* I realized, lying in the hospital bed, that my recovery and the power to be transformed were waiting for my acceptance of them.

Lying there, in the hospital bed, my beloved Denise's face hovering above me, I remembered an incident that I had allowed myself to forget. The Great Blue Heron is a personal totem, and this is the reason why. My lover and I have a small cabin on Walpole Island in Ontario. This island is an Indian reserve and is primarily marsh land. Denise and I love to canoe along the little channels and watch birds. One day we found a small patch of land that was dry. A tree was still growing there and gave us shade and a lovely place to eat our lunch. We wanted to make love and so we did. As I felt the first tremors of orgasm, a Blue Heron entered my mind and body. She started to unfold her great wings to take flight. As each pulse of the orgasm took hold of me, she raised herself higher and higher, her wings flapping with incredible strength. She was in flight and opened her long yellow beak and let out a cry. Later, I asked Denise if she had heard the Heron's voice. She replied, "no dearest, I heard only yours."

I have thought about that Heron since my operation and especially during this week. The transformative power of sex, the complete magic of sex that has been denied us, or trivialized to the point of denying meaning. The transformative power of being Native lesbian at this time and for all time.

My cry of *no,* my cry of love, is the cry of a Blue Heron—unconfined, true, power-filled. The Heron taught me that recovery is transformation. Transformation is an act of love. Lesbian and gay Natives will become the elders of our people. We will be giving counsel of love and wisdom. Indian people bring a particular kind of beauty to this world. Lesbian and gay Indians expand that beauty by bringing our transformative love to those who would receive it.

Thank you.

Notes

1. The Basket and Bow Conference took place June 18–19, 1988. For further info, call Lee Staples (612) 870-4848.
2. Barbara Cameron is the cofounder of Gay American Indians (GAI). She has been a source of inspiration and love to all Native lesbians, by being the strong, unafraid woman she is. Writer, activist, mother, and speaker—she was the one that women like me could point to and say, "She did it, it must be possible for me to do it also."

Taking Risks
The Creation of Feminist Literature

Judith McDaniel

It is ironic. Sanctuary is about living dangerously. Sanctuary is about
taking risks beyond the ordinary. Risks of class security or race
security. Risks of the heart. Physical risks. I have never in my life
felt as secure in myself as during those twenty-nine hours of captivity
on the Rio San Juan. I knew well I might be killed. But I also knew
more clearly than I had ever known before that I was in the right
place. I was in the right place in that jungle and I was in the right
place in myself. Taking the risk allowed me to be the person I had
always wanted to be (from *Sanctuary: A Journey*, Ithaca, NY: Firebrand
Books, 1987, p. 147).

I became a serious writer when the risks I was taking in my life began
to have "real" consequences in both my life and art and when the risks
I was taking in my art began to have "real" consequences in my life.
Taking risks, it has been suggested to me, is a literary cliche, the stuff
of undergraduate poetry workshops. Or, I've been told, taking risks
is what those early feminists did in the sixties and seventies, and our
job now is not to take risks but to consolidate our access into the

"Taking Risks: The Creation of Feminist Literature," is reprinted from *The American
Voice,* No. 17, Winter 1989, pp. 102–9.

system. After a year of traveling all over the United States, reading and talking about sanctuary and taking risks, and about my own experience of being captured by U.S.-backed Contras in Nicaragua while working with Witness for Peace, I am convinced that we need to continue the discussion of risks, perhaps reminding ourselves now and then that the original meaning of risk was "danger and loss." The risks I refer to are risks that lead to a profound change in our landscape, both the personal, emotional landscape of our lives and the physically present landscape.

*   *   *

I began writing poetry seriously in 1975, the same year I affirmed, both publically and privately, my lesbian identity. I didn't change the pronouns in my poetry, didn't try to pretend the "you" in my love poems was other than my woman lover. For the first few years I wrote poetry, I felt generally supported. I was, after all, a novice and didn't expect notices about my work in the *New York Times*. I gave a couple of readings, attended by faithful, but honest, friends and began to get feedback. A new lesbian journal, *Sinister Wisdom,* published two of my first poems in 1976. Other poems and publications came slowly; I was primarily a college professor, teaching other people's literature, and it was nearly seven years before I had enough poems I was pleased with to consider publishing a chapbook. Even then, I thought myself fortunate. A local arts group was starting a publishing venture and offered to publish my first chapbook, *November Woman.* They received a small grant from the Arts Council and began the process. Just before we went to press, they asked me to come for an editorial conference. One poem, they felt, didn't fit, wasn't as good as the others, was off tone. "Acadia" was, of course, the only explicitly lesbian and sexual poem in the collection. I withdrew my manuscript from consideration; after several difficult conversations—and circumstances that made it impossible for them to publish any other book with the funds they had received—they agreed to publish my book in a reduced print run on less expensive paper. You see, they wanted to use up the grant money but had no intention of trying to sell the book locally and so did not want any of their money tied to this venture.

While these negotiations were going on, I was also in the process of a tenure decision at the college where I had been teaching for six years. After even more unpleasant and extended interactions, I was told that I was being denied tenure. Not because I was a lesbian, of course, not because I had been politically active around gay and lesbian issues in my community and in my national professional organization, but because they had decided I was a poor teacher, a deficient scholar, a naive and unsophisticated poet, and an inadequate colleague.

I was in those years feeling rather sorry for myself, but that's not why I'm telling this story today. Nor, today, do I feel sorry for myself. I was an adult, acting with a certain amount of political consciousness, making choices that would have an impact on my professional life, choices that would carry consequences in a real world that is—as I certainly knew—less than perfect.

I would like to digress for a moment and present a poem written in the same genre as "Acadia," that is, a lesbian love poem. It was written in 1935 by poet and feminist antiwar activist Barbara Deming.

> she held the flower cold up against her cheek
> bones in the dark the petals flattened cold up
> against her cheekbones this flower your
> fingers you had danced with this flower in your
> mouth your tongue had been pink like a cat's
> tongue and slender touching the petals you had
> dance with this flower in your mouth held in
> your teeth your teeth biting the petals the
> petals cold up against her cheekbones she held
> the flower cold up against her cheekbones in
> the dark.

This poem is, I think, quite wonderful. It is written as though one spontaneous breath, written without punctuation and without self-consciousness. It uses enjambment and syllabic stress to create the breathy rhythm and contains no punctuation, asking the reader to create the emphasis and pause usually given by punctuation.

Many people have known Barbara Deming from her book, *Prison Notes,* an account of her struggles during the civil rights movement, a struggle which found her in Birmingham, Alabama, and Albany, Georgia, jails with Martin Luther King and others. Some may have known her from her book *Revolution and Equilibrium,* which recounts the antiwar struggle during the Vietnam years, including her trip to Hanoi during the height of the U.S bombing of that city. Others first knew her when they read *We Cannot Live Without Our Lives,* an early book about feminism which was published in 1974 and dedicated "to my lesbian sisters." And women who were at the Seneca Women's Peace Encampment in upstate New York in the summer of 1983 may remember Barbara Deming herself as she walked from the Seneca Falls Women's Hall of Fame toward the Women's Peace Encampment at the Seneca Army Depot, was stopped—with many other women—on a bridge in Waterloo, was arrested with fifty-four other women, and thus became one of the "Jane Doe's" of the Peace Encampment. But few, I think, remember her as a poet.

I am now the literary executor of Barbara Deming's estate, and I found the poem that I have just read among manuscripts containing many other poems and letters.* When she wrote it in 1935, Barbara was seventeen years old and having her first love affair, her first sexual experience with a woman. She fell in love with her neighbor, Norma Millay, sister of Edna St. Vincent Millay, a woman twice Barbara's age. In a letter written to her mother in 1974, responding to her mother's criticism of Barbara's dedication of her new book "to my lesbian sisters," Barbara writes: "I have always been grateful to you for the fact that when you first told me about homosexuality you spoke of it very simply and did not condemn it to me as anything ugly. Because of this, when I fell in love with Norma I felt no hatred of myself. My first experience of love was free of that poison. I've always been grateful to Norma, too—for *she* taught me no shame. But I learned it all too soon."

That must be true—that she learned it all too soon—for in the upper right hand corner of that poem written in 1935, and on dozens of other love poems like it, is pencilled in Barbara's handwriting the word *omit*. Omit. Omit this poem from being sent out to journals for publication, omit this poem from the collection she was putting together, and from all collections after this. I have been reading the poems Barbara published during her lifetime and the poems she didn't publish, and if I didn't know something about oppression and the way it inhibits the risks we can take, I think I might simply conclude that Barbara Deming failed to become a "great" poet because she never developed the faculty of self-evaluation—where her poetry was concerned. But today I believe Barbara Deming had no forum in which to truly test her poetic powers, no magazine or journals to which she could even submit a lesbian poem, no identified audience to whom she could read a lesbian poem, and therefore no feedback about which poems "worked" and which did not.

I was more fortunate than Barbara when the quality of my poem was challenged. I had read "Acadia" in front of an audience of several hundred women earlier that year at a National Women's Studies Conference event. I knew from the reaction of women in that audience, women about whose opinion I cared, that "Acadia" was not the problem with my book of poems. So even if I had not been able to judge the poem for myself, exercising that elusive faculty of self-evaluation, I had information that would help me decide whether or not to omit that poem from my book. It was a risk, there were consequences; but

---

* The Barbara Deming archive papers are now available for study and use at the Schlesinger Women's History Library of Radcliff College, Boston, MA.

I knew it was not a risk that would annihilate me and I knew that not to take the risk would carry far more serious consequences to my work. Those are the consequences Barbara Deming experienced. If we do not choose to take some risks, or if we are forbidden to take them, then we are denied the chance to test ourselves in the world; and that denial leaves us less skilled, generally, I believe, leaves us in a child-like or adolescent state rather than letting us experience ourselves as adults.

What makes an action risky is a question I have asked myself many times. I know I am facing a risk when I feel fear, and that fear is not always of the same things nor do all fears feel the same. In *A Burst of Light,* poet Audre Lorde writes about living for the last three years with liver cancer. She says in her journal, "I want to write down everything I know about being afraid, but I'd probably never have enough time to write anything else. Afraid is a country where they issue us passports at birth and hope we never seek citizenship in any other country" (Firebrand Books, Ithaca, NY, 1988, p. 53). When we choose a risk, we are choosing to face down a fear, or at least to walk with it past the boundaries of our experience.

Sometimes art is that risk and sometimes art makes it possible for us to face the fears that are inhibiting our journey. I began this reflection with the assertion that I became a serious artist when the risks I was taking began to have "real" consequences in my life. One of those consequences was being denied tenure, losing the career and definition of self that I thought would always be mine. To stay sane I began to write down what I was feeling. I couldn't yet put the words down about my own feelings and my own experience, and so I created a fictional college professor, a young woman named Anna who was a poet, a good poet, and I gave her a teaching position at a college like one I had been at many years before, and then I fired her. And this professor who was not me could have all of the feelings I was afraid of until I was able to have them myself. I wrote every day for three months, usually about three pages a day, and before I left my job I had a draft of my novel *Winter Passage,* and I had a grasp on myself.

I had a very similar experience in writing my second book of poems about recovery from alcoholism, *Metamorphosis and Other Poems of Recovery.* I was afraid sometimes of being overwhelmed by the feelings I was learning, beginning to experience. I do not advocate art as therapy or presume that every self-expression which may be therapeutic is therefore art, but I have found that poetry and fiction are excellent places to begin to walk past the boundaries of our lives. The explosions and flying shrapnel of our emotional lives are not usually fatal in art.

And the risk we experience when we tell our stories truly is the risk of change: the risk that we will be changed by the telling and the risk our audience similarly experiences, that they will be changed by the hearing. In some traditions, this kind of truth telling is called witnessing. I had to think about this process when I began to work with the Sanctuary Movement in 1984, began to meet refugees from El Salvador and Guatemala who believed that their work was to tell the story of what was happening in their country. It wasn't enough to be safe, the refugees were saying, they had to work for the people they had left behind who were not safe, and their work was to tell the story of what had happened to them for North Americans to hear and—hearing—to understand our role in the refugees' suffering. For it is our government, primarily, that is supporting the Central American military dictatorships with arms and assistance.

As I was hearing and responding to (being changed by) the stories of refugees from Central America, I realized that this process had happened to me before:

> Those of us who are feminists, who have lived the experience of feminist process, know the power of witnessing. That was what we did when we heard one another's stories of oppression or connection with the kind of attention that is nearly passion. We always knew the truth of a story, knew when the speaker had found the core of what she was seeking to express. I know my life is not the same today as it would have been if a feminist poet had not stood in front of a group of academic women and challenged them to hear their own hearts by exposing hers. My decision to live openly as a lesbian in the moment I claimed that identity was only possible because I had met other women who were living openly lesbian lives.
>
> Witness, I learned again in my life, is a circle. I heard Pedro tell his story and my consciousness was changed by hearing him. I decided to go to Nicaragua. When I returned I told my own story. If other lives are changed by the hearing, and others feel moved to act differently, there will be new witnesses to that experience (from *Sanctuary: A Journey*, p. 128).

And with *Sanctuary: A Journey* I began to understand risk in a new way. I began to understand the artistic risk of political writing and I began to understand that while physical risks and emotional risks are not the same, they are sometimes joined.

What I understood in that new way in Nicaragua was that my political life, my artistic life, my emotional life, and my spiritual life could not be separated and that they all grew from the same source. When I began *Sanctuary: A Journey,* the first poem I worked on was the long poem about beginning the journey called "Leaving Home." In the last section of that poem I wanted to say something about the journey. I had been writing about home, trying to understand some of the things home can be and what it cannot be. In the poem I remember:

There are words you must never use
in a poem I have told students
soul love and yet I have found
no image to bear the weight of knowing
that home is the place of the heart . . .

Love was the word that followed me during the writing of this book. It was a risk for me artistically—the word LOVE, I mean—I knew that certainly, as do any teachers who have tried to wade through amateur poems that proclaim "love" rather than demonstrate it. And it was a risk for me personally. I had tried always to understand my relationship to the world in political terms. I went to Nicaragua as a feminist to make a political statement. I believed that. But after our release and in the months following my return from Nicaragua I was forced to look differently at what I had done. Finally, I had to realize that *Sanctuary* was a book about love and the risks we take for love, even when we call it something else.

Palestinian Women
Building Barricades and Breaking Barriers*

Rita Giacaman and Penny Johnson

Umm 'Uthman (the mother of 'Uthman) is forty-six years old. A member of the black community of the Jericho area, she is tall, fine-boned, almost Ethiopian in appearance. She lives in 'Ayn Duyuk, a small community of about 1,000 persons, where the race divide of black and white still dominates economic and social relations, a rarity in Palestinian society. Umm 'Uthman is to us Umm Ruqayya, because we came to know her through her radical and activist daughter.

Ruqayya, twenty-six years old, is a worker at one of the sewing sweatshops in nearby Jericho. She is reputed to be one of the main figures fueling the activism of the local chapter of the Seamstresses' Union. As her friends and family put it: "She has driven the owner and administration of the workshop mad with her clever strategies and plans for improving work conditions." Ruqayya is also well educated, modern, and "cultured" (muthaqqafa). She reads regularly, writes well,

* Reprinted with permission from *Intifada: The Palestinian Uprising Against Israeli Occupation,* ed. by Zachary Lockman and Joel Beinin, A M.E.R.I.P. Book, Boston, South End Press, 1989.

argues points beautifully and, in sum, represents the best characteristics of a new generation of progressive women political activists.

With innate characteristics not so unlike her daughter's, but without having had the chance to grow up in an era when these characteristics could develop, Umm 'Uthman is haggard, very tall, and very thin, except for that pouch of a belly, the nagging evidence of many pregnancies, twenty-two in all. About half were lost before birth or early in childhood. Twelve children remain, with the oldest aged twenty-eight and the youngest a mere six months old. She has no regrets about having had so many children because children, she says, "are needed, especially in these days of strife, when every Palestinian counts." Umm 'Uthman's sense of responsibility toward family and community is embodied in her awareness of her important role as a mother, a role enhanced in her mind and the community's by the current uprising.

We went to visit her on November 6, 1988, when we heard that the family house had been demolished by the Israeli army. Hers was one of more than 100 houses destroyed in the northern Jordan valley, leaving about 1,000 persons homeless and devastated. The army's rationale was collective punishment of these remote communities for allegedly having hidden in their midst someone who had thrown a Molotov cocktail at an Israeli bus, resulting in the deaths of an Israeli mother and her three young children. In fact, the Israeli army had apparently been intending to empty that particular area, a sensitive security zone, of its inhabitants.

We found Umm 'Uthman seated on the floor, clutching her breast-feeding infant with one hand and a cigarette that she puffed deliberately and systematically with the other. Chairs were quickly brought to seat the guests, and Umm 'Uthman began to recount her story:

> It was on the night of October 30 that our lives were pulled upside down. That evening, just a day or two after the bus incident, we heard helicopters flying in the sky. They came down towards our village at the same time as soldiers began to move in. We immediately closed our door, put out the lights and went to bed, wondering to whose neighbor's house they were heading. So you can imagine our shock when they began to ferociously bang at our door. They came in and began to break everything they had in front of them. They took away my five sons and informed me that I had ten minutes to pack my belongings because they were going to demolish the house. But there was no one to help me pack because they had kept away all the villagers and had succeeded in isolating us and our house. I was alone with my youngest child. I was hardly able to carry some clothes for my baby with me when I was pushed, shoved and forced out of the house, and the house with everything in it and all our belongings were dynamited.

Of all the members of this community, it was Ruqayya who mobilized immediately in response to the destruction of her house, three more in the village, and many others in the valley, as well as the arrest of her five brothers. When we arrived Ruqayya had already left for Jerusalem to talk to lawyers, the Red Cross, and any other institution or agency capable of assisting the family and the community in these hard times. Within a day, she had single-handedly "moved mountains," utilizing her skills and contacts developed through her activism in the local women's committee and her Seamstresses' Union.

Ruqayya's activism and her education thus gave her a considerable amount of power, not only within the world of women, but with her entire village. Although a woman, Ruqayya was indispensable to her community during this crisis. She could serve her community in areas where no one else could, so why bother about the fact of her womanhood? To the community, what mattered most was survival in these times when the formal networks of support were breaking down and when conditions were creating new and pressing needs. Survival dictated a changing attitude toward the activism of women in general and to Ruqayya's full participation in political life in particular.

Ruqayya is one of many women forging a new chapter in the history of the Palestinian women's movement. She is the antithesis to the image of obedient wife and mother, of the silent woman who executes the wishes of husband and kin without a word uttered. *Tum bila lisan* (a mouth without a tongue) is how traditional society usually characterizes "good" women. Ruqayya exemplifies an emerging new consciousness regarding the status of women in Palestinian society and their participation in political life. Ruqayya is the daughter of the uprising, having risen to the status of a community leader of both men and women just during the past several months.

Observers of the intifada have tended to focus on its impact on the Palestinian political agenda, as exemplified in the decisions of the November 1988 meeting of the Palestine National Council in Algiers. But equally important for the lives of the Palestinian people, in particular women, are the transformations the uprising has wrought in the forms of struggle. Mass insurgency and collective defiance in the context of a popular revolt have become the new cornerstones of political action, a change from the previous emphasis on armed struggle, shuttle diplomacy, and limited mass action. The development of the popular and neighborhood committees and a partial shift in the locus of authority and action from formal institutions and networks of political action to the streets have also had far-reaching social ramifications. In the framework of the new informal and popular networks of community support and action, important shifts in women's participation in political life have taken place.

On the basis of interviews with women activists, particularly leaders and activists in the women's committees, as well as the authors' own observations and conversations with women in camps, towns, and villages during the course of the uprising, we have tried to explore how the dramatic political changes outlined above have affected the position of Palestinian women in the world of politics—both formal and informal. We wanted to delineate the various roles women are playing in the uprising: in confrontations, in political organizations and political decision making, in community survival and in community organization. We have only tentative answers for some of our questions, including the all-important question of whether women's political role in the uprising will lead to permanent changes in women's participation and status in the society of the future. That question remains to be asked—and ultimately answered—by Palestinian women themselves.

The Palestinian women's movement

From its inception in the 1920s, the women's movement in Palestine was the product of the economic and social changes set into motion by the opposing forces of colonialism and nationalism. Women as a group began to be involved in political action in the context of the national struggle.[1] In other words, women were propelled by their nationalist sentiments—and in many instances encouraged by society—to deviate from their traditional roles by protesting and even establishing their own organizations. This development was not, however, necessarily accompanied by autonomy for the new women's organizations.[2]

After 1967 Palestinian women responded to the nationalist movement and to the new conditions generated by occupation. Structural economic changes, particularly the employment of Palestinians inside Israel, also affected women, whether directly as women workers or as the wives, mothers or sisters of male workers. Another important development, not directly related to the occupation, was a dramatic increase in the education of women, including higher education.

Women were politically active from the very beginning of the occupation. As early as February 1968, for example, several hundred women demonstrated in Jerusalem against land confiscation and deportation. A few even joined the armed groups that formed in that period. However, the major framework for women's organization and activity were the over one hundred traditional charitable societies located in the towns. Among the most successful of these were In'ash al-Usra (Family Rehabilitation Society),[3] which grew from two rooms in 1965 to a large modern building with over 100 employees, an orphanage, and a wide variety of programs, and the Arab Women's Union in Nablus, which runs a hospital. These societies were motivated by nationalist as well as charitable sentiments and were led largely by urban middle-class women, although in some cases these women were actually major-domos for male leaders. While these societies were very active in serving the rural and refugee poor, they did so largely without their participation.

In the late 1970s, a new generation of young activists launched a number of grassroots committees and movements in the West Bank, and to a lesser extent Gaza, including the volunteer work committees (begun as a voluntary work movement in 1971–72), trade and student unions, youth movements, and a grassroots health movement. A new generation of women, many of whom had been politicized in the student movements at Palestinian universities, founded grassroots women's committees that, in contrast to the charitable society network of women's organizations, sought to involve the majority of women in the West Bank who lived in villages—along with women in camps, the urban poor, and women workers as well as intellectuals and urban middle-class women—in a united women's movement. Reflecting the leftist ideas current in student circles and political organizations, the first two committees—the Women's Work Committee and the Working Women's Committee—began by focusing on the conditions of women factory workers. The first project of the nascent Women's Work Committee, for example, was a 1978 survey of women textile workers in the Ramallah area. These committees, joined in 1982 by the Palestinian Women's Committee and in 1984 by the Women's Committee for Social Work, launched a series of projects serving women: literacy, small-scale production training, nurseries and kindergartens, and health education. These projects were animated by the desire to mobilize women and raise their nationalist consciousness. Three of the committees articulated a program of improving women's status in society, although national liberation remained the overriding concern. The four committees reflected the four main political streams in the nationalist movement, a factionalism which created competition and occasionally hampered their attempts to respond to local conditions and women's needs.

By the eve of the uprising, the women's committees had developed to include seasoned women leaders and a base with firm roots in towns, villages, and camps. While not the generators of women's mass participation in the uprising, the committees played a major role in shaping that participation.

From home to community:
women's expanded role during the uprising

"We told the shabab (young men), 'Stay home and sleep, today we're in charge.' "

These words were spoken by a smiling young woman from the Ramallah-area village of Kafr Na'ma as she described a march by several hundred women from the village in celebration of International Women's Day, March 8, almost three months into the uprising. It was Kafr Na'ma's first local celebration of International Women's Day. In previous years women activists from the village might have traveled to celebrations held by the women's committees in Jerusalem, but this year women from the village actually demonstrated twice, going in the morning to Ramallah to join ranks with urban women teachers, grandmothers in peasant dress, and blue-jeaned teenagers for an impressive march through the center of town.

By March 8, a qualitative change had taken place in women's participation in public and political life, although whether this change was (or is) obvious to the largely male leadership of the uprising remains a question. Images of daily life in this period attested to this change: a middle-aged woman in Ramallah helps young men build a barricade, a woman in Aida camp fights and even bites a soldier who is trying to take her son, women in Gaza carry trays full of rocks on their heads to supply demonstrators, women in camps under extended curfew defy the military to smuggle food and fuel into the camp. Even women's language, as one activist noted, had begun to change: "Women now sit together and talk about the uprising, about politics: who was detained, what the latest communique says, strike days, curfews. They no longer chat about petty concerns."

Urban women organized their own protest activities, for example sit-ins at the International Red Cross to protest mass detentions and prison conditions. However, many of the political actions that engaged masses of women—particularly informal actions—were not the province of the urban women who have traditionally been the most active in women's organizations, or even necessarily of students, who have often carried the banner of political mobilization in the occupied territories. Women in refugee camps and villages have in fact been more active than women in towns, reflecting the uprising's focus on the central role of these communities. This constitutes a historical reversal in the orientation of the women's movement in Palestine, although it is not yet reflected in women's leadership, since decision making still remains largely in the hands of urban middle-class women.

In the widespread participation of women some have discerned an emerging new role for women in society. For example, Birzeit University Dean of Arts Dr. Hanan Mikhail-Ashrawi argues that women's activity in the uprising "has removed the basis of authority of the male. Traditional hierarchies are challenged by new hierarchies." Some have gone even further. Israeli journalist Ehud Ya'ari, for example, has described the uprising as a gender rebellion, "an internal revolution of children against fathers, women against husbands, poor against rich, refugees against the propertied classes."[4]

Careful scrutiny of the kinds of actions women have most frequently taken during the course of the uprising suggests another hypothesis, though Ashrawi's point about new hierarchies is provocative and important. Although it is often asserted that women's traditional domestic role in the family is an obstacle to public political action, that the world of the home and the world of the polity are sealed off from one another,[5] these barriers seem to have become permeable for Palestinian women during the uprising. Women, and particularly those not already organizationally identified with a political movement or group, have enlarged or extended their traditional role rather than adopting a completely new role. Many of their forms of political participation are based on aspects of this role, particularly defense of family, nurturing and assisting family members, and mutual aid between kin. These aspects of women's role have become a source of resistance because women have transformed their family responsibilities to encompass the entire community. In a real sense, particularly in villages and refugee camps where the community is closely bound together, the community has become the family in this time of sustained crisis.

A clear example is offered by the myriad accounts of women struggling with soldiers to reclaim young men whom soldiers have seized to beat or detain. The common refrain, echoed by a multitude of women as they attempt to snatch a youth from the clutches of the army, has been, "He's my son!" Initially a spontaneous response, some women have made it a "profession," in the sense that they are on the streets ready to confront the army. In Ramallah, Akram, the son of Jamila, was detained near the mosque on January 29 after Friday prayers. Jamila, a youthful middle-class woman and a U.S. citizen, struggled in vain to free her son, who was surrounded by a group of soldiers who were kicking him with their boots and pounding him with their rifle butts. Then, one elderly woman in peasant dress got hold of Akram and smothered him in a huge embrace while soldiers tried to beat him back.

"He's my son!" she cries, "don't you touch him!"

"Liar," says a soldier, barely out of his teens, "how can you be his mother?"

"They are all my children, not like you motherless lot!"

Another women's activity that clearly derives from their traditional role is visiting the sick and wounded, which is now not restricted to relatives or immediate neighbors and can even become an organized activity of a women's organization, such as a visit to a village that has been attacked by the army. Attending funerals of martyrs—the equivalent of a demonstration—is the most politicized version of this activity.

Confronting soldiers during army raids (usually at night) when they come to detain youths, is yet another activity of women that has been extended from the family to the community, to the extent that women call each other to confront the army as it enters a camp or village. Women have also been involved in smuggling food and other provisions into refugee camps under curfew, a major contribution to sustaining the uprising.

The courage of women confronting soldiers in the most difficult of conditions—unprotected, late at night, in remote villages and curfewed refugee camps—is uncontestable. Three women in the northern West Bank village of Ya'bad told us of an older woman, Umm Kamal, who during a massive army raid against the village in February tried to block the soldiers' entrance into her house and was clubbed and teargassed. A younger married woman, Umm Mahmud, alone with her children and her elderly father, gave a lively account of soldiers invading her house in the same dawn raid: they smashed her solar heater and the concrete steps leading to her house, dumped her household possessions outside, and pushed her with clubs. Her answer was simply: "I am not afraid." A teenager, her hand bandaged, described with some relish an irritated solider, stick poised to beat her because of her defiant behavior (she had thrown a brick from the roof), angrily saying: "What's this? You are trying to defeat the occupation all by yourself?"

This kind of women's activism is not reflected in the gloomy statistics of deaths, woundings, and detentions. Of 204 Palestinians killed in the West Bank (excluding Gaza) by soldiers or settlers and documented by al-Haq, the Ramallah-based affiliate of the International Commission of Jurists, fifteen were women or girls. An estimated 300 women have been detained for longer than a day or so in the course of the uprising, compared to about 20,000 males. Al-Haq recently reported that thirteen Palestinian women were placed under administrative detention (imprisonment without trial, usually for six months), in contrast to 3,000 to 4,000 men.[6] Since these indicators are also used by Palestinian society to measure activism, it is unclear how visible or valued women's activities are in the collective assessment of society.

The assessment of the family, of course, is often the individual woman's most important measure. Women's movement from family to community has broken one major barrier for many women: the barrier of shame, of family restrictions on the movement of women. This critical transformation is evidenced by the participation (and even leadership) of unmarried women in mixed settings, whether demonstrations or neighborhood committees. Such participation is made easier when the community is close knit, as in villages. Still, although some women find that their families (and especially their fathers) are proud of their new political activism, others still face conflict with their parents over political participation.

Demonstrations are perhaps the clearest of political actions, and the least tied to traditional women's roles. Demonstrations of women in towns reached their peak in February and March, when marches from mosques on Fridays and especially churches on Sundays drew the widespread participation of women not necessarily bound by religion. In Ramallah, for example, many women attended both Friday and Sunday marches. Other protests, particularly at the village and camp level, drew strength from communal and family roots. During a visit in late October to the Nablus-area village of Kafr Thuluth, 'Aziza, a youthful married woman, barefoot in a bright blue dress accented in red and black, confidently discussed the complicated political situation of her village while her husband served cola and occasionally chimed in. She is a new activist in the Women's Work Committee and has apparently developed by leaps and bounds in the course of the uprising. When she calls women to demonstrate against soldiers, she begins with her sister, aunt and cousin—a sort of family demonstration unit. As a Birzeit University faculty member put it, "The extended family has been put to use."

For Palestinian women under occupation, the conditions of the past twenty-one years have consistently thrust them into politicized situations, and their roles, and perhaps the functions of the family itself, have stretched accordingly.[7] In the absence of a state and in the presence of an implacably hostile authority, the family's role as protector, arbiter, and social authority has undoubtedly been important, and this has made it more resistant to other social forces undermining its authority. Women's role has "stretched" to include numerous encounters with the army, miliary courts, prisons, and police as women have, for example, taken on the responsibility of caring for imprisoned family members. As attorney Lea Tsemel notes in a recent book:

> I often see women because during the years of occupation they have
> become the most active ones over the everyday problems of detention.

> They go to the police, they ask for permits—it's not traditional, but they have become very active. They're more stubborn than the men.[8]

The politicization of women has resulted from both the repression of males and the new consciousness engendered mainly by the new generation of educated women, which includes young women in camps and villages, since under occupation higher education expanded far beyond the middle class. It has led to women taking on greater political responsibilities. With so many men under detention, women have been propelled into new political roles and have often replaced the lost cadre. The case of Ruqayya cited in our introduction is one example of female community leadership in a situation of crisis. To what extent this leadership exists at formal rather than informal levels is another question.

Women as political leaders

In the town of Ramallah last April, a middle-class music teacher, joined by other women in the neighborhood, worked tirelessly to set up a full alternative curriculum for children and high school students in her neighborhood, because all schools in the West Bank were closed by military order on February 2, 1988. Her tasks ranged from calling and chairing meetings of the newly founded neighborhood committee to hauling blackboards and finding school supplies. A neighborhood away, an older woman summoned the other women nearby to a sex-segregated neighborhood committee to plan classes and plant a community garden. In the next street, a Birzeit University student became the acknowledged dynamo of her "coed" neighborhood committee and was appointed to the committee that guards the neighborhood at night, a previously unheard-of role for a single woman.

Women have been prominent, and sometimes leaders, in the neighborhood committees which sprang up in many locations in the occupied territories in March 1988, paralleling the establishment of the more political popular committees.[9] The community service functions of the neighborhood committees and their all-inclusive and democratic form encouraged the participation of women. While many of the activities of these committees, for example teaching and home gardening, are not explicitly political, the self-organization of the community and the philosophy behind it—to disengage from existing Israeli structures and to build Palestinian alternatives—make the neighborhood committees political instruments in a broad sense, as their banning by the military authorities on August 18, 1988, attests.

It is not only the extension of the family role to the community that explains women's heightened activity in these committees and other forms of public action. Paradoxically, it is precisely women's inferior social status which gives them greater flexibility to respond swiftly to new situations and new needs, even when the action is foreign or "beneath" them. For example, women seem to have done the bulk of the alternative teaching, although professional teaching in Palestinian society is the domain of both women and men. On the other hand, the rigidity of men's role in society clearly made it harder for adult men—as opposed to the youth confronting the army—to adapt to new roles, for example, community service functions.

Neighborhood committees are the clearest example of how the new forms of authority born of the uprising include a greater role for women than do the more traditional structures of power, including the nationalist institutions. It is difficult, however, to gauge the real extent of women's empowerment or how this new empowerment affects the older structures of inequality and domination. Palestinian women in the occupied territories are, after all, clearly not in possession of instruments of power, such as wealth, control of institutions, or legal authority. To a lesser extent, despite the dramatic rise in education among women, many of the necessary political and professional skills remain in the male domain.[10] Thus, women are still many steps behind men: even their institutions are in part miniature versions of those of men, and they are still struggling to formulate an alternative agenda that defines gender (and class) as legitimate issues along with the national cause.

Despite these handicaps, women have taken on political tasks that require a substantial amount of authority—usually associated with males—such as distributing clandestine leaflets or telling shopkeepers to close their shops during a strike, although single women are more active in these more organized roles than married women. Whether even highly politicized women in the political organizations have leadership roles or remain implementors of male decision is less clear. Some activists assert that women should play a greater role in decision making, while others point out that, as one put it, "in any case men in the West Bank and Gaza Strip do not make decisions either. The decisions are made outside and we inside . . . we execute." This comment underlines how the understanding of political dynamics, in this case what is called in Palestinian politics the relationship between "inside and outside," has a direct bearing on women.

Neighborhood committees are the only semivisible new structures of organization where women's role can be gauged, because the popular committees and the other local middle-level formations that guide the uprising are clandestine. At this level, and in the more flexible grassroots formations like student and union groups and the health movement, women seem to be playing increasingly important roles.

But there is no evidence that women have an increasingly important role in established nationalist institutions like the universities and the press. Nor (with significant exceptions) do activists from the women's committees believe that women are represented in the Unified Leadership of the Uprising. Indeed, women have been barely mentioned in the almost thirty clandestine communiques from the Unified Leadership, despite repeated appeals and commendations to other sectors of society—merchants, prisoners, workers, students. An exception is Communique No. 29, the "Call of Celebration of the Independent State," which offers "congratulations to the mother of the martyr, for she has celebrated only twice: when she gave her son and when the state was declared."

The "mother of the martyr," a heroic role enshrined in Palestinian history and the Palestinian present, has the qualities of stoical courage but not necessarily of active resistance. In the Declaration of Independence, which affirms equality between men and women, women are praised but nonetheless portrayed in a static role: "We render special tribute to that brave Palestinian woman, guardian of sustenance and life, keeper of our people's perennial flame."

The prevalence of these two images in nationalist consciousness suggests that women's current role has not been adequately assessed and may not be sufficient to improve her status in the future.

The pattern of women's mobilization during national liberation and backsliding after liberation is well-known: Algeria is the example best known among Palestinian women. The form of mobilization itself may well inhibit further development. Examining the role of Palestinian women in Lebanon, Rosemary Sayigh noted "how crisis continually recommits women to struggle, how its form prevents them from consolidating or 'feminizing' their struggle, with national priorities forcing it to remain spontaneous, auxiliary."[11]

Many women activists in the occupied territories are well aware that the role of women in a Palestinian state will be determined before, not after, liberation. As one remarked:

> I feel that if we do not raise the issues relevant to women now we
> will never raise them, for now is the time. I am afraid that if we do
> not raise the social issues now during national liberation, women's
> position will regress after liberation.

Toward a women's liberation strategy for the nascent state

The conditions and consequences of the uprising have already had a considerable influence on the women's committees' short- and long-term strategies for women's and national liberation. Women's political action has passed through roughly three phases, parallel with the stages of the uprising itself. From January through March/April, women's political action was primarily, although not solely, characterized by direct and immediate confrontations with the Israeli army at the level of the street. Women were at the barricades, organizing sit-ins at the doorsteps of humanitarian and human rights organizations, and staging demonstrations which grew in size and impact, reaching a peak on March 8, 1988, when demonstrations were held in most of the major towns and localities of the West Bank and Gaza Strip.

The second phase lasted until around September and was dominated by the building and consolidation of the network of neighborhood and popular committees. Slogans such as "Expanding and Strengthening the Popular Committees in All Areas" and "Neighborhood Committees: Organizing for Self-Reliance" reflected the core strategy of the women's committees in the arena of politics. As a result, by August 1988, women probably formed the organizational core of the neighborhood committees. On August 18, 1988, the popular and neighborhood committees were declared illegal by the Israeli military, and membership in, assistance to, or even contact with them could bring a sentence of up to ten years in prison.[12] This considerably curtailed the visible activities of neighborhood committees and, consequently, dampened women's committees' efforts to continue building and consolidating them.

By November 1988, a new phase began, in which political and social action was being evaluated in terms of future state structures. Some leaders of the women's committees now began a serious examination of the ways in which the women's movement could consolidate the gains of the uprising to achieve permanent changes in the social and political status of women. As one leader of the women's movement put it, "What is needed now is to unite all women to keep the gains once statehood is achieved."

The Palestinian women's movement today faces at least two strategic problems that might make unity difficult to achieve and could therefore not only hold the whole women's movement back but also limit the possibilities of radical change in the positions of women in all spheres of life. First, there is the divergence of perceptions and therefore strategy and tasks among the different women's organizations. While the three committees on the left clearly stress the need for action to achieve social change and call for an agenda for women's liberation that is separate from national aspirations, the fourth committee is characterized by "mainstream" views and equates national liberation with female liberation in a mechanistic way. As one Women's Committee for Social

Work activist asserted, "with liberation we should be able to attain all of our rights as women as well, so there is no need for feminism."

The other problem is structural: the fact that the women's movement was conceived and born as part of a nationalist struggle may make it difficult for it to develop a balanced feminist agenda. This dilemma surfaced in the first few months of the uprising, when service provision to women—up to that point the main focus of the women's committees' activities—declined considerably because of the avalanche of national political work that women activists had to take on. As one committee activist noted:

> We even closed down some of our kindergartens and nursery schools, temporarily of course, because we could not succeed in combining the new political work that fell on our shoulders and our previous activities. Now we are beginning to be aware of the need to work on both types of work together, but this is very difficult.

It is of course understandable that the women's committees opted for national-political over feminist work when they were no longer able to cope with everything at once. Women could not have easily forsaken the new political role that they were suddenly able to play for the more ordinary work of providing services. Indeed, such service work was not at the center of most women's concerns during this period, especially in view of the increasing awareness that effective long-term change in the status of women must be preceded by women's taking over important political positions. On the other hand, nursery schools and kindergartens form the framework for mobilizing the potential constituencies of the women's committees in the villages, refugee camps, and town to participate in political and social action. To suggest that both types of activities are needed is obvious. Less obvious is how to reconcile the two when resources are limited.

A purely radical feminist agenda for the women's movement is also problematic in the Palestinian context, as it is in other settings. As Michele Barret notes:

> In posing women's oppression simply as the effect of male domination, it refuses to take into account the widely differing structure and experiences of that oppression in different societies, periods of history and social classes. [13]

A brand of feminism that reduces everything to equality between men and women without taking sufficient note of the fact of power relations and structures not only fails to serve the national political struggle which dominates the lives of Palestinian women but is bound to fail because it does not take into consideration what can realistically be achieved. This leaves us, once again, with the problem of reconciling national, class, and gender issues in a new synthesis that could guide the women's movement and inform its strategy. The task ahead is a difficult one.

In the Palestinian setting, a radical change in economic relationships may be difficult to achieve in the immediate future. However, the basis of authority of men over women can nonetheless be challenged by demanding transformations in law and education, through the struggle for civil law and equality as sanctioned by law, the right of equal inheritance, the right to own, the right to travel, and the right to vote—to name only a few pressing demands. This is why activists and leaders from three of the four women's committees cite the legal status of women and the replacement of the shari'a (Islamic law) with civil legislation as a critical area. The problem of gender-based division of labor in the home, in child care and housework, can also be addressed by calling on the new state to provide state-subsidized nurseries, bakeries, restaurants, and laundries. Equal opportunity in work is another demand voiced by some women activists.

Guided by the Declaration of Independence, which proclaims the new Palestinian state to be based on the principles of "equality and non-discrimination" between men and women, the women's movement could now embark on the path of providing the mainstream and progressive nationalist camps with a critique of the flaws in their conceptions of the status of women, making it clear that the removal of national oppression alone will not solve the problems of women. Radical change in the status of women in Palestinian society is also linked to broader changes in society, especially at the level of the economy. A strategy must therefore be formulated to foster the building of autonomous women's organizations that participate in the national and class struggles.

In this respect the story of Ruqayya is telling. Ruqayya, the daughter of the uprising, develops and struggles in the contexts of home, community, and workplace. Both the national battle against occupation and the desire for economic and personal rights mobilize her, while the grassroots organizations she belongs to—her women's committee and her trade union—provide a forum for action. She and the many other women like her, the breakers of barriers and the builders of barricades, have emerged as political actors. Their rights in the future will rest on their ability to consolidate this new position in the form of permanent and far-reaching changes in the position of women in Palestinian society.

Notes

1. Al-Khalili, G. 1981. *The Palestinian Women and the Revolution*. Acre: Dar al-Aswar (in Arabic); and Peteet, Julie. "Women and the Palestinian Movement: No Going Back," *MERIP Middle East Report*, No. 138 (January-February), 1986, pp. 20–24.

2. See Kumari, Jayawardena. 1986. *Feminism and Nationalism in the Third World.* London: Zed Press. And Davis, Miranda. *Third World, Second Sex.* (London: Zed Press, 1983).

3. Most of the premises of In'ash al-Usra were closed down by the military authorities for a period of two years on June 20, 1988.

4. *The Atlantic,* June 1988.

5. For a critique of this perspective see Rassam, Amal, "Toward a Theoretical Framework for Women's Studies." "To begin an inquiry into the subject by taking the public/private scheme as a 'given' is to run the risk of distorting data by forcing them into one or the other of the two categories, and more important, it draws attention away from the central fact that Aram men and women live in one world, no matter how much it seems to be separated into two domains."

6. Al-Haq, 1989. *Punishing a Nation.* Boston: South End Press.

7. Sayigh, Rosemary. 1984. "Looking Across the Mediterranean," *MERIP Middle East Report,* 124 (June).

8. Lipman, Beata. 1988. *Israel, The Embattled Land: Jewish and Palestianian Women Talk About Their Lives.* London: Pandora, p. 153.

9. Popular committees, which often include representatives of the different PLO factions, have guided the uprising on a community level, while neighborhood committees took on the tasks of survival and community development: alternative teaching, home gardening, protection of the neighborhood, food storage, first aid and health. Sometimes a single committee handles all these functions, but often they are separate. At their peak of public activity, neighborhood committees were most widespread in the towns, particularly Ramallah, Beit Sahur, and Nablus.

10. In Palestinian society men can have authority over women even if there is no material base for it; for example, a younger brother may have authority over a sister who is supporting him. This authority is sometimes understood as deriving from the *shari'a* (Islamic law), which makes men the guardians of women.

11. Sayigh, Rosemary. Op. cit., p. 23.

12. *The Jerusalem Post,* Aug. 19, 1988.

13. Barret, Michele. 1980. *Women's Oppression Today: Problems in Marxist-Feminist Analysis.* London: Verso, p. 4.

III

Building Women's Multicultural Alliances for Social Change

Ⅲ

Introduction

Lisa Albrecht and Rose M. Brewer

The seven articles in this final section suggest that alliance building is not a fixed entity. It is rooted in the lived experiences of the alliance builders.

Why do historically oppressed groups come to alliances? Often, it is literally a survival mechanism. Roxanna Carillo's work informs us that women in Central America have come together at *encuentros* to talk about their common experiences with the impact of colonialism and sexism and to understand how they are different. In Guida West's essay, we learn that women are in alliance to press for social equity, not to become best friends.

Marginalized groups often bring a history of anger and resentment toward privileged groups. Sometimes when this anger is present, it is misread by people with privilege, who see it directed at them personally. However, when alliances do reproduce the oppressor/oppressed dynamics, anger can emerge (Kaufman, 1988). It is critical that we not forget that women who have been exploited historically have profound visions of change in the midst of their anger. They know that we are all in this together. This anger should never be denied, and the alliance work should go on.

It is also important for us to remember what Gloria Anzaldúa writes about in her essay. The metaphor of women of color as bridge, drawbridge, sandbar, or island represents choices that women of color constantly make. Above all, these choices need to be respected; we cannot always expect women of color to want to align with white women or other women of color. At times, we need to be and work only with those women with whom we most closely identify. This is about a deep need for solidarity and safety, and it is a valid survival mechanism. Anzaldúa urges women of color to choose carefully and white women to be aware of these choices and be respectful.

Why do historically privileged groups come to alliances? Some women with privilege have principled reasons for working in alliances for social change. They are aware that for global social justice to happen, we must all be free from oppression. If we work together in alliance, we can create a vision of the future where equality is central and where we view our diversity as truly enriching. Miranda Bergman writes about white Jewish women from the Break the Silence Mural Project. They are good examples of women who risk life and limb to work with Palestinian people to end the Israeli occupation and work toward a two-state solution.

On the cynical and superficial side, for privileged women working in alliance is the politically correct thing to do. The party line of feminist and progressive politics says we have to build alliances with people of color, gays, lesbians, working class people, and so on. But, oftentimes it is little more than lip service. Real alliances do not get built. For example, middle and upper middle class people may bring a missionary mentality to the table with the attitude of, "I want to help these people because it would make me feel better about my class privilege." White feminists who work with women of color want tremendous amounts of acceptance without confronting the kind of discomfort that goes along with doing this work. Women of color get caught in the trap of wanting to make it okay for white women. As Gloria Anzaldúa points out, "Some of us [women of color] get seduced into making a white woman an honorary woman of color—she wants it so badly."

How do you break from privilege when you are implicated? Why would someone want to give up any privilege? Why move from the comfort zone? It seems to us that privileged people often attempt to distance themselves from their privilege to have greater legitimacy within the group, and perhaps to feel less guilty. However, this doesn't take the privilege away. For example, heterosexual women sometimes pretend they are not connected to men when working in women's groups with lesbians. The key may be for those women with privilege to use it to advance the struggle for social equality and justice.

To accommodate the kinds of diversity we envision in alliance, new social structures have to be created. For example, from within the Canadian national system, feminist social service collectives attempt to build alternative institutional structures. Janice Ristock looks at the impact of these structures on women of different racial, class, and sexual identities. In another example, Audre Lorde demands that African-American women must connect local struggles to the broader diaspora. She urges us to support institutions which make visible the voices of women of color, especially publishers such as Kitchen Table: Women of Color Press in North America, Sheba Publishers in England, and Sechabe Publishers in South Africa. She draws on her own experiences meeting Afro-German women to illustrate the vital connections possible between African women all over the world. North American Black women have too often narrowly defined their struggles without tying them to international resistance movements. Clearly, the possibilities for global feminism are given form and content in this last section of the anthology. In the appendix that follows this section we include two pieces that provide us with necessary information to do some of this work. Virginia Cyrus' piece gives us valuable information for global networking. The Ford Foundation lists national projects to integrate gender and multiculturalism into the undergraduate curriculum.

As we have said throughout this collection, meaningful social change can only occur if it touches each of us personally while dismantling institutional structures. This means that we cannot compartmentalize our political lives. Generating social change engages our entire being; we cannot neatly carve up our lives into alliance work as if it were separated from our personal, family, work, and social lives. Nor can we presume that any single-issue politics is enough. Even if we come together around a single issue in coalition, we must recognize the nuances, permutations, and the whole range of connections any single issue has with other issues, coalitions, and alliances. Alliances move us from a place within ourselves to a place outside ourselves—from local to international, from one color to many colors, from our individuated selves to a new center that situates what was once the periphery at our core.

Touching each other is at the core of alliance building; we must forge human connections which will tie us together—women, men, and children. The spirit of this section is that powerful alliances are currently bringing about some of the kinds of changes that a fair and just social order demands. These alliances foreshadow the even greater degree of struggle that must happen globally if we are all to survive.

References

Kaufman, Jonathan. 1988. *Broken Alliance: The Turbulent Times between Blacks and Jews in America*. New York: New American Library.

Cooperation and Conflict among Women in the Welfare Rights Movement

Guida West

Twenty years ago Johnnie Tillmon, the leader of the national welfare rights movement—the first movement of poor women on AFDC (Aid to Families with Dependent Children), spoke before a national meeting of feminists and called on women to rally around welfare reform. She argued that "welfare is a women's issue" and that many "women are one man away from welfare." Welfare, she noted, was a dehumanizing system of public assistance for poor women and their children and needed to be radically changed. It was a sexist and racist system which also exacerbated the divisions between women (West, 1981). In October 1988, the United States Congress passed the most sweeping welfare reform bill in fifty-three years—The Family Support Act of 1988 (FSA)—largely shaped by Senator Daniel Patrick Moynihan (D-NY). The new plan, according to the national legislators, was designed to eliminate the seemingly intractable "problem of dependency" of AFDC mothers. Thus, as the decade ended, the problems of poor women became defined by policymakers (mostly male and white) as one of "dependency" rather than "poverty" or lack of income.

Many feminists and welfare rights activists view this national legislation with alarm, having witnessed the early results of similar policies implemented and tested as "demonstration projects" in many states (with special waivers from the federal government). Historically, the struggle for welfare rights and welfare reform reflects the ebb and flow of the tide of political support for state intervention in the lives of the poor in general and poor women with dependent children in particular. The question addressed by this paper is: how have women from diverse groups been involved historically in this welfare rights struggle?

This paper is part of my continuing work on leaders of the welfare rights movement and women in protests around the world. I focus here on the welfare rights protest that took place between 1966 and 1976 and the cooperation and conflicts that emerged among women striving to reform the welfare system in the United States. Many feminists today are concerned about building coalitions across class and race divisions that continue to divide women (Abramovitz, 1988; Ackelsberg, 1988; Ackelsberg and Diamond, 1987; Bookman and Morgen, 1988; Cole, 1986; Giddings, 1985; Hull, Scott, and Smith, 1982; Jones, 1985; Davis, 1983; Joseph and Lewis, 1981; Lorde, 1984; Lefkowitz and Withorn, 1986; Piven, 1985; West and Blumberg, 1990, forthcoming). This article adds to this literature by exploring some successes and failures at bridging these chasms between women in the welfare rights movement.

The paper is divided into four sections. First, I discuss the origins of the welfare rights movement and the alliances among diverse groups of women. Second, I explore the interracial bonding *within* the welfare rights organizations (WROs) and the cross-class and cross-race alliances *between* WROS and middle-class women's organizations (traditional and feminist groups). Third, I describe the nature of conflict *within* welfare rights mothers groups and *between* them and middle class women's organizations. Finally, I conclude by identifying some signs of increased cooperation and signs of tension today in the continuing welfare reform struggle. I explore their implications for feminists interested in shaping the outcome of this major welfare reform policy that will have an impact on the lives of women and children for decades to come.

Data are based on my research and participation in the Welfare Rights Movement from 1966 through 1978 and a survey of fifty-eight WRO women leaders/organizers in 1984–85 (West, forthcoming). In addition, other data have been gathered through continued informal contacts and observations in meetings and conferences in New Jersey and other parts of the country.

Some theoretical considerations

Within my theoretical framework, social protest is dynamic and continuous, characterized by a fusion and fission of groups with varying interests and resources to achieve or resist some redistribution of power within the system. Under "friendly" conditions, the protest becomes salient and active within the political arena. Under increasingly "hostile" conditions, the protest becomes less visible, sometimes adopting new profiles and agendas to minimize the risks in a more punitive environment. Some have labeled this latter stage the "becalmed stage" of a movement (Zald and Ash, 1966). Others have identified it as "in the doldrums" (Rupp and Taylor 1983). What is significant is that scholars are increasingly documenting that movements do not necessarily die and disappear. More often they adapt to survive the buffeting of political tides (Morris, 1984; West and Blumberg 1990, forthcoming). Also, feminist researchers argue that the absence of data should not necessarily be interpreted to mean that movements no longer exist. What many agree is that "silence," or the nonexistence of data, should alert us to interpretations other than that the movement has collapsed, given the pervasive male and elitist bias in the literature. Thus, changing political conditions within and outside social protest movements both mold and mirror their development, especially the alliances that arise, develop, disintegrate, or reemerge at different periods of time.

Existing theories grounded in historical data also suggest that alliances within a social protest movement generally add to its resources (people, money, time, skills, commitment, solidarity, as well as material items). At the same time, internal conflicts over goals and strategies combined with adverse external political conditions may result in reduced resources and power for the movement (Oberschall, 1973).

Cross-racial and cross-class alliances among women in their historical protests have been documented, along with estrangement and alienation that ruptured ties and divided African-American and white women in the abolition and suffrage movements and poor and middle-class women in progressive reform movements in the nineteenth and early twentieth centuries (Aptheker, 1982; Balser, 1987; Cole, 1986; Giddings, 1985). Protest literature suggests that one of the most common strategies used by dominant groups to control and reduce the power of challengers of the system is to "divide and conquer." By exacerbating differences—especially racial and class differences—authorities have often succeeded in defusing the power of protest movements (Piven and Cloward, 1977; West, 1981). Thus, for those of us seeking to bring about social change, it is important to understand the nature of the issues and processes that continue to divide us and to work to bridge those gaps.

Origins of the welfare rights movement and coalitions among women

The welfare rights movement emerged in 1966 as the first social protest of poor women on AFDC (Aid to Families with Dependent Children); its goal was to replace the existing welfare system with a guaranteed jobs/income system in the United States. It was a spin-off protest from the civil rights and the poverty rights movements in the 1960s and united over 25,000 AFDC women in local and state welfare rights organizations (WROs). While this paper focuses on the interactions among women, it is helpful to note that some men were also part of the welfare rights movement.

Men, both Black and white, participated as paid and volunteer staff and organizers, and, with some exceptions, were generally from the middle- or working-class. Ironically, although the welfare rights women were the elected leaders and represented the female-based membership, the men (both Black and white) as staff and organizers wielded significant power despite their relatively few numbers. Most visible was the leadership and power of George Wiley, NWRO's Executive Director, officially hired by the women to direct the day-to-day activities of the movement. Many observers, however, ascribe to him a much more important role. He is often described as the founder and the most prominent leader of NWRO, which he defined as a movement of poor people, not of poor women. The women leaders respected him and took pride in the fact that he headed the movement. He was an African-American man, a professor of chemistry who had sacrificed his career first for the Black struggle and then for welfare rights movement. He attracted people, money, and followers to NWRO and conveyed a deep sense of commitment to the cause that made him a very special person in the eyes of the welfare rights women and allies (West, 1981).

Other men, both Black and white, were part of the movement as paid or volunteer staff and as organizers in the field. The data suggest that while men in the movement were assigned to supportive roles, in practice they tended to take control. Thus, at least in the early days, this movement of poor women was significantly led by mostly middle-class men, both Black and white. It is not surprising, therefore, that issues of immediate concern to women were often ignored or interpreted from a male point of view. Only as the women gained political awareness of how the welfare system oppressed poor women in particular did they begin to question and oppose male dominance within the welfare rights movement. With raised consciousness and new skills, national women leaders finally rebelled and took control. But by then, the political tide had turned and the resources once available to NWRO disappeared (West, 1981).

NWRO also attracted support from various white middle-class liberal sectors: mainline Protestant denominations, some activist groups within the Catholic church, various foundations, a few labor groups, and some Black and women's organizations. Its middle-class allies were called "Friends of Welfare Rights" (FWROs), and in some parts of the country, Friends' groups organized in support of local and state welfare rights organizations. Most of these groups were dominated by white middle-class women, with a sprinkling of white men, mostly ministers, priests, students, and social welfare workers.

The national welfare rights movement collapsed in 1975 as the political climate shifted from the more friendly Democratic era of Johnson's "War on Poverty" to the more hostile Nixon days, which called for punitive measures to reduce the welfare rolls. This change exacerbated internal and external pressures on the movement. Supporters dropped by the wayside. Money vanished. Harassment of leaders by the state and internal conflicts rocked NWRO, leading to the demise of the national movement organization.

Some local and state welfare rights organizations, however, weakened and scattered from the larger movement; they remained autonomous units, struggling independently at the grassroots level. Thus, the configuration of the movement changed, but the movement itself survived, despite various reports that it had died.

Several factors converged to facilitate interracial and interclass bonding within the movement. Cooperation across racial lines among women in the welfare rights protest emerged because of the structure of poverty and the AFDC program, both of which were and still are multiracial and overwhelmingly female. At all levels AFDC was made up of poor women and their dependent children, although the law did not restrict eligibility by gender. Benefits were available to any single-parent family with children in need. (In the 1950s AFDC-UP was extended to two-parent families with dependent children—which could theoretically have increased the number of men receiving this kind of assistance—but only twenty-five states chose to adopt it.) In the mid-1960s about one-half of the AFDC mothers were white, slightly less than fifty percent were African-American, and the remainder were Hispanic and Native American women.

In contrast, NWRO's membership did not reflect this fairly even racial split between Blacks and whites. NWRO attracted a constituency that was overwhelmingly Black. Estimates suggest that NWRO was approximately eighty-five percent Black, ten percent white, and five percent Hispanic (or Latinas) in the late 1960s (West, 1981:45). Black female prevalence in NWRO stemmed not only from the structure of poverty in the United States and the organizers' concentration in urban areas but also from white AFDC women's reluctance to become associated with a militant Black movement in the late 1960s. As economic and political conditions changed, more poor white women joined NWRO in the 1970s, even as the movement was declining as a national protest. Thus, racial diversity within the poverty population, the AFDC rolls, and to a lesser extent within NWRO's constituency provided opportunities for racial interaction and bonding.

Interclass ties in the welfare rights movement emerged between poor women and their middle-class allies. Cooperation between poor women and their more advantaged allies became a reality in part because the emerging War on Poverty and the declining civil rights movement in the mid-1960s channeled white middle-class organizers, supporters, and their money into the inner cities to mobilize the poor, who were mostly Black women. As a consequence, the welfare rights movement developed a constituency and supporters' base that included Blacks and whites, as well as representatives of the poor and the middle class.

The ideological principles of NWRO also facilitated interracial and interclass linkages among women. Coming out of the integrationist wing of the civil rights movement, NWRO called for racial cooperation within its own organizations and its coalitions with white liberal allies. Despite its high Black profile, movement leaders made it clear that NWRO represented not only Black women but women of all colors and white women. From the very beginning NWRO leaders called for racial integration and cooperation within and across class lines. Johnnie Tillmon, an African-American AFDC mother from the impoverished Watts area in Los Angeles and the first elected chair of the national movement, liked to point out that their movement was unique because of its interracial base. This, she emphasized, was what scared the politicians more than anything else. She described NWRO as a movement where white women from Kentucky had united with Black women to work for common goals. She insisted that if it ever became "all Black or all brown," she would quit (West, 1981:44).

In addition, the existence of middle-class women's organizations (both Black and white), especially those grounded in religious or quasireligious tenets that espoused cooperation across race and class, as well as the rise of feminist organizations in the 1960s and 1970s with similar rhetoric, created the structural opportunities for cross-class and cross-racial alliances. Finally, cooperation among women occurred across racial and class barriers as a result of NWRO's deliberate strategies to organize the poor *and* nonpoor to enhance the chances of achieving its goal of welfare reform.

NWRO thus can be conceptualized as multiracial and multiclass, although its constituency was primarily Black and poor. It was a movement made up of diverse types of welfare rights groups. Some were racially integrated; some were all Black; a few were all white. While the number of welfare rights groups has fluctuated over the years, NWRO's racial profile has remained fairly stable. In the late 1980s welfare rights women leaders from across the nation reorganized as National Welfare Rights Union in an attempt to empower and coordinate groups in various states. Reflecting NWRO's original commitment to interracial cooperation, they vowed to uphold inclusive principles for membership in the movement. Its leadership and base constituency are racially integrated, and its program and activities call for cooperation across racial, class, and gender lines.

One important bond that unites these women is their common experience of being or having been poor and dependent on a punitive welfare system that punishes rather than supports those in need. Another is their collective involvement and the growing awareness of the national and international scope of the problem of poverty in general and its affect on women and children. Finally, some are committed welfare rights women who continue in the struggle for economic security. In the 1960s they were in the front lines demanding "$5500 or Fight!" as a minimal guaranteed income for their families. In the 1990s, the demands continue. Only the slogan has changed: "UP AND OUT OF POVERTY!"

In brief, both external political conditions and internal structures and principles helped to bring together diverse women's groups in this struggle for welfare reform. Black and white women united within the welfare rights movement to fight to change the welfare system in the late 1960s and early 1970s. Cooperation between NWRO women and middle-class women supporters emerged primarily as a result of organizers' efforts to mobilize the resources of white liberal groups. This led to coalitions, in some instances, between WROs and Friends of Welfare Rights. Coalitions created ties across race and class among women in this movement, as I discuss later.

Cooperation among women in the welfare rights movement

Cooperation among women *within* the welfare rights movement occurred at many levels, two of which were mobilizing members and leaders and confronting authorities to change the system. Most racially integrated groups made a point of sharing leadership so that the racial diversity of their membership was visibly represented at the policy-making level. It was a statement of principle as well as a means of recruiting a broad-based constituency. For example, at the national level, leadership was deliberately integrated on the basis of race. While all women were poor (poverty-level status was a criteria of membership), the nine-member, all-female Executive Committee of the National Welfare Rights Organization (NWRO) included Black, white, and Hispanic women. While Black women clearly maintained control as representatives of the Black majority in the movement, they insisted on representation from other racial and cultural groups. Black women were always nominated for the top posts; the other positions were filled by white and Hispanic as well as Black women.

Welfare rights women also worked across racial lines in planning strategies against the authorities. Collectively, in many parts of the country, they took over welfare offices, demanded clothes, food, shelter, and higher benefits and forced the state to increase funds for their families and children. Within local welfare rights groups, common economic experiences united women across race in their fight against the welfare departments. In Boston, for example, one Black leader recalls that they mobilized women for "endless marches" which "changed the whole system." She noted that "what was different about us, was that we were a young group of mothers, very militant . . . three Black and two white leaders" (West, forthcoming).

In other joint strategies, Black, white, and Chicana women welfare rights leaders joined nationally in class action suits against the government, and traveled to state capitols and to Washington, D.C., to make their voices heard. They demanded and forced the transfer of millions of dollars in cash, furniture, clothing, and food stamps from the welfare departments to poor people. The women won, through class action suits with legal services lawyers, the elimination of residency requirements and "midnight raids" that violated their rights under the U.S. Constitution. They also won the right to fair hearings before termination of benefits. In Congress, welfare rights mothers and their allies mounted and succeeded in a broad-based campaign to "Zap FAP"—the Nixon/Moynihan 1968 version of "workfare" called the Family Assistance Plan (FAP)—while liberals and conservatives joined to defeat this legislation in 1972.

Confrontations against the state also united women. In California, for example, Black, white and Hispanic women, outraged at the continuous barrage of insults from high state officials about AFDC mothers being tax cheaters, organized a special confrontation in May 1971 against the highest official in the state—its governor. Targeting the American Legion Dinner, where he was the keynote speaker, they marched in together, dressed in their "Sunday best," to present him with an award.

As the Black woman leader moved toward the stage holding high a framed plaque, she called out to the guest of honor—Governor Ronald Reagan—that her group wanted to give him a special award. As an long-time activist in welfare rights, state welfare officials quickly recognized her and tried to warn the Governor. But it was too late. She was already at the microphone, and all the cameras turned to focus on her as she began to read the award:

THE HIGHEST PAID WELFARE RECIPIENT AWARD

"On this, the 24th day of May 1971, the California Welfare Rights Organization hereby certifies GOVERNOR RONALD REAGAN as the highest paid welfare recipient in the state of California as evidenced by the fact that he was paid $76,500 in state funds and did not pay one penny of state income tax."

As a result of this guerilla theater, these women gained international and national press coverage, mobilized new supporters, and put a stop to the Governor's tirades against AFDC women in his state. Later, other welfare rights women confronted President Nixon and gave him a "Noble Prize" for tax evasion. For a time, high government officials reduced their public attacks on welfare mothers as "tax cheaters." In addition, this collective strategy gained greater visibility and recognition for the entire movement.

In short, cooperation among women *within* welfare rights groups emerged across racial lines, reflecting their integrated membership base. Together they mobilized, shared leadership, confronted the state at various levels, and brought about some reforms in the welfare legislation. However, as the political climate changed and became more conservative in the 1970s, they lost members, supporters, and money, resulting in the collapse of the national movement.

Cooperation also emerged *among* welfare rights women and middle-class Black and white women's traditional and feminist organizations. Given NWRO's overwhelmingly female base, gender solidarity was a potential source of added support for the movement. As we shall see, however, while some ties did emerge, they were largely negligible, partly because of race and class conflicts.

Black women's traditional organizations provided only symbolic support to NWRO and only in its final years. While cross-class alliances have been documented historically between middle-class Black women's service organizations and poor Black women, long established organizations eschewed linkages with organized groups of welfare mothers. While the movement had been active since June 1966, the two largest Black women's groups—the National Association of Colored Women and the National Council of Negro Women—only linked up with the welfare rights movement seven years later. Even then their ties were largely symbolic. In 1973 they sent representatives to the NWRO convention and contributed about $500 to the depleted coffers of the struggling movement. While the data are sparse, the ties between Black women in the welfare rights movement and Black women in traditional middle-class organizations failed to materialize at the grassroots level. Gender and motherhood failed to provide the necessary incentives for cooperation. In New Jersey, for example, attempts to establish ties across class were met at best with lukewarm responses. A common explanation offered by welfare rights leaders was that the pervasive stigmatization of welfare mothers in American society worked to undermine common gender and racial bonds.

In contrast, as Black feminist organizations emerged in the mid-1970s, they made a point of highlighting their solidarity with welfare rights women. Their philosophy was one of inclusiveness. For example, the National Black Feminist Organization (organized in 1973) and the Coalition of 100 Black Women (organized in 1974) openly and publicly announced that they were inviting welfare rights women leaders to join in planning and promoting their agenda. Welfare reform issues were included in their goals, and welfare rights women leaders were invited to join policymaking boards. Financial support for the movement, however, did not materialize because the newly founded groups were hard-pressed for funds at the same time that NWRO was trying to mobilize money and supporters. Another possible explanation is that it was well known within the movement that men—both Black and white—had dominated the welfare rights movement and its agenda for many years, a factor that was not acceptable to feminist organizations.

Thus, Black traditional women's organizations failed to establish alliances with NWRO and only provided symbolic support in NWRO's final months. In contrast, Black feminists developed some ties with welfare rights women across class lines as soon as they organized, but these were limited and short-lived because of limited funding, wrong timing, and perceived male dominance in NWRO.

Similarly, few of the traditional white women's groups supported the welfare rights women's movement. National church women's organizations in liberal Protestant denominations (such as United Methodist Women) provided some money in the early years. National church and YWCA women also attempted to mobilize and broaden support for the movement by holding educational/political meetings with their predominantly white and middle-class constituencies around the country in cooperation with local welfare rights groups. In addition, they used their publications and other media to attract supporters to the welfare rights cause and lobbied in Washington.

This general model of cooperation was adopted by many of the national women's liberal Protestant church groups. Friends of Welfare Rights were individuals and groups scattered throughout the country— mostly white, and mostly women—who paid dues, provided resources to the national and local welfare rights organizations, and sometimes participated with NWRO in direct actions to change the welfare system. A welfare rights leader described the support of Friends as follows:

> [Friends] were middle-class people much like yourself who first said they didn't know that welfare existed and were really shocked when we would go and talk to them in different groups and churches. [Then], they would ask how they could help . . . we told them . . . and they became supporters.

She noted that when Friends became involved in the struggle against the Nixon FAP plan, it gained visibility, or as she put it, "it became much more noticeable." Together, they participated in public forums, explained the issues, and mobilized other allies. Thus, in some cases middle-class white women, as Friends, contributed to the protest of the welfare rights mothers by providing some resources and enhancing the base of opposition and the visibility of the issue within the political arena.

Women's groups in the peace movement in the 1960s and 1970s were one of the few continuous and visible allies of welfare rights groups at the national and local levels. They invited national welfare rights women to join peace missions traveling abroad. They highlighted welfare rights leaders prominently in their programs. NWRO acclaimed its ties with peace activists and their mutual slogan of "welfare not warfare." In New Jersey, women in welfare rights, peace, and "Friends" groups united in the early 1970s for a week-long event around "welfare not warfare" to raise money and to mobilize more middle-class support for the movement. This joint effort, along with others, contributed to the passage of some legislation that helped to attenuate the negative impact of welfare cuts by the Cahill administration in New Jersey (West, 1981:192). Thus, while such coalitions did not achieve the welfare rights goal of a new and better economic security system, they may have helped to lessen state repression against welfare mothers at that time.

The League of Women Voters never allied itself with the national welfare rights movement except in the final moments of the struggle against the Nixon/Moynihan Family Assistance Plan. As a primarily white middle-class women's organization, at best it helped to enhance the debate within the political arena. However, it never linked up with the welfare rights movement, working independently on policy analysis and solutions for "the problem of welfare." Many times, while their analysis coincided with that of NWRO's, their policy choices differed dramatically from that of the welfare rights women, who criticized the League for its paternalistic strategy of deciding what was best *for* poor women, rather than *with* poor women.

Finally, in the late 1960s and early 1970s a number of feminist movement organizations attempted to establish ties with the welfare rights movement at the national level. The results were not very successful, although many feminists as individuals were involved in the welfare rights struggle. Among them were prominent activists such as Gloria Steinem, Florence Kennedy, Bella Abzug, and Robin Morgan. Organizationally, however, the links between feminists and NWRO were fragile at best, nonexistent at worst, despite their common female-based constituencies.

The National Organization of Women (NOW), established in June 1966—the very same moment in history as NWRO—recognized welfare as a women's problem and included a task force on poverty to address this issue. NOW, however, was only peripherally involved in the welfare reform struggle of the 1960s and 1970s, concentrating its resources on the Equal Rights Amendment fight.

Some ties did emerge. In 1968 NOW invited Johnnie Tillmon, as the head of the national welfare rights movement, to speak at one of its conventions and tried to explore other ways of linking up with NWRO. These efforts proved to be fruitless, however, because, according to the president of NOW, feminists were turned off by the sexist attitudes and agenda of NWRO's then male-dominated staff. By 1977, after the collapse of NWRO as a national movement, NOW began to take a more visible but independent role in welfare reform, as reflected in the speeches of its national leaders, newsletters, and participation in congressional hearings (West, 1981:258–59).

Similarly, the ties with the National Women's Political Caucus (NWPC) were few and fragile. NWPC did invited NWRO to join its coalition of women's groups and adopted as part of its agenda a guaranteed income plan and the defeat of "forced work" for AFDC mothers, two very important objectives of the welfare rights movement. Beulah Sanders, the second national chair of NWRO, joined and represented welfare rights in this feminist coalition. In 1975 Audrey Rowe Colom, a former member of the welfare rights movement and staff, was elected the first Black president of the National Women's Political Caucus.

Debates between feminists and welfare rights leaders emerged over definitions and solutions of welfare. The NWPC, a middle-class feminist organization, emphasized employment and work rather than welfare as the solution to women's lack of income to support their families. This led to some conflicts between poor and middle-class women. In addition, Beulah Sanders, NWRO's leader, was highly critical of NWPC's relationship with NWRO. While the NWPC strategy supported women of all colors and classes running for office, few welfare rights women had the resources or the opportunity to move into the political arena through the electoral process. A few did, but they were the exceptions. In the 1970s (when NWPC emerged), NWRO women were more concerned with defeating Nixon's Family Assistance Plan—a policy that could easily reduce even further their minimal resources from the state—rather than running for office. Long range structural change in electoral politics was not a matter of life and death for them. Welfare benefits, food stamps, and protection from state harassment were. Despite common grounds, the differences in short-range and long-range strategies to solve the welfare problem were significant. Class and race intersected to widen the gap between women working around common struggles for survival. Consequently, coalitions at all levels between feminist groups and NWRO were rare.

Briefly, both traditional and feminist middle-class organizations (both Black or white) established only limited ties with NWRO and participated only minimally in the welfare reform struggle of the 1960s and 1970s. The impact of their cooperative efforts in general or on the Family Assistance policy struggle in particular is difficult to assess, but nonetheless important, as I have argued elsewhere and will review at the end.

Conflict among women in the welfare rights movement

Conflicts emerged *within* racially integrated and racially separated groups of WRO women, primarily in situations where they competed for limited resources offered by the state or by their allies. Competition for a few crumbs disrupted many groups and served to divide and undermine the movement—the pernicious "divide and conquer" strategy of those in power. Racial differences at the national level also led to conflict and some reorganization within the movement. For example, one of the changes that occurred, as a result of Chicana women demanding more control, was the spin-off of the Chicana Welfare Rights Organization (West, 1981:45). Separation provided them with more independence and control over their own agenda. They did, however, continue to maintain ties with NWRO and were considered an integral part of the movement. In this situation, internal conflict was resolved without reducing the resources (membership constituency base and solidarity among women) of the movement as a whole. At the local level, as political and economic conditions changed and brought more white women into the movement, some other racial tensions emerged (West, 1981:48–9). One area of conflict was the priority of agenda items. In some areas white welfare rights women argued for a primary focus on educational rights—the right to college assistance from the state, something that was generally excluded by the welfare system. Many came from working-class backgrounds, and welfare was viewed as a temporary setback due to divorce, family crisis, or loss of jobs. Without having to face the realities of racism in the marketplace, jobs and careers seemed a viable way of moving out of poverty. Black welfare rights women supported the fight for educational rights to better their own economic condition. However, they were quick to point out that in a racist society, Black women (especially those raised in the South) had been so seriously disadvantaged that they could not compete in that arena. Their immediate and most pressing needs were for cash and health benefits (provided by Medicaid) to ensure survival of their children and families. This differential in priorities created tensions in some integrated groups around the country.

Another area of tension emerged over leadership. While the principle of sharing leadership remained well ingrained in the ideology of the movement, in practice and at the local level fear of dominance by white women periodically emerged in integrated welfare rights groups. One white woman explained that in her group, Black women "just saw us as coming and trying to take over because we were white, without ever finding out who we were as people." She added, "Right away, they lined us up with those 'feminists' . . . [because] of their class . . . and didn't see that there were far more poor whites in this country than there ever had been poor Blacks." In sum, historical patterns of racism in American society that provided differential access to jobs and leadership for Black and white women were reflected in the movement and helped to exacerbate the tensions between them.

When we examine conflicts *between* welfare rights and middle-class women, we find ample evidence from the perspective of both sides. Welfare rights women, when questioned about what they thought about middle-class women in the movement, were generally outspoken in their hostility and anger. The most common statement was that middle-class women lacked any understanding of what it was like to be poor and on welfare and yet insisted on acting as experts and deciding what had to be done. They spoke critically about coalitions with "the so-called Friends who could completely exorcise . . . their guilt by contributing fifteen minutes a day to various 'gimmicky' promotions to raise money and participate in a movement of poor folk." They resented paternalistic support represented by the "Friends" who turned out to be just "basket ladies" rather than real political allies.

Middle-class Friends were accused of supporting the "status quo" rather than real change in the welfare system. Some welfare rights leaders felt that Friends reflected the dominant view that welfare dependence by women was inherently bad and something to be rejected at the very first opportunity. Said one Black local leader, "As soon as times start getting a little better, the message comes through loud and clear from middle-class women that you definitely ought not to be depending on welfare or even wanting welfare. That was one thing that I had a hang up about with Friends. It's not that I disagree with the concept, but they just didn't understand how difficult it was for poor mothers on AFDC." Others expressed anger over the Friends' lack of staying power and commitment to the long struggle. Friends could do their thing and go home to suburbia, said one WRO leader. Welfare mothers, on the other hand, lived with the system twenty-four hours a day. One Black leader's feeling typified those of many others. She said, "They didn't need us and they didn't stay with us," said one. In her opinion neither Friends' groups in her area, nor other women's (Black or white) groups, had helped the local welfare rights organizations. She added, "Some individuals were very helpful; but as a group—it just didn't work."

On the other hand, middle-class white women, as Friends of WRO, were critical of the alliance with welfare rights mothers. They stated that they resented being treated as a social welfare department, useful only in terms of the money, furniture, transportation, and child care they were willing to provide. They complained that they were not willing to take on only the "service" role in a political movement. Many, with raised feminist consciousness, rejected this traditional role and demanded action in planning and implementing strategies. Politics was the name of the game, especially for those who had been involved in the civil rights movement. Middle-class Friends thus wanted to be partners in the struggle and/or "to do their own thing"—besides providing basic resources to the welfare rights groups. These clashing expectations about what their roles should be within the movement— "service/resource providers" *versus* "political partners" in the struggle- created tensions within some of these coalitions. On one hand, welfare rights women felt deserted and betrayed; on the other, Friends felt confused and resentful. Clearly, a lack of or breakdown in communications exacerbated the conflicts within these alliances.

Feminists as supporters were also criticized by welfare rights women for a variety of reasons: their emphasis on the ERA, their neglect and lack of understanding of poor women's economic issues, and their failure to commit themselves to this struggle. The women I interviewed almost unanimously supported the ERA, but not as a top priority issue, arguing that its passage would "never put more food on [our] tables" or get them more cash benefits or jobs to help them support their families.

Welfare rights women also highlighted the lack of understanding among middle-class feminists about what it was like to be poor, to be a poor woman, and to be a poor woman trying to raise children as a single parent. Black and white welfare rights women expressed similar views about this area of conflict. One former recipient and white woman, for example, pointed out that "feminists have never been particularly sensitive to the needs of poor women." She expressed outrage at their lack of support, stating:

> Until this more recent [talk about] feminization of poverty, until middle-class women started seeing themselves end up like poor women . . . they've never seen the necessity [for welfare reform] and even now there's a kind of apathy [among them]. [It makes] you want to take people by the collar and say, "Listen, bitch! You know, we've been putting up with this all our lives. Where the fuck have you been?"

She continued, highlighting what she perceived as elitism and racism among white feminists:

> Some woman came here speaking on the feminization of poverty [and said] that people didn't do anything before this. Well, that's crap. Where were all these middle-class bitches when we was putting our asses on the line and going to jail over welfare issues? They don't have nothing to do with us poor son-of-a-bitches and they certainly didn't want nothing to do with a primarily Black organization.

Another area of contention between welfare rights women and middle-class feminists was how the issue of "mothering" was to be handled in public policy. Some feminists, defining reproduction and child rearing as the major sources of women's oppression, did not want "mothering" to be identified as a job to be subsidized by the state. They were wary of dependency on the state and reinforcing traditional sex roles in public policies that undergirded the idea that only women can or should "mother" and raise children. Paying women to stay home did not mesh with the agenda of some feminists in the welfare rights struggle in the early 1970s. Yet, one white middle-class woman, who had been active in NWRO and identified herself as a feminist, acknowledged that her views about "mothering" had changed dramatically after she had become a mother herself. She explained:

> I have a much better understanding of welfare rights since I've had my kids . . . Only since I have had my own, have I understood what welfare rights was all about . . . mothers not wanting anybody to shit all over their kids. I really didn't understand that at a gut level

> when I was in the movement. Women organized and were in the movement to protect their kids [and] their kids' interests.

Welfare rights women wanted "mothering" to be defined as as valued occupation and a "job choice" just as it was for more privileged women. They viewed it as a valuable contribution to society and could not understand why feminists did not accept their views. Staying home was a full-time job, especially when a women was raising children as a single parent. One white welfare rights mother and leader argued passionately for the right of women to choose their jobs in or out of the home with these words:

> I thought that women [with dependent children] already had a job and that they should be recognized as having that job if they chose it. Now, if they chose to have a different job, that is their business. But they have a job—and that is called being a mother . . . Getting a job was not clearly the objective of most of the welfare mothers that I knew . . . in that moment in time. Not that people don't get there . . . and want to leave and do something else, but they want for a certain period to do right by the kids. I don't necessarily think leaving them to the whim of whatever kind of shit child care they could get is the best thing for them. Maybe being poor isn't good, but it may be better than having most of the waking hours of their children in the hands of someone they don't trust . . .

She concluded: "I wanted to be a mother and I am a mother taking care of this kid and I don't have any rights to survive. What kind of crazy world is this?"

It is important to note that in the 1977 Houston National Women's Conference representatives of poor women rejected the proposed feminist resolution and redrafted their own—"Women, Welfare and Poverty"—which spelled out very clearly that *"just as other workers, homemakers receiving payments should be afforded the dignity of having that payment called a wage not welfare"* (emphasis in original) (West, 1981:266). Throughout the movement, and still current among existing welfare rights groups today, is the slogan that reflects this critical theme: "Every mother is a working mother!"

Many welfare rights women also emphasized the tensions around what they perceived was the lack of action and recognition by feminists that "welfare is a women's issue." She noted that for several years she had tried to get the feminist movement involved in her work of organizing welfare women and confronting the state around welfare reform. But, she added, "they didn't want to deal with it . . . that welfare was a women's problem." At one point she was asked to address a NOW meeting, but with specific instructions "not [to] try to analyze her situation in a political way." She continued in outraged tone:

Can you imagine? What they wanted was [a welfare rights mother] to just stand up and make a brief statement about what the women's movement had done for her! I was so angry that I said, "How dare you come and ask for a person on that kind of a basis? We are an organization. We have an agenda. We have a theory around this stuff. And we are not going to stand up and say what you have done for us."

Her protest led to the welfare rights group organizing about forty women—Black, Hispanic, Asian, and white—and taking over the meeting. Feminist leaders tried to defend their position that they already had poor women on their agenda because they were fighting for Medicaid abortions. The response of the welfare rights mothers group was: "Who the hell are you to decide for us what our agenda is? Which is not to say that we think you shouldn't be supporting Medicaid abortions." They told the assembled middle-class feminists not to be "so damn patronizing." "You're just like men," they said, "telling us what you do for us. We will tell you and then—and only then—we can be together. Otherwise, it will not work." Reflecting on the relationship between welfare rights women and middle-class feminists in her area, she said that it had been fraught with "lots of struggles" because of "total lack of understanding" of what welfare is all about.

The issue of "jobs" for welfare mothers and "workfare" also became a bone of contention between welfare rights women and their more privileged allies. Workfare— mandatory employment to work off your welfare benefits—was first introduced as a "solution" to the welfare problem by policy-makers in the Work Improvement Program— WIN—in the late 1960s. Immediately, NWRO criticized the principle of mandatory work at minimum wage for women in exchange for minimal benefits, and without the safeguards afforded to regular workers. Moreover, NWRO leaders argued that women were already working raising children and, more importantly, forcing anyone into dead-end jobs to pay off their benefits would never solve the "problem of dependency" it was supposed to cure. NWRO women also pointed out that the initial 1935 AFDC legislation had as one of its basic principles the right of caretakers (read "mothers") to choose to stay home or to join the labor force based on what they considered to be in the best interest of their children.

Welfare rights women immediately labeled WIN and its mandatory work provisions as "slave labor." While they wanted the choice to determine what was in the best interest of their children, they also wanted jobs with decent wages, adequate benefits, quality child care, and real opportunities for advancement. Said Beulah Sanders, one of the national welfare rights leaders, "If you're going to slave for nine hours a day and get nothing but the same welfare check . . . you can sit home and take care of your family, instead of paying someone else to take care of them for the same nothing" (West, 1981:89).

Feminists, according to WRO women, did not seem to understand the punitive aspects of "workfare," even in the early days of WIN, when it was less restrictive than it is today. A Black welfare rights leader, actively engaged in mobilizing white middle-class feminists, recalled that when "WIN came on the scene," feminists viewed it as a "solution," buying the dominant argument that the state was providing job opportunities for poor women. As such, she added, they demanded that "everybody . . . be referred to the WIN program regardless of whether or not their children were under or over the age of six." They did not understand, she stated, the many facets of WIN and how it denied women equal jobs, how it pushed poor women into low-paying service jobs, and how it gave men all the good referrals." She continued:

> They just kind of went crazy on that issue, without realizing that they were supporting the expansion of workfare—workfare in its most repressive way. They wanted to take Reagan's California Work Experience Program (CWEP). I mean, really, you wept, if you got in there. They wanted to take that program and implement it, plus implement Title IV-D, which is the child support enforcement act. Both of those things—workfare and enforced child support—were detrimental to the welfare rights women and the movement.

This same Black woman concluded that feminists were "working at cross purposes" with poor women, adding that they just did not realize that AFDC mothers did not want "to go back to the old system of having to sign a complaint against your husband, or get no welfare." The facts were, she noted, that in the late 1960s and early 1970s feminists just "did not understand that what they were supporting was the termination of welfare grants to women who refused to go out to work" [under the WIN/workfare program]. She pointed out that middle-class feminists had "marketable skills and they could go out and do something," while welfare mothers had very few skills and were relegated to dead-end jobs in the WIN program. Thus, the consequences of this policy were devastating for poor women. She concluded angrily: "To assume that you are suddenly speaking for all women, just because you call yourselves feminists, was wrong. There had to be another voice, a different voice. . . . There had to be somebody telling those people about the real world."

Although the data are sparse, some of the feminists involved with welfare rights women in the early years expressed similar feelings of confusion and resentment over the attacks on their role in the welfare reform struggle. They criticized the expectation that they take on the traditional service role and respond out of guilt to appeals for support. In their view, they wanted to be independent allies, working separately and together with welfare rights women, depending on the opportunities and the resources available. Once again, the data indicate minimal communication as a potential source of conflicts in such coalitions, exacerbated by historical race and class schisms.

Summarizing, conflicts *within* welfare rights groups generally reflected societal tensions of racism and classism, with some tensions emerging between Black, Chicana, and white women, as well as between Black women from very poor backgrounds and white women who had "slipped into welfare" and came from a working-class background. Conflicts between welfare rights women and middle-class women's groups (traditionalists and feminists) also were present within the movement and seem to have inhibited cooperation to a much greater extent. Black and white welfare rights women were highly critical of the predominantly white middle-class Friends groups for their lack of commitment to the struggle of poor women and their lack of understanding of what it was to be poor. But, as one welfare rights leader concluded, there was still time to learn. "We need to get people so they understand each other. Everybody has to get into the head of someone else, to take that person's perception and frame of reference and look at the information . . . All of us have different perceptions of what is going on, and, if we start doing this, then we would be able to build coalitions and we would have peace in the world."

Signs of continuing cooperation and tensions among women in the welfare reform struggle

I want to end by sharing some encouraging and distressing things I see happening around the country in women's alliances within the welfare reform struggle. These are informal observations as well as data from conversations with women in the past year or so.

It is encouraging that the feminist movement seems to be integrating women and poverty into its agenda in many new and diverse ways today. Some of the signs are: the proliferation of articles and books on women, welfare, and poverty by women of all colors and classes; the inclusion of welfare rights women in Black feminist conferences, such as the May 1988 Black Women's Conference at Ohio State University; the adoption by Black Women's Summit and the Black Women's Agenda of a broad proposal for welfare reform; inclusion of "welfare reform" in the expanding "women's agenda movement" in many states across the country; the action of the Massachusetts NOW against the 1988 Moynihan welfare bill and its workfare principles; the efforts of university feminists to bring new educational opportunities for welfare mothers, such as the programs at Smith College, the University of Massachusetts, University of Wisconsin, and in New York City; the establishment of the Poor and Working Women's Caucus in the National Women's Studies Association; the new mobilizations around welfare reform, such as the May 1987 meeting in Boston organized by white and Black feminists in the group called Women for Economic Justice; the reemergence of a national coalition of welfare rights groups around the country; and their first convention in September 1988, bringing together women of different colors and classes.

Some of the distressing happenings are: the failure of many old and new coalitions to integrate as a matter of principle AFDC women into their boards and groups and the continuation of paternalistic models of speaking *for* instead of *with* women on welfare; the limited attention of feminist groups (both Black and white) to the welfare reform struggle and their absence from new coalitions to monitor the most sweeping welfare reform policy in the last fifty years; and the muted voice of feminists in the forums on welfare reform to counter the groundswell by policy-makers to define the welfare problem as one of "women's dependency" rather than one of "insufficient income."

Clearly, the signs suggest rising opportunities for cooperation, as well as some basic threats to solidarity among women in the welfare reform struggle. As we have seen, conflicts are not necessarily destructive, if creative resolutions are found to reinforce and reshape alliances between women. A united stand by diverse women's groups is a vital "missing resource" in this historical struggle. In this arena women in the past have tended to be reactive rather than proactive. Men have defined welfare problems and solutions rather than women setting their own agenda in an area that dominates their lives.

My long-range agenda is to find ways to strength women's alliances to bring about an economic security program for everyone. To do this will require the insights and experience of a broad diversity of women who are knowledgeable in this area or care about becoming more informed.

What can we learn from the past few decades of trying to work together across race and class barriers? What have we learned about bridging some of these chasms? Under what conditions are such alliances possible, and why do some succeed where others fail? All these are important questions that need answers. The study of women in the welfare rights struggle suggests some answers but leave many unanswered, as yet.

We have learned from the alliances in the welfare rights movement that communications between women of different classes and races have to be improved. We have to begin listening to each other, "talking across the table," as Withorn and Lefkowitz (1986:341-355) suggest.

We need to invent new ways of organizing not only to facilitate, but to guarantee, that we have the opportunity to meet, talk, debate, disagree, and agree with women from diverse groups. Our fear of differences—largely reinforced by the patriarchy—has to be transformed into our celebration of our diversity. When we define our diverse talents, experiences and understandings of these problems into positive assets and resources, we will be less vulnerable to divisive attacks. Most importantly, if we develop opportunities and structures grounded in diversity, interracial and interclass communication is bound to expand.

We also need to examine and debate the differences of our "staying power" with various issues, especially those that affect the lives of the most disadvantaged among us. Another aspect of this same problem is learning how to accept the challenge of never-ending struggles. As one feminist said, "We are in for a very, very long haul. . . . " and somehow this needs to be discussed more frequently in light of creating far-reaching alliances and coalitions with diverse groups. Perhaps the idea of building and weaving strong networks—rather than joining temporary coalitions—is needed to keep us on the track.

Finally, in my opinion, to work together we must commit ourselves to organizing together. If our foundations are diverse and representative of diverse groups, the various agendas will emerge. Those of us who are more advantaged in society bear the responsibility for redistributing resources within the movement to enable *all* women who are interested to participate. In the long run, this kind of solidarity, I believe, is what will ultimately help women achieve their long-range goals. It is a resource yet largely untapped.

In contrast to taking action, words are easy to formulate. Nonetheless, ideas are the essence of any revolution. We must be creative in how we organize and communicate so that we find ways to work together as "sisterwomen." Only then can we hope to tap our latent political power to transform the welfare system and implement a real women's agenda in the United States.

References

Abramovitz, Mimi. 1988. *Regulating the Lives of Women: Social Welfare Policy from Colonial Times to the Present*. Boston: South End Press.

Ackelsberg, Martha A. 1988. "Communities, Resistance, and Women's Activism: Some Implications for a Democratic Polity." In *Women and the Politics of Empowerment*, ed. Ann Bookman and Sandra Morgen. Philadelphia: Temple University Press.

Ackelsberg, Martha, and Diamond, Irene. 1987. "Gender and Political Life: New Directions in Political Science." In *Analyzing Gender: A Handbook of Social Science Research*, ed. Beth B. Hess and Myra Marx Ferree. Beverly Hills, CA: Sage Publications.

Aptheker, Bettina. 1982. *Woman's Legacy: Essays on Race, Sex and Class in American History*. Amherst, MA: University of Massachusetts.

Balser, Diane. 1987. *Sisterhood and Solidarity: Feminism and Labor in Modern Times*. Boston: South End Press.

Blumberg, Rhoda Lois. 1980. "White Mothers in the American Civil Rights Movement." In *Research in the Interweave of Social Roles: Women and Men*, ed. Helena Z. Lopata, Vol. 1, pp. 22–50.

Bookman, Ann, and Morgen, Sandra, eds. 1988. *Women and the Politics of Empowerment*. Philadelphia: Temple University Press.

Cole, Johnnetta B., ed. 1986. *All American Women: Lines that Divide, Ties that Bind*. New York: The Free Press.

Davis, Angela Y. 1983. *Women, Race and Class*. New York: Vintage Books, Random House.

Giddings, Paula. 1985. *When and Where I Enter . . . . : The Impact of Black Women on Race and Sex in America*. New York: William Morrow and Co.

Ferree, Myra Marx, and Hess, Beth B. 1985. *Controversy and Coalition: The New Feminist Movement*. Boston: Twayne Publishers.

Hull, Gloria T., Scott, Patricia Bell, and Smith, Barbara, eds. 1982. *All the Women Are White, All the Blacks Are Men, But Some of Us Are Brave: Black Women's Studies*. New York: The Feminist Press.

Jones, Jacqueline. 1985. *Labor of Love, Labor of Sorrow: Black Women, Work and the Family, from Slavery to the Present*. New York: Vintage Books, Random House.

Joseph, Gloria I., and Lewis, Jill. 1981. *Common Differences: Conflicts in Black and White, Feminist Perspectives*. Garden City, NY: Anchor Press, Doubleday.

Lefkowitz, Rochelle, and Withorn, Ann, eds. 1986. *For Crying Out Loud: Women and Poverty in the United States*. New York: The Pilgrim Press.

Lorde, Audre. 1984. *Sister Outsider*. Trumansburg, NY: The Crossing Press.

Morris, Aldon. 1984. *The Origins of the Civil Rights Movement: Black Communities Organizing for a Change*. New York: The Free Press.

Oberschall, Anthony. 1973. *Social Conflicts and Social Movements*. New York: Prentice-Hall.

Piven, Frances Fox. 1985. "Women and the State: Ideology, Power, and the Welfare State." In *Gender and Life Course*, ed. Alice S. Rossi. New York: Aldine Publishing Co., pp. 265–87.

Piven, Frances Fox, and Cloward, Richard A. 1977. *Poor People's Movements: Why They Succeed and How They Fail*. New York: Pantheon.

Rupp, Leila J., and Taylor, Verta. 1988. *Survival in the Doldrums: The American Women's Rights Movement, 1945–the 1960s*. London: Oxford University Press.

West, Guida. 1981. *The National Welfare Rights Movement: The Social Protest of Poor Women*. New York: Praeger Publishers.

West, Guida. Forthcoming. *Protest Leadership Outcomes: Leaders in the Welfare Rights Movement Two Decades Later*. New York: Praeger.

West, Guida, and Blumberg, Rhoda Lois. Forthcoming. *Women and Social Protest*.

Withorn, Ann, and Lefkowitz, Rochelle. 1986. "Talking Across the Table: Possibilities for Dialogue and Action Between Poor Women and Feminists." In *For Crying Out Loud: Women and Poverty in the United States*. New York: The Pilgrim Press.

Zald, Meyer N., and Ash, Roberta. 1966. "Social Movement Organizations: Growth, Decay and Change." *Social Forces* 44 (3): 327–41.

Canadian Feminist
Social Service Collectives
Caring and Contradictions

Janice L. Ristock

Marie: "I worked in a collective years ago—but never again! It was one of the worst experiences of my life. I was so devastated and hurt—these were supposed to be my sisters—but I had a disagreement with the group and before I knew it, I felt like I was 'the enemy'. I thought we needed to spend more time on our budget. What a mistake—suddenly I was identified as being too task-oriented, if not patriarchal in my thinking. . . . well I just couldn't cope anymore with life in the collective." *Joan:* "You're kidding, it sounds so awful— yet I feel that I would give anything to work with a group of women. Women helping women, working for social change, all within an alternative collective structure—it's my ideal!" Marie: "Well it may be the ideal but I know that I'm not the only woman who has had bad experiences within collectives—I just wish that I could explain why things go wrong when our intentions are so good."

Working collectively is a common organizational form for many feminist groups. It is a structure that allows our feminist ideals and practices to be integrated within our work environment. In Canada, there are a number of feminist social service collectives that offer services such as transition hostels, shelters for battered women, and rape crisis centers. I recently conducted a national survey of these services which elicited information about their social service work, their processes and difficulties, and their social change role (Ristock, 1987). I also interviewed eight women from four different collectives. The national survey provided broad-based, descriptive information, while the interviews and case studies allowed for an in-depth, critical evaluation of the work of collectives. I began this research project because I felt there was little information available that systematically and empirically documented the struggles and successes of this feminist approach to organizing. My research questions were shaped by my own experiences as a former collective worker and by my training as a community psychologist.

I compiled a list of sixty-seven self-defined feminist social service collectives. Questionnaires were distributed and thirty-four of the sixty-seven were returned. Most of the collectives in my sample have formed primarily as a response to violence against women. In addition, these collectives are found in every province in Canada and in both urban and rural settings. Ninety-four percent (32/34) of the respondents in this sample see themselves as providing an alternative service and feel they are changing the position of women in our society through the work they are doing. Thus these collectives have a dual role of providing needed social services for women while working for social change.

But these collectives also have their difficulties. Many report difficulties in decision making, group conflict, and factions within the collective, to name a few. As my opening scenario indicates, many women feel frustrated with collectives and are tired of the continual problems that all too often result in certain collective members leaving their jobs. Yet feminists continue to use the collective structure because it offers consistency with feminist theory. In particular, feminist social service workers want a work environment that will be responsive to their needs and the needs of women using the service. Thus it is important to have a structure where decisions and responsibilities are shared by the very women who are in contact with the service users. The organization, then, operates based on women's experiences and knowledge, and this is in keeping with the feminist adage that the personal is political. But what specifically are the tensions in collective work? How do they get created? First, it is important to understand and acknowledge that the services provided by these collectives remain embedded within the mainstream oppressive social service system because of their reliance on government funding. This is problematic because the values and goals of feminist collectives are in direct opposition to the values and goals of the government funders. What emerges, then, is an area of contradiction and tension that is felt inside the collective. These contradictions experienced within social service collectives are also related to the dichotomy between feminist values and societal values at large. Thus despite our desire to be and act as consistent feminists we bring with us a history of childhood socialization based in traditional, nonfeminist values. It is the effects of this overarching area of tension that give rise to many of the internal difficulties women experience within collectives.

In this paper I will present some of the internal and external difficulties faced by feminist collectives that were revealed to me both in the interviews I conducted with collective workers and through the national survey. In addition, this paper will show that an analysis of our contradictory positions within society is a necessary and positive step in order to build solidarity and foster alliances among women who work in these important, alternative structures.

External relations: feminist collectives in the Canadian context

According to the survey results I compiled, 100 percent of the collectives in this sample receive all or a portion of their funding from the government (e.g., provincial ministries of Community and Social Services). The Canadian system of universal access to health care and social services has many advantages, but feminist agencies within this system are often in a precarious position. For instance, sixty-five percent of the collectives in this sample report that their funding is inadequate and insecure. Often they have to rely on volunteers to help provide all of the services (ninety-four percent report using volunteer/support workers), and this adds an additional component and power imbalance to the ideally flat organizational model. As well, collectives are forced into a relationship with the state. This relationship involves power that further impacts on their direction and structure. For instance, the service mandate is prescribed by the funder, a board of directors is required, and the name of an executive director might also be required. The collective structure then begins to resemble a hierarchical structure. The women I surveyed who currently work in collectives are well aware of this contradictory location as indicated by the following comments:

> "We are an alternative feminist service, yet we are embedded within a mainstream, oppressive social service system." "A contradiction exists between what our feminist theory and practices say and our reality of accepting government funds, using volunteers and having a board of directors." "Our social service work is 'band-aid' work that doesn't address the root of the problem . . . . The irony is that we are supposed to be working for social change. Also we experience another contradiction between the power we have as workers and the lack of power of the women who use the service—since our goal is to make the service empowering for women."

This work context, then, is filled with tension and struggle. The collectives were quick to point out, however, that they do strategize to get around some of the imposed restrictions on their work. For example, they will have an executive director in name only, they will hand pick a board of directors that may also function as a collective or serve only as a "rubber stamp." In addition, the collective provides services that go beyond their service mandate (see Ristock, 1987). But despite these strategies, the possibility of their funding being revoked or cut back at any time always exists.

I describe this context because it becomes clear that these feminist collectives are embedded within a hierarchy of power relations and that many contradictions inevitably arise. In particular, the feminist goals of empowerment and social change become difficult to achieve because so much of the collective's energies are directed toward maintaining their external relations. They want to preserve both their salaries and the service. Internal tensions, then, are also created because of this complex and contradictory context of feminist social service work.

Internal relations: contradictions within collectives

Internal tensions such as power within collectives, differing feminist analyses, tensions between lesbian and heterosexual women, white women and women of color, and service providers and service recipients are issues that reflect the felt contradictions experienced in this work. There is a gap between the ideal vision of what it means to operate as a feminist collective and the real practices women engage in within collectives.

These tensions are always felt but are difficult to acknowledge and respond to. In fact, the reaction that I have both experienced, observed, and engaged in is to try and create a homogeneous collective that then pits itself against the external forces (such as government funders). That is, the collective becomes "us," and it is against "them." This tactic allows collectives to feel strong and united. But with this creation of homogeneity comes the denial of differences. Women's personal sense of self is expected to fit within the "cohesive" collective's identity in a way that is often prescriptive. Social psychological research has shown that highly cohesive groups are known to exert power and control over their members' behavior. They want individuals to conform to the norms of the group. Diversity and difference are perceived as threatening to the larger goal of a collective identity. Thus the ultimate threat of a nonconforming group member becomes ostracization. Some of the interviews that I conducted echo the felt internal difficulties and also reflect the creation of an "us" and "them" dichotomy within the collectives themselves because of this focus on creating a cohesive, homogeneous collective. One woman described the way in which "our political ideology (feminism) is often used to hide truth" and to reinforce the existence of an "in group" and an "out group" within collectives.

She says: "We accommodate superficial differences but what that amounts to is real differences remaining hidden. The accommodation is just to allow women into the fold to make them become one of 'us,' but differences in feminist analysis, skill, and identity remain unacknowledged."

Another collective worker also commented on differences not being acknowledged and her analysis of the situation points to the way in which a a feminist ideology can be misused:

> Factions exist within our collective between lesbians and heterosexual women, between the politically correct and the politically incorrect. Some identities and differences are perceived as having more value— all this does is reinforce a hierarchy of feminism.

Another woman also experienced the often prescriptive mandate of what is required to remain as part of the 'in group' within collectives. She comments: "I often feel silenced because I am not a lesbian, nor am I a woman of colour. I am a white, middle-class, heterosexual who often feels less valued because of who I am."

Donna Barker, a Black woman, recently wrote about her experiences within a white feminist collective where she too experienced practices that did not acknowledge the differences that do exist amongst women (Barker, 1987). She writes:

> Being the only Black working among white people is always a drag, but working with a white feminist collective is particularly treacherous. Treacherous because white feminist rituals include openly expressing feelings and emotions and sharing personal information so that when the inevitable attack comes, they are deeply painful. Painful because we want to believe that their pronouncements about our common womanhood and anti-racist feminism will be expressed in their behaviour. We usually go with hope and the smashing of that hope is devastating (p. 12).

These women's comments reflect the all too often destructive experiences that occur within collectives. Feminism is typically cited as the reason for these difficulties. Individual women are judged as less feminist or as holding the incorrect feminist views when they are different. Thus a feminist ideology is often transformed into an oppressive rule-setting, prescriber of acceptable attitudes and behaviors.

Janice Raymond, in *A Passion for Friends,* also writes about the way in which feminist theory can be transformed into prescriptive rhetoric within collectives.

She states: "Under the rhetoric of 'collective', 'noncompetitive' and 'equal', women who achieve, who are ambitious, and who are successful in what they do are relegated to the status of pariah" (p. 195). She further makes the point that women within collectives often become alienated from their own sense of personal and political power, thus endowing the collective with false power (Raymond, 1986).

As part of my research, I reviewed the internal documents (e.g., basis of unity statements and job application forms) of the thirty-four collectives in my sample. In each of these diverse services the documents reflect the emphasis of certain feminist values. Words like *empowerment, equality* and *choice* consistently appear, with only a few documents making reference to women's diversity. The job application forms also stress a feminist analysis as being central to collective work. Questions such as, "What is your definition of feminism?" and "How does feminism inform your work?" are examples from all of their forms. Many of these services do not even want to see a resume of women's previous work history or educational background. Not surprisingly, then, feminism and the emphasis of certain feminist values are the major criteria for hiring a new collective member and for remaining as part of the collective. Thus the basis of unity for collectives becomes an assumed shared ideological commitment. When a woman shows diversity or difference, then, it is her feminism that is called into question. She is seen as a deviate threatening the unity and power of the collective. This analysis of some women not being "feminist enough" merely individualizes the complexities of collective difficulties and, as Raymond suggests, it fills the collective with a sense of power that is not based on the strength of its members' diversity. The desire to have a homogeneous collective identity is understandable given the struggles and tensions within the social service context. Women want and need to feel united because their type of service and feminist analysis is marginalized within the mainstream social service system. And it almost goes without saying that it is desirable to work with women who share your vision of the world. But it is necessary to acknowledge the social construction of the collective identity and the constraints that this construction has for women. Women might resist the notion of a heterogeneous collective, with openly acknowledged differences in feminist analysis, skills, roles, and identities because they feel it might be filled with conflict and the collective would crumble in the face of external struggles. A closer examination of internal practices and assumptions points to the contradictions and power differences that are already in existence within collectives because some identities, locations and political analyses are valued over others. In other words— homogeneity is a myth! For example, eighty-eight percent of the collectives in this sample report use the consensus decision making practice. In this process everyone has an opportunity to discuss an issue until a decision is reached that everyone can agree with. This is seen as preferable to the majority vote process, where a minority voice is oppressed. In addition, this process is used so that authority and leadership can reside with all group members. Nancy Hartsock has written about the alternative form of leadership and authority within collectives (1974): "To lead is to be at the centre of a group rather than in front of others. Authority is based on skill and knowledge and is compelled to demonstrate its force to those concerned in terms which they can grasp, and by dint of being so compelled, is made in some real measure responsible to them" (p. 116).

Decisions by consensus, however, are also based on some false assumptions which challenge these ideal alternative notions of authority and leadership. One assumption is that everyone in the group is equal in terms of sharing power and having equal skills for the process. It also assumes that decisions by consensus are empowering because no one is forced by the majority into a decision. Yet many women describe that in reality it is those who are more articulate, who have been with the collective longer, and who are louder when voicing their opinions that benefit from this decision-making process (Ristock, 1989; Zaremba, 1988). As Zaremba explains: "In feminist consensus organizations . . . the underlying issue is virtually always control over the organization. Under an overt majority rule structure, the question of control is out front and power can change hands within the accepted process. . . . But under a consensus system there is no process for control to pass from one group or faction to another" (p. 4). The consensus process itself is not necessarily inadequate; but the denial that power relations can operate during this process is the problem.

Another process used by collectives that reveals power relations is the practice of sharing and rotating all jobs. Over half of the collectives in this sample (fifty-three percent) engage in this practice. The ideal is that responsibility, knowledge, and accountability will be shared equally by all members. No one is placed in the position of being "expert," and everyone is assumed to want to engage in all of the tasks equally. Yet this practice denies that certain women have strengths, skills, and preferences for certain areas. This practice forces a blending of these differences. What emerges, then, is unacknowledged power struggles between members around issues of accountability. In fact, eleven percent of the collectives in my survey sample were critical of the job-sharing practice and have specialized job roles as an alternative. In addition, it is often with these internal practices that deny differences, that the effects of homophobia, racism, and classism are felt. For example, many collectives use the model of "nonviolent communication" as a vehicle to express constructive criticism and held resentments to one another. But this process has also caused some collective members to be silenced. One collective reported to me that they were having difficulties with the model. In their collective one of the difficulties was with the word *resentment*. Some of the collective workers were Chilean, and the word resentment had a very strong connotation, implying intense dislike or hatred. Thus they found the process to be destructive. Later they changed the language in the model to expressing a *held concern*. This was a beginning for them to review the underlying assumptions in their collective processes which are often based on white, middle-class privilege. For example, the nonviolent communication process assumes a certain level of rational, verbal, and analytical abilities based on Western values. Critiquing the underlying processes and assumptions within collectives practices will allow us to create new ways of working together.

Women may find tackling the difficulties between us to be frightening and experience the complexities as great. But diversity can also bring innovation and growth and change within our work settings that is creative. Bell Hooks (1984) discusses the necessity of grappling with differences in order to build solidarity and foster alliances. She asserts:

> Women do not need to eradicate difference to feel solidarity. We do not need to share our common oppression to fight equally to end oppression . . . we can be sisters united by shared interest and beliefs, united in our appreciation for diversity, united in our struggle to end sexist oppression, united in political solidarity (p. 65).

Working toward alliances

Collectives are slowly reflecting on their practices and making changes that will acknowledge the rights and diversity of all women. Most Canadian social service collectives formed in the early seventies at a time when feminism was emphasizing our commonality as women. The women's movement has been criticized for reflecting the values and experiences of a minority of women—that is, young, white, middle-class, heterosexual women. There has been a recognition of the need to represent the majority of women and their struggles in the mainstream agenda of the women's movement (Hooks, 1984). Factors that affect women's life experiences, such as class, ethnicity, sexual preference and age, need to be taken into account. Slowly, feminist theory has been evolving to acknowledge women's diversity. One collective recently reported this change in their thinking: "Reflecting upon the diverse needs of women on the frontline meant we could no longer gloss over the differences between us as collective members. Our differences reflect very real differences in power and privilege in society. We had to apply our learning not only to our counselling techniques but internally as well." In particular, many of the Canadian rape crisis and sexual assault centers have begun to challenge and expand the collective structure through the use of problem-solving tools such as constructive criticism and appreciation.

The Toronto Rape Crisis Centre (TRCC) is one collective that has changed their collective structure to begin to address diversity, power, and privilege. They have included the components of caucus and group within their collective structure. They define caucus as "a mechanism for women dealing with an additional facet of oppression to take care of each other, discuss areas of shared reality and to work on policy and action plans as a whole" (p.71). Thus caucuses are given power and leadership in a particular area. They have caucuses of working-class women, women of color, lesbians, and Jewish women in their collective. The collective then is prepared to deal with criticisms from the caucuses and give serious weight to any recommendations that they make. In order to involve all collective members in this process, they have groups that correspond to and counterbalance the caucuses. They have groups for heterosexual women, gentile women, and middle-class women. The women in groups examine the reality of living with privilege and support each other in changing behaviors arising from that privilege. They describe women in their collectives who cross a number of privilege/oppression lines (e.g., a white, middle-class, lesbian), which ensures that members know both the impact of being in a caucus and the responsibilities of being in a group. (Toronto Rape Crisis Centre, 1988.) I interviewed two women from the TRCC who commented on implementing the caucus/group system:

> It was so amazing when we implemented this structure. For the first time we recognized major differences and similarities amongst us.

> When we first brought this structure back to the collective after learning about it at a conference for sexual assault centres—it led to probably the worst split that the collective ever had. It brought up other issues—do we see ourselves as primarily providing a service or as community activists? It brought up scary issues for many women— How do you work on differences? How will it change the collective? The split for the collective broke down along the privilege lines. The women who left, with the exception of one, were all middle-class and all white women. I don't think that it was a coincidence. It was scary for them at the time to work on what those differences meant.

The caucus/group structure within their collective openly acknowledges the power and privilege differences between collective members. Thus the unity of the collective was threatened because the collective's assumption that all women are equal was changed. Yet despite the split, they have continued to develop this system.

Further changes in the collective structure have included the development of working teams. Many collectives are now finding that in order to grow and change it is important to offer women a chance to work in particular areas. For example, some of the shelters now have teams for diverse areas of work such as housing, fund-raising, community outreach, and internal services. Collective members are able to work on a team of interest. This new development in the structure means that women have to give up ownership of all parts of the service and trust co-workers to handle specific areas. Teams then report on their work at collective meetings and make recommendations for decisions based on their more in-depth knowledge of their work.

Finally, work is being done by other collectives to develop additional tools so that internal processes can also reflect the changes in the assumptions about what it means to work collectively. These are just some examples of the positive steps women are taking to grapple with differences within collective structures.

The efforts of these collectives reflect women's continued desire to have their work structures consistent with their feminist values. Some of the changes being made within the collective organizational model challenges the view that there is a static, unitary collective model. Our feminist organizations are challenged by the struggle to work with diversity and foster alliances. Collectives will continue as a viable organizational form if they are responsive to the needs of workers, the context of their work, and if they remain committed to an ever-evolving feminist ideology. We need to reevaluate our ideas of collectives in the 1990s and ensure that a politics of difference, a vision of heterogeneity, and an analysis of the relations of power are central to our structures, practices, and agendas for social change.

References

Barker, D. 1987. "Anatomy of Working With A White Collective." *Our Lives* 2(2–3): 12–13.

Hartsock, N. 1974. "Political Change: Two Perspectives On Power." *Quest* 1:3–19.

Hooks, Bell. 1984. *Feminist Theory: From Margin to Centre*. Boston: South End Press.

Raymond, J. 1986. *A Passion for Friends*. Boston: Beacon Press.

Ristock, J. 1987. "Working Together for Empowerment." *Canadian Women's Studies* 8(4): 74–76.

Ristock, J. 1989. "Feminist Collectives Spring Up Across Canada." *Worker Co-op* 8(3): 10–11.

The Toronto Rape Crisis Centre (working class caucus). 1988. "Around the Kitchen Table." *Fireweed* (winter/spring): 69–81.

Zaremba, E. 1988. "Collective Trouble." *Broadside* 10(1):5.

Opportunities and Challenges
The Role of Feminists
for Social Change in Hong Kong

Chi-Kwan A. Ho

As reunification of Hong Kong with socialist China by the year 1997 draws near, the economic-political-socio-ideological systems in Hong Kong inevitably are undergoing major, if subtle, changes.[1] What feminists in Hong Kong should be concerned with at this historical juncture is whether they can seize this opportunity to include a feminist perspective in the reconstruction of Hong Kong's future. The purpose of this paper is to assess where the women's movement in Hong Kong is and suggest strategies in bringing about a feminist agenda for social change in the context of coalition building. Specifically, I am including in this paper first, a brief description and analysis of the existing economic-socio-ideological-political conditions of women in Hong Kong; second, a presentation and assessment of some of the major women's groups in Hong Kong, followed by an analysis of these groups along a continuum of feminist consciousness; third, corresponding

Special thanks to Evelyn Torton Beck for her support and reading of an earlier draft. Thanks and appreciation to my sisters in Hong Kong whose sweat and tears made this article possible.

strategies feminists in Hong Kong can employ to facilitate a coalitionfor social change. For the purpose of this paper, feminist consciousness is defined as the ability to understand the causes of structural sexism and a readiness to challenge and eliminate institutional patriarchy on both personal and structural levels.

Existing realities of women in Hong Kong

The status and position of women in Hong Kong, in general, have improved since the late sixties due to changes in demographics, economic priorities,[2] migration, and new legislation enacted by the (British) colonial government in the face of mounting social pressures. Some of these gains include increasing rates of female employment,[3] rising educational standards for women, equal pay for equal work since 1981 for government employees, the elimination in 1971 of the concubinage system,[4] (conditional) legalization of abortion in 1973 and 1981,[5] a trend toward free and later marriage, formation of the nuclear family, which gave "wives" a relatively greater sense of freedom as opposed to being "daughters-in-law" in a patrilocal extended family system, technologization of housework, and availability of fertility control practices. Despite these changes, women in Hong Kong are far from being liberated. A closer examination of the reality reveals that the gap between females and males has remained in all major aspects of life.

The economic sphere

A high degree of segregation based on sex in the labor market persists as the social production of women continues to be regarded as a secondary and supplementary activity. As a result, although more women have been absorbed into the labor market, most of these women have low status and low-paid jobs. In 1981, for example, while 67.2 percent of the total 92,968 workers in the electronic industry were women (62,467), more than 94 percent of these women worked on the operative and unskilled level, doing low level, nontechnical jobs on the assembly line (HKCSD 1981:19). In the plastics industry, the second largest manufacturing industry—which absorbed a large number of women wage workers—there were in 1981 32.9 male employees for every female employee at the technician level (Report of Manpower Survey of the Plastic Industry, 1981). According to the 1981 census, a majority of the 53 percent of women who labored as wage earners were working either as outworkers—housewives who bring home crafts distributed by factories so that they could undertake wage labor, child care, and household chores simultaneously—or part-timers (HKCSD, 1981). As part-timers or outworkers, many women were rendered extremely vulnerable in the wage labor market, as they were not entitled to rights and protection covered by the Employment Ordinance. The subsidiary position of Hong Kong women in the wage labor market resulted from the fact that females continue to be preordained as chief agents of reproduction, defined as including both biological reproduction and the reproduction of labor power (Mackintoch, 1981:3) and assigned the role as a secondary or reserved labor force in the wage labor market.

Sociocultural legacy

The high degree of segregation based on sex in wage labor suffered by women is reflected in the distribution of females and males in the educational system. Whereas over the years the number of females of school-age groups approximated the number of males in elementary and high school, the gap between the two sexes in higher education continued. For every female studying in higher education, there were 19.2 males in 1976 and 19.5 in 1981 (HKCSD, 1977; 1982). This gap is also reflected in educational careers: whereas there were more female teachers than male ones in elementary grades, this ratio reversed as one moved up the educational pyramid (Chan, P.K., 1983).

Despite the dissolution of the patrilineal system of descent and increased practice of neolocal residence resulting from migration and urbanization in a highly industrialized city like Hong Kong, women continued to be ideologically tied to traditional gender role expectations. Whereas most women no longer adhered to traditional Confucian rules and regulations, such as the "Three Obediences", whereby a woman was supposed to obey her father when young, obey her husband when married, and obey her son if widowed, many women knew and very often internalized societal expectations that females should play the part of a submissive, dependent, self-sacrificing paragon (Leung, 1984). Socialized and coerced into accepting marriage as their ultimate goal and success in life, many women still feel they are primarily responsible for the success of their marriages and the caring of their family. More than 60 percent of the 951 women interviewed in a 1985 survey expressed willingness to sacrifice their careers for the sake of the family. These women also stated that familial satisfaction was the kind most valuable to them (Report on Women's Participation in Public Affairs, 1985).

Traditional sexual division of labor persists as women continue to be charged with the ultimate responsibilities of child rearing and caring of the family. Besides adding a burden to female wage earners who are wives and mothers, this preoccupation with the family was found to be one crucial stumbling block for local women to participate in community and public affairs (Report on Women's Participation in Public Affairs, 1985.)

The political arena

The gap between females and males in the government structure remained wide even as people applauded the increasing appointment of women into the legislative and decision-making bodies of the Hong Kong government. For every female, in 1983, there were nineteen males on the commissioner level (Government Information Service). In 1986, there were eight males in the Legislative and the Executive Councils, six males in the Urban Council, and 10.4 males in district administrative boards for every female (compiled from the 1987 Hong Kong Year Book). More important than this numerical fact, however, is the lack of concern for women's issues among the appointed council women. None of them had ever questioned existing sexist laws and/or sex discriminating social policies in Hong Kong. Instead, many of these women supported the status quo and continued to reinforce the traditional sexual division of labor. In 1987, one young legislative council woman openly expressed to representatives of a women's organization that she would not hesitate in giving up her job and office if her husband so wished. Many of the other council women perpetuated the myth of "superwoman" by boasting publicly their triple roles as able stateswomen, virtuous wives, and good mothers. Some recently elected female district board members proved to be more concerned with women's issues. But their number is minimal when compared to their male, and patriarchalized female, colleagues.

As a result of the overemphasis of women's reproductive role, accompanied by the devaluation of work related to this role and the assignment of supplementary quality to their social production power, women in Hong Kong are kept in low-paid, low status jobs. This chaining of women to their reproductive responsibilities exists in all aspects of life and explains continual subordination of females to males in the economic socio-cultural-political spheres. In the face of this reality, what have women's groups in Hong Kong done about it? What can they do?

Women's voices, feminist outcries

For all movements working for social transformation, a shared vision, united effort, and strong support/power base are necessary preconditions for possible success. In this respect, do we have a consolidated women's movement with a feminist agenda for social change to speak of in

Hong Kong? My own experience with and observation and assessment of the various women's groups active in Hong Kong raised both doubts and optimism. Differences in the analysis of the causes of women's oppression, diverse focus and style of work, the differences in access to economic socio-political resources, and ideological persuasions of the various groups make unity at this point difficult. However, breakthroughs in the context of communication and small-scale cooperation among some of these groups since 1985 give me hope that the seed of unity has been sewn and is indeed germinating. What is to be done next is to cultivate this budding seedling with more care and conscious efforts. Before I proceed to discuss strategies for forging a more consolidated women's movement for social change in Hong Kong, I am going to sketch below the main features of the major women's organizations there and assess these groups along a spectrum of feminist consciousness to see where the movement is. As mentioned in the introduction, feminist consciousness here refers to the understanding of the root cause for institutional patriarchy and the realization of the necessity to fight it on both the personal and structural level.

Women's groups: a review and assessment

The Hong Kong Council of Women

Being one of the oldest women's organizations concerned with women's status and their position in society and the family in Hong Kong, the Hong Kong Council of Women (HKCW) was founded in 1947 by middle- and upper-class local and Eurasian women. In the sixties, the Council was in the forefront of a coalition of more than 140 groups campaigning for the abolition of the socially sanctioned concubinage system. This first significant effort of the alliance among women's and other groups resulted in a change in the marriage law in 1971. The Marriage Reform Ordinance officially proclaimed monogamy as the only legal form of marriage. The HKCW then became relatively silent in the early seventies and was revived only in 1975 as the United Nations declared International Women's Year. Membership then was made up mostly of expatriate women, a majority of whom came from England and the United States to stay in Hong Kong temporarily, either because of their own jobs or those of their husbands. Important concerns of the Council during this period included "the status of women, working women, social problems, film censorship and prostitution," but the primary focus was "consciousness raising" (Annual Report, HKCW, 1986:1.) The main thrust of work was to set up different rapport groups, such as the mixed marriage (usually white women married to Chinese men) groups, single women's workshops, and the women's health education committee. In 1977, some active members of the Council became more issue-oriented. A series of War-On-Rape campaigns were launched in cooperation with the Family Planning Association, the United Christian Hospital, the Samaritan Society, and the Salvation Army. This campaign resulted in the introduction of women police officers, female probation officers, and a family planning service to assist victims on the legal front.

However, in the process of campaigning in local communities on the issue of rape, the inherent weakness of the HKCW was exposed. The Council's active membership was largely made up of middle-class, expatriate women who enjoyed some forms of special privilege in colonial Hong Kong. Ignorant of the socio-economic cultural dynamics of the local community, many of the Council's proposals on the prevention of rape were found to be impractical, especially in the low-cost housing areas where rapes happened most often. HKCW members also failed to develop a sensitivity to the reservedness of local women in talking publicly about one's personal life and sexual practices during consciousness-raising sessions. As a result, many local women felt threatened by the aggressive and confrontational approach advocated by the Council and became alienated from the War-on-Rape campaign. At the same time, the Council was suffering from a lack of personpower because of the high turnover rate of its active members, whose duration of stay in Hong Kong depended on extraneous circumstances. These realizations pushed the Council in the late seventies into a conscious membership drive among local women. The very fact that English continued to be the language used in all meetings, however, automatically barred many local women from participating. Chinese women who joined the Council came mainly from the well-educated, often overseas-trained, middle class.

Into the eighties, work of the Council continued on issues that affected women's well-being and began to take more interest in serving its socio-economically less fortunate sisters. By 1985, the Council established a hotline service on legal advice, opened a Women's Center in a low-cost housing estate (complete with a small library, a conference room, and a paid staff) and set up the first and only refuge home in Hong Kong for battered women.[6] The Council has a current membership of over 150, most of whom are from the middle class. Its direction and work are largely service oriented, focusing on empowerment of women as individuals. Recognizing that it is indispensable to fight sexist discrimination and male chauvinism on a personal level, the Council certainly could make greater contributions to the budding women's movement in Hong Kong if and when it equipped itself with a more structural macroanalysis of patriarchy.

Women's clubs of the "rich and famous"

A few women's organizations, such as the Chinese Women's Association (CWA) and the New Kowloon Women's Association (NKWA), were established in the sixties by wives of rich celebrities for social networking and public demonstrations of their philanthropy and commitment to charitable work. Sharing their objectives in the seventies, wives of members of the Lion's Club International, Local 303 (Hong Kong), started clamoring for their own chapters in Hong Kong. A total of nine such chapters have been set up since. In 1970, the Zonta International also established a chapter in Hong Kong, which developed into four chapters by 1988. Similar to the ideology and practice of the mother organization, the Zonta chapters in Hong Kong invite as its members only successful top executive women from different professions within the status quo. Their members are hailed for their achievement at work but more so for their adherence to the traditional role of *yan qi liang mu* (Mao, 1981:13.) To be a *yan qi liang mu*—virtuous wives and good mothers—is a role that members of the other women's clubs mentioned earlier also took pride in perpetuating.

Professional women's groups

By the late seventies, many women were moving slowly into traditionally male-dominated professions. How to survive and succeed in a sexist, male-dominated world became a real and urgent need for many of these women. As a result, occupational organizations for women in different professions such as the Hong Kong Federation of Women's Lawyers (HKFWL) and the Hong Kong Association of Professional and Business Women (HKAPBW) began to shoot up. In general, these groups served as old girls' networks and did help professional women lend support to each other in the pursuit of their careers or fighting sexism in the work place. But except for a few individual members, these groups seldom challenged the institutionalization of sexist inequalities on a larger scale. Most of these women fit well into the status quo. Many times, members of these organizations helped advocate the "strong/masculinized female" image.

The Yan Ngai Society

This women's organization was established in 1981 at the initiation of the government. Housewives in the middle-lower socio-economic communities were tapped to help organize other women in their own often far-off neighborhoods with inadequate facilities and poor services. True to its name, which means virtue and perseverance, the society perpetuates the traditional female gender roles of enduring wives and sacrificing mothers. Needs prioritized for these women by the government focused on help for child rearing and management of familial problems. Recreational activities for members included picnics and interest classes on cooking, knitting, and flower arrangements, while visitations to hospitals are taken as community participation (Report on the Yan Ngai Society, 1982.) In many aspects, the Yan Ngai Society (YNS) was created in the image of the women's clubs such as the Zonta Club, only this time, it is for the lower socio-economic class. The Society also was meant to serve as a safety valve to contain frustrations and anger of women being left alone in far-off, underdeveloped, minimally facilitated satellite towns in the New Territories.

Women workers and community groups

Groups concerned about conditions of women workers and women in grassroots communities also have sprung up in the seventies alongside the upsurge of community and social movements in Hong Kong. The major ones include:

1. The Committee on Women Workers (CWW) of the Hong Kong Christian Industrial Committee (HKCIC) and the Electronic Workers' Union (EWU) have spearheaded, since the late seventies, demands for paid maternity leave and improvement of women workers' benefits and working conditions. One characteristic of these groups is their prioritized concern for workers' issues. Problems may occur when issues concerning women's rights are pitted against benefits of the workers in general, especially in times of economic recession.

2. The Youth and Community Development Division (Y&CD) of the Hong Kong Young Women's Christian Association (HKYWCA) had initiated research and service projects for housewives and working women in the lower socio-economic communities in Hong Kong. In recent years, they have also been receptive to working with other women's groups on issues such as pornography and the denouncement of beauty pageants. However, much of the present active participation of the HKYWCA(Y&CD) against sexism and concern for the well-being of community women seemed to have stemmed from the leadership of their well-respected veteran Director, Ko Siu Wah, who is herself an advocate for women's welfare. Whether the Board of Directors of the YWCA or the next Executive Director of the Division will continue such a line of work after Ko's soon-to-occur retirement remains to be seen.

3. In recent years, a few self-initiated women's groups in some low-income communities have sprung up. Two outstanding examples of

these grassroots women's organizations concerned with both women and community issues are the Tai Hang Tung & North & South Estate Women's Group and the Li Chi Society in Tun Mun. Both groups work around activities that cater to the concrete needs of community women, such as adequate child care and better community facilities. At the same time, they worked on women's leadership training and participation in community affairs. In 1985 and 1988, one member from each group was elected and reelected to their local district board respectively. Both carried on their platforms women's concerns and the commitment to work for women's rights.

Feminist outcries

1. The International Women's League. The first women's group with a clear feminist ideology was organized in the late sixties largely by expatriate women from the West. The League, however, was dissolved shortly afterward. I could not find any documentation on the reason for the disbandment except that a few of its members later joined the HKCW.[7]

2. The Women's Rights Editorial Committee. In 1973, another women's group with clear feminist ideology, this time composed mainly of local women, was formed. The Committee's main activities rally around the publishing of its monthly magazine *Women's Rights,* which exposed and analyzed causes of patriarchy, sexist discrimination, and women's oppression. The target audience of the group was women workers of the lower economic class. The Committee was short-lived, however, and disbanded a year later, partly because of an ideological rift among some of its key members. According to a recent private conversation with an ex-member of the group, the conflict was on leadership style between some members who are active anarchists and others who wanted a more focused and structured format for the group. The ex-member added that the group eventually dispersed also because the anarchists in Hong Kong were undergoing their own "organizational" crisis around that time.

3. The Association for the Advancement of Feminism. If the formation of the Women's Rights Editorial Committee marked the first round of feminist consciousness among local women challenging sexism on the structural level, the birth in 1984 of the Association of the Advancement of Feminism (AAF) signified the second wave toward the goal of analyzing and challenging structural sexism, classism, racism, and homophobia in all aspects of life. By naming themselves publicly as a feminist group, the founding members of the AAF demonstrated a readiness to fight patriarchy. Their ideological struggle against the negative labeling of feminism as being too radical ushered

in a new stage for the germinating women's movement in Hong Kong (Chan, S.H. 1988). The AAF as an organization does not follow any particular ideology, although a few of its founding members carry socialist-feminist inclinations. Two characteristics of the Association, however, stand out among other women's organizations. First, there is an identification of institutionalized patriarchy as the root cause of women's oppression and a need to fight it on both the personal and the structural levels (AAF Constitution, 1984). Second, AAF is conscious of the importance of working in alliance with other women's groups or individuals for a consolidated feminist movement in Hong Kong (Annual Report, AAF, 1988).

Since its inception in March 1984, the Association has worked on several fronts: launching ideological struggles against sexism, classism, racism, and homophobia in newspaper columns and magazines; working in alliance with community centers and women's groups on the grassroots level to reach out to women of the lower socio-economic class; conducting research and publishing information on women's needs, attitudes, and conditions, such as the survey on Women's Participation in Public Affairs, 1985; developing print and nonprint media on, for example, sex discrimination in Hong Kong, a resource guide on services for women, a critique of the social welfare policy on women, a monthly *Women's News Digest,* and making educational videos on child care and battered women (Annual Reports, AAF, 1985, 1988).

The AAF is also active in the political arena. This group was, before the June 4 massacre in China,[8] the only women's organization that has expressed publicly its view on the reunification of Hong Kong and China. The group recognized the sovereignty of China over Hong Kong (welcoming an end to British colonial rule) and advocated that Hong Kong should reunify with the People's Republic of China with a high degree of autonomy in all local affairs. Members of the AAF also rallied for an inclusion of clauses guaranteeing equality of the sexes in all spheres of life and freedom of sexual preference in the drafting of the Basic Law—the mini-Constitution of Hong Kong after 1997 (Recommendation on the Drafting of the Basic Law for Hong Kong, AAF, 1987). As an organization, the AAF also participated in the Coalition for the Promotion of Democratic Structures in Hong Kong since 1987[9] and the Hong Kong Alliance in Support of Patriotic Democratic Movement in China (HKASDMC) since May, 1989.[10] The Association also advocated participation of more women in public affairs and supported female candidates advocating women's welfare in district elections. Starting with twenty-two founding members in 1984, the AAF now has over eighty members from all walks of life.

Multiformity and variations

Voices and outcries of women's groups in Hong Kong are indeed varied. To sum up where these organizations are in relation to each other in the formation of a feminist coalition for social change in Hong Kong, I will present a continuum of feminist consciousness.

Spectrum of women's groups in Hong Kong

Conservative		Liberal		Progressive
Strived for and supported by the status quo, reinforcing traditional gender role stereotypes; would not be included as part of the women's movement. Examples: CWA NKWA Zonta Club Yan Ngai Society	Professional interests: survival and success in a male-dominated world without challenging sexism and the status quo. Examples: HKFWL HKAPBW	Feminists concerned with women's issues on a personal/ individual dimension. Example: HKCW	Grassroots community-based groups working with women of the lower socio-economic class. Examples: HKYWCA (Y&CD) HKCIC (CWW) EWU Committee on Women Workers' Organizers	Equipped with a feminist analysis of structural patriarchy and launching an ideological critique of sexual division of labor and policies; call for both personal and structural changes to eliminate women's oppression. Example: AAF

Given this diversity in focus, interests, and multiformity of feminist consciousness among the various groups, it is too early to speak of the existence of a consolidated women's movement in Hong Kong.

Coalition building for social change

Concrete collaborations

Though varied and different in their analysis and focus of work, some efforts at collaboration among the liberal and progressive women's groups along the spectrum outlined above have taken place since 1985. Some forms of communication among women's groups both on the organizational and individual levels have been established. Joint committees working on specific issues among varying groups at different times also have taken place. Some successful examples of this form of ad hoc coalition on specific issues among women's groups in Hong Kong are listed below:

- A joint committee on "Concern on Pornography and Violence in the Mass Media" was formed in 1985 composed of members from the HKCW, HKYWCA(Y&CD), and AAF.
- A joint statement against exploitation of women in pornographic magazines issued by the "Anti-pornographic Media Campaign," initiated by members of the above Joint Committee, was co-signed by nine other women's groups in 1986.
- A joint declaration against molestation of women in public transportation (subways) was issued in 1988 by the AAF and the Women's Center (WC) of the HKCW.
- Joint declarations and surveys to study and promote female worker's rights, such as demands for implementation of paid maternity leave, for rights in refusing overtime work, and caution against absorption of females as reserved labor at times of labor shortages have been undertaken by the HKCIC(CWW), EWU, AAF and other women workers' groups and the Committee on Women's Workers Organizers (CWWO) since 1985.
- A Celebration of the 1988 International Women's Day was organized jointly by the AAF, HKCW-WC, HKFCW, Federation of Textile Workers, HKCIC, Kwun Tong Pastoral Church, Industrial Relations, and the CWWO. The peaceful march was disrupted by the police.
- A forum on civil rights to free assembly and free speech was jointly organized by the groups sponsoring the Celebration of International Women's Day in April 1988.
- A joint declaration and petition to the Hong Kong government for separate tax filing for women was undertaken in April 1988 by the AAF, HKCW's WC, and HK Federation of Christian Women (HKFCW.)
- A joint message of solidarity in support of the patriotic Democracy Movement in China in May 1989 by the AAF, HK Women Christian Council, HK Women Workers' Association, HK International Women's Council, HKCW-WC, and the Garment Manufacturing Workers' Union.
- A coalition, the Women In Support of Democracy in China, has been formed by some active members of the AAF, HKFCW,

and HKCW(WC) and other women in response to the repression of the Patriotic Democracy Movement in China in June 1989. The main task of the group is to organize women in Hong Kong to support the development of democracy in China and Hong Kong.

The advantages of issue-specific coalitions among women's organizations at this historical juncture are several. The first and the most obvious advantage is the creation of opportunities for dialogues and understanding among women's groups. No matter how different the analysis and strategies for change are, these opportunities for exchange will help to foster friendship, trust, and a better appreciation of what other groups are doing. This is especially important at this early stage of movement building. Second, alliances also signify the pulling together of limited human and material resources which demonstrate the strength of unity in a very concrete way. Third, they help to create a pool of similar experience as a basis for reflection, communication, and consciousness raising. For example, police intervention in the peaceful march in the Celebration of the 1988 International Women's Day provided both the organizers and the participants with an experience of the abuse of power by law enforcers. This collective experience united them in rallying later for respect for free assembly and free speech. Four, working together provides a platform for struggling with ideas upon which genuine unity can develop.

Future tasks

In light of what has taken place, many tasks still await action before a consolidated women's movement in Hong Kong can materialize. Whereas continuation of issue-specific coalitions among different women's groups should be facilitated whenever circumstances and resources allow, there is a need to start strategizing on advancing the movement into the next stage. Toward this goal, I suggest that first, feminists in Hong Kong should be more conscientious in gathering like-minded individuals for mutual support and as catalysts for feminist consciousness-raising in our respective groups.

Second, capitalizing on gains made in previous issue-oriented collaborations, they should begin paving the ground for building strategic alliances—collaborations that challenge the cornerstones of structural patriarchy. One such focus is the subordination of women perpetuated by a patriarchal dichotomy of women's social production and reproduction and the low status assigned to reproductive labor. This dichotomy cuts across class and race, although concrete manifestations of the exploitation do take different forms and can provide an important strategic platform. Another outgrowth of patriarchy that we will want to challenge is the "victimization" of women as the chief caretakers of children, the family, the sick, and the elderly. The exclusion of women as a separate entity in the present social welfare system in Hong Kong (Women and the Welfare Policy in Hong Kong, AAF, 1987) can be a very appropriate entry point. Or, building on the wide support generated from various women's organizations of all persuasions against pornography, we may want to upgrade our work to expose and challenge the social forces working to perpetuate fetishism of the female body in a consumerist, patriarchal society.

Third, there is always the need to continue launching ideological discussions and feminist critiques on sexism, classism, racism, and homophobia. Furthermore, it is necessary to struggle with women's groups like the Chinese Women's Association, the local women's chapters of the Lions Club International, the Zonta Club, and Yan Ngai Society to combat their perpetuation of the myth of women's "comfort captivity."

Alliance with other groups working for social change

The determination of the People's Republic of China to regain sovereignty over Hong Kong by the year 1997 forced the otherwise complacent people in Hong Kong to reexamine the kind of values and society they wanted. Whether motivated by anticommunist sentiments, a sense of desperation to keep a familiar lifestyle, a belief in genuine democracy, or a commitment to eliminate injustice and sexist discrimination, there has been since the mid-eighties a collective awakening for greater political participation among the people in Hong Kong. The recent student-led Patriotic Democratic Movement in China and the subsequent June 4 massacre orchestrated by the current Chinese regime revealed yet another fundamental dimension in the struggle for social change in Hong Kong. More people realize now the future of Hong Kong is bleak unless feudal dictatorship in China is eliminated. In order to facilitate a feminist agenda on social change at this historical juncture, feminists in Hong Kong should do three things. First, we should reflect and define clearly for ourselves the dialectical relationship between the feminist struggle and the movement for democracy in China and Hong Kong. Second, insofar as we agree that the struggle for social change needs to be fought both within and outside the institution, it is time for us to consider choosing and developing our own candidate or candidates to run for elections at all levels as the political structure in Hong Kong inevitably undergoes changes. Third, we should extend our alliance to other groups working for economic, political, and social transformation. Two particular groupings in this context should be targeted for coalition building. One, community and mass organizing groups working at the grassroots level; two, the more progressive forces within the Hong Kong Alliance in Support of the Patriotic Democratic Movement in China. It is true that male chauvinism and sexist practices are very much alive among many members of these groups. However, to choose to adopt a separatist stance at this historical moment will be both politically and organizationally unwise, since that will only work to limit the scope and participation of the women's movement in structural change. In my opinion, what we should do instead is to ally tactically with these groups for two basic objectives: first, to insist and struggle with them for an inclusion of a feminist agenda for social change, and second, to force on them a feminist presence, which also is an educational process for all parties involved. Knowing how or when to choose our battles with these groups in the face of sexist discrimination may help minimize frustrations.

Of course, in the final analysis, the primary task of feminists in Hong Kong is to strengthen our own forces. In this respect, conscientious efforts to develop more and facilitate unity among like-minded women cannot be overstressed.

The differences in focus, analysis, and work of women's groups in Hong Kong remind me of varied pieces of threads that yet need to be woven into a kinetic tapestry. Although the process has started, a more conscious strategy of coalition building (like the one I have just proposed) should be devised to facilitate a feminist agenda for social change both in Hong Kong and China.

WE HAVE COME A LONG WAY
MUCH IS YET TO BE DONE
LET US SPEND THE REST OF OUR LIVES IN THE BEST OF STRUGGLES!

Notes

1. Hong Kong is comprised of Hong Kong Island, Kowloon Peninsula, and the New Territories. In 1986, a total of 5.53 million people, 95 percent of whom are Chinese, lived in this total land area of about 1,060 square kilometers (Hong Kong Census and Statistics Department, 1987). Hong Kong Island and the Kowloon Peninsula were ceded in 1842 and 1860 to Britain by the Ching government in China as the result of the Opium Wars and the treaties signed. The area was extended in 1898 by a 99-year lease of the southern part of the New Territories. In 1984, the People's Republic of China and Britain signed a joint declaration to return Hong Kong to China's sovereignty by July 1, 1997. The Joint Declaration proclaimed Hong Kong a special administrative region under PRC and guaranteed her a high degree of autonomy and the maintenance of her existing capitalist structures under China's

socialist rule. But influence and pressure from China already is felt, and changes are bound to occur, especially after the June 4 Massacre in Beijing.

2. Primarily an entry port concentrating on handling re-exports before World War II, Hong Kong has since the seventies developed into a manufacturing, commercial, and financial center. With the government's laissez-faire economic philosophy, low standard of labor laws, a weak trade union movement, and being enmeshed in a world economic order, Hong Kong is, like many Third World countries, vulnerable to the exploitation of transnational corporations.

3. The crude female labor force participation rate of the population aged 15 and above in 1961 was 36.8 percent. This rate rose to 42.8 percent and 49.5 percent in 1971 and 1981 (HKCSD, 1981). These rates only reflect the percentage of women entering the wage labor force. The labor of homemakers, the majority of whom are women, is dismissed as "economically inactive" and is not included as part of this working force. Furthermore, female participation in wage labor is concentrated in the manufacturing (16.5 percent), construction, and service (50.8 percent) sectors. Eighty-three (83) percent of women wage workers earned a monthly income of HK$2,000 (approximately US$250) or less in 1981 (*Beyond the Women's Decade*, AAF, 1985.)

4. The concubinage system legitimizes a man to have as many second wives called concubines as he likes and can afford to have. Concubines are supposed to assume an inferior position to the first wife (usually addressed as the Big Sister.) In many cases, concubines are treated as maids in the family until they bear a male heir.

5. Legislation was passed in 1973 legalizing abortion if and when certified by two physicians that continuation of the pregnancy would endanger the physical or psychological well-being of the pregnant woman. This legislation was amended in 1981 to include legalization of abortion for victims of rape or incest and females under sixteen years of age.

6. Initially sponsored by the Hong Kong Women of Council, the Harmony House—the refuge home for battered women—was incorporated in April, 1986, and since then has been an independent organization with its own governing board and staff (Annual Report, Harmony House, 1987.)

7. At the time of writing this paper, I have no way of tracing or interviewing, for clarification of the disbandment, any of the ex-members of this group. This piece of information is important both in terms of its own historical value and the lessons from which feminists may possibly draw. It should be pursued in the future.

8. Since mid-April 1989, hundreds of thousands of students demonstrated in Tiananmen Square in Beijing, Shanghai, and other cities of China demanding their right to participate for freedom of speech and an end to bureaucratic incompetence and the elimination of corruption. The Chinese government responded to their demands by branding the students' actions as subversive and called for a clampdown to end the "unrest." Thousands of students started staging a hunger strike on Tiananmen Square on May 13 to protest the government's stance, demanding a direct dialogue with the government to discuss their demands. This student movement soon turned into a spontaneous people's movement, as millions of sympathetic citizens, workers, intellectuals, civil servants, and some members of the Communist Party marched in support of the students' demands. The government proclaimed martial law on May 19, and troops were sent into Beijing. Tens of thousands of workers, women, and other Beijing residents proceeded to peacefully halt the advance of the army but only for a few days. On the night of June 3, soldiers were ordered to use whatever means to "recapture" the Square. Hundreds of tanks and armored combat vehicles and thousands of troops forced their way into the Square after midnight, shooting indiscriminately along their way. Gun shots were fired almost nonstop during the first hours of June 4. It is estimated that thousands were massacred and many more wounded.

9. The Coalition was officially formed in 1987 and is composed of more than a hundred organizations clamoring for democratization of the political structures of Hong Kong. At present, there is no direct elected representation in any political organ in Hong Kong except the Urban Council (primarily responsible for environmental sanitation, cultural service, recreation, and amenities) and the District Boards, which have functioned as consultative bodies in district administration since 1981.

10. The Alliance was formed in late May 1989 in support of the student-turned-spontaneous people's movement for freedom of the press, participation in decision making, and an end to corruption and bureaucratic incompetence. The Alliance, with over 200 member organizations, continues to support Chinese dissidents and works for democracy in China and Hong Kong. They have been severely criticized by the current Chinese regime and branded as a subversive force not to be tolerated.

References

Annual Reports. 1985 to 1988. Hong Kong: Association for the Advancement of Feminism.

Annual Report. 1987. Hong Kong: Harmony House.

Annual Report. 1986. Hong Kong Council of Women, Hong Kong.

Beyond the Women's Decade. 1985. Association for the Advancement of Feminism, Hong Kong.

Chan, Po King. 1983. *The Subordination of Women in Reproduction: the Case of Married Women of Childbearing Ages in Urban Hong Kong in the Years 1971–81.* Unpublished dissertation, University of Kent at Canterbury, England.

Chan, Shun Hing. 1988. *The State of the Women's Movement in Hong Kong.* Speech at the Conference on Women in Transition, Hong Kong, March, 1988.

Government Information Service. 1983. Hong Kong.

Hong Kong By-Census. 1976. *Basic Tables.* 1977. Hong Kong: Hong Kong Census and Statistics Department.

Hong Kong 1981 Census. 1982. *Basic Tables.* 1982. Hong Kong. Hong Kong: Hong Kong Census and Statistics Department.

Hong Kong Yearbook. 1987. Hong Kong.

Labor Force Survey: Preliminary Report, 1981. 1982. Hong Kong: Hong Kong Census and Statistics Department.

Leung, J. 1984. *South China Morning Post.* Hong Kong: April 28, 1984.

Mackintoch, M. 1981. *Gender and Economics: The Sexual Division of Labor and Subordination of Women.* In K. Young et al., eds.

Mao, Y. K. 1981. "Not a Barren Ground: Introducing Women's Organizations in Hong Kong." *Intervention,* No.2. Hong Kong: Mass Cultural Action Group.

Recommendation on the Drafting of the Basic Law for Hong Kong. 1987. Hong Kong: Association for the Advancement of Feminism.

Report on the Yin Ngai Society. 1982. Hong Kong.

Report on Manpower Survey of the Plastics Industry. 1981. Hong Kong.

Report on Women's Participation in Public Affairs. 1985. Hong Kong: Association for the Advancement of Feminism.

Women and the Welfare Policy in Hong Kong. 1987. Hong Kong: Association for the Advancement of Feminism.

Abbreviations

AAF	Association for the Advancement of Feminism
CWA	Chinese Women's Association
CWWO	Committee on Women Workers' Organizers
EWU	Electronics Workers' Union
HKAPBW	Hong Kong Association of Professional and Business Women
HKCIC(CWW)	Hong Kong Christian Industrial Committee, Committee on Women Workers
HKCSD	Hong Kong Census and Statistics Department
HKCW	Hong Kong Council of Women
HKCW(WC)	Women's Center, Hong Kong Council of Women
HKFCW	Hong Kong Federation of Christian Women
HKFWL	Hong Kong Federation of Women Lawyers
HKYWCA(Y&CD)	Hong Kong Young Women's Christian Association, Youth and Community Development Division
NKWA	New Kowloon Women's Association

Feminist Alliances
*A View from Peru**

Roxanna Carillo

I welcome and congratulate the organizers of this conference for their
initiative and for envisioning these plenary sessions as a way of making
sure that new women's voices are heard. My many years in the women's
movement have taught me how important, indeed crucial, it is to
listen to what women are saying. Our survival as a global movement,
our viability as a political community, is deeply interrelated with our
capacity to continually listen to new voices, to process and respond to
the challenges and questions they pose, and to change our initial
assumptions and prejudices as we see their limitations on our visions
and strategies for change.

Today I am speaking as a feminist organizer from Peru, as an activist
involved in the process of building the women's movement in Latin
America, and as a sister that believes in the need for dialogue between
South and North, between Third World women like the speakers on
this panel and women from industrialized countries. I am aware that
this dialogue is not easy, that there are many barriers and obstacles
that can interfere with such exchange. Nevertheless, I believe that such

---

* Speech at International Plenary session of National Women's Studies Association
Conference. University of Minnesota, Minneapolis, June 22-26, 1988.

dialogue is both possible and urgent. Some problems that obstruct our alliances are rooted in the patriarchal system we have all been brought up under. Others arise from our fear of differences, from our guilt and inability to realize that our diversity is, more than anything, a source of strength and that we can use it to our advantage. Still other obstacles to a better understanding of each other come from ignorance, particularly from the failure of many women to seek out more accurate information about those whose lives are not reflected in the dominant media portrayal of reality. Mainstream media don't tell you much, if anything, about the vibrant women's movement globally. Most often what gets across about women in the Third World are distorted images that portray us either as exotic creatures, most useful for entertainment or research purposes, or as passive victims unable to do anything to change the situation we live in. The response that such a view brings out in northern women is usually a distant one, at best rooted in compassion and a feeling of solidarity, and all too often one of charity and condescension. These responses are not enough and do not necessarily lead you to see the connections between your oppression and ours, between your lives and ours. I want to use this opportunity to bring you a different picture, I hope a useful one.

I am keenly aware of the need to work politically in alliances and coalitions. My personal history as a feminist organizer in Peru taught me this necessity, and the very nature of politics demands that we pool our resources to bring about more comprehensive changes. Without that understanding as the first step to working politically, all our efforts toward making change are intrinsically weaker. Nobody is the owner of all the truth—not even Third World women. We need as many women's perceptions of reality as possible if we are to put forward visions and strategies for change in the world that include the diverse needs of women in a wide variety of circumstances.

My first contact with feminism in my country came in the early 1970s when several women's groups organized marches and demonstrations against the Miss Peru beauty contest. I was a bright kid making my way up as a journalist and didn't have any political consciousness about how difficult life could be for a woman in a male-defined society. Frightened that it would put me in a vulnerable position with my male colleagues, I refused to join the campaign, giving some silly excuses. The attacks that the press launched against these courageous women were so brutal and vicious that they left a deep impression on me. I knew from then on that in working for the liberation of women and making public—thus political—their concerns, these women were touching one of the most sensitive chords in Peruvian society. I knew, but I was not quite yet ready to join them, nor to endure the sarcasm and the many arguments that male politicians and intellectuals, particularly progressive ones, used to de-legitimize and minimize the relevance of women's demands. These men's styles were arrogant, even fascist in their unwillingness to consider the arguments put forward by women, and in many ways their attitudes reminded me of the reaction of the old oligarchies and owners of haciendas when their large properties were turned into agrarian cooperatives by the Land Reform Bill.

In 1975, the United Nations International Women's Year conference took place in Mexico City. Much of the later development of the women's movement in Latin America—and I think throughout the Third world—is connected to the widespread effects of that gathering. In Latin America, the conference received extensive media coverage—after all, it was taking place in one of our countries. Further, the very fact of the conference legitimized and acknowledged the feminist claim that there was indeed a "women's problem" in every single society on the planet. This gave visibility to women's efforts to address these issues and thus gave us an enormous boost of energy and conviction in order to face the adverse reactions to the women's liberation movement we found in our countries.

After the Mexico City conference, the United Nations launched a Decade for the Empowerment of Women, a useful though limited umbrella under which numerous projects and institutions addressing women's needs were begun. In the late seventies, and after months of endless collective meetings trying to define more precisely our vision and to strengthen our political positions, I co-founded—along with a dozen other women—Centro de la Mujer Peruana Flora Tristan (Flora Tristan: Center for Peruvian Women.) This is a multipurpose women's center which now owns a house in Lima, with programs on women's work, legal services, leadership training, health and reproductive rights, women's alternative media and publications, a research unit about women's history, and so on. It has played a crucial role in the development of a feminist movement in Peru.

From the beginning, we saw that our work at Flora Tristan would have to be done through alliances with other women's groups, most of which came into existence around the same time we did. Living in a small country with very limited resources teaches you that surviving politically requires adding up your efforts in order not to disappear. Peru is also a country in which a large majority of women live in poverty—most of them of Andean descent—which makes us aware that if we are to work for the development of a strong women's movement, we must cross the class and race barriers that divide our country. Thus, much of the organizing carried out by feminist groups in Peru in the last decade—and this is true for most of the countries of the region—has happened in the slums or shanty towns that surround the major cities, where an interesting and potentially powerful political chemistry is creating new political consciousness and alliances among women.

I have seen this potential, for example, in the development of women's movements around *comedores populares,* a kind of communal dining rooms or soup kitchens where women join together to prepare food and feed their families in common. This is an initiative born from women who have to face the reality of stretching meager resources to feed large families. It is a strategy that has brought women together, breaking the isolation of the individual units they live in, socializing the domestic chores, and starting a process of organizing that has transformed their lives. It has opened the door to challenging other aspects of the oppression they experience daily, such as battery and sexual assault. Increased political involvement has grown out of this challenge. Shelters for battered women and health and legal services are some of the projects that have developed as a result of these organizing efforts, as well as women's demonstrations against food prices and against the state's violation of human rights.

Every other year since 1981, feminist activists from throughout Latin America have gathered together for a conference that represents a wide alliance of groups doing political work in the region. The regional gatherings started on the initiative of a handful of Latin Americans who attended the U.N. Mid-Decade International Women's Conference in Copenhagen in 1980. Confronted with difficulties in their efforts to articulate a feminist discourse of meaning to their region within that predominantly North American and European context, and fascinated by their discovery of other feminists coming from the same continent, they called for a regional meeting in which Latin American feminists were, as Peruvian activist Virginia Vargas put it, "to define feminism in our own terms."

The *encuentros* (encounters), as these events are known, are a significant step in a continent that has experienced all types of nationalist conflicts and several wars between its competing militaristic governments during its republican history. In spite of those historical barriers, feminists have moved beyond the patriarchal nationalist divisions and have been able to work together putting forward a vision of change that emerges from our political understandings as women. The reason that we have been able to work across national boundaries is the recognition of our common oppression as women and of our cultural identity as Latin Americans and the need to develop a feminist discourse that builds on the experiences in the many projects that have sprouted throughout the region.

To sketch the process of growth and development of the movement in the continent as illustrated by the *encuentros,* I will begin with the first meeting in Bogotá, Colombia, in 1981, with 200 women of different Latin countries. It was marked by debates about our political identity—from what reference point did we start our organizing. The issue here was autonomy, particularly from the left, who until then had absolute ideological hegemony over the analysis of reality among groups working for social change in our region. In the left's analysis, women kept playing a secondary role and this *encuentro* challenged that assumption by declaring the independence of the feminist movement from control by any other groups.

The 1983 *encuentro* in Lima, Peru, furthered that autonomous identity by focusing on an analysis of patriarchy and its different forms and institutionalized expressions throughout the continent. These forms were identified in discussions of violence against women, of literature, power, religion, economics, sexuality, the family, media, health, and—for the first time—an open debate about the previously taboo topic of lesbianism, and workshops that acknowledged—also for the first time among feminists—the problem of racism in Latin America. The third *encuentro* took place in Brazil in 1985, with an emphasis on body politics: we were discovering our own bodies as women and examining the interrelation of *lo cotidiano y lo social,* that is to say the relation between our gender and the social and political forces, seeing how the personal is political. This meeting with its 1,000 participants also brought to the fore the insights and concerns of women's culture and spirituality.

The fourth *encuentro* celebrated in Taxco, Mexico, in 1987 was attended by over 1,500 women and reflected the enormous growth of feminism during the decade in both numbers and complexity. It explored the issues of diversity, particularly around class, race, and sexual preference, as well as the difficulties surrounding the interplay of feminism and national liberation movements. This meeting was the first with significant participation of women from Central America, including forty Nicaraguans, challenging all of us to discuss concrete policies and changes that women want from governments committed to a radical transformation of society. It also included a large and energetic presence of women from *sectores populares* (popular sectors), the most clear reflection of the amount of work done by feminist organizers across race and class lines. A week prior to that *encuentro* the First Regional Lesbian Feminist Meeting took place and resulted in the conformation of a network of Latin American lesbian feminist activities.

But although there have been significant advances in the development of the women's movement in Latin America, we have also had difficulties in dealing with issues of power and leadership among ourselves. A group of women who had been active feminists for many years in different countries presented a document* at the *encuentro* in Mexico where they raised these issues in the region and discussed the negative consequences of not dealing with them more directly. They questioned the often unspoken assumption in the movement that women are not interested in power and challenged the tendency to see feminism as a vision of women for women only. They noted that we must rather construct a feminist power base that can transform social relations, addressing both women and men from a feminist perspective that will help to build democratic and participatory societies. They also pointed to the growing diversity of women involved in the feminist movement in the region and called for an alliance, a regional pact founded in the recognition of differences as a source of strength that can be a step forward in the achievement of our political goals. Above all, this paper led to a recognition among feminists that we must face the question of power between women and leadership in a more conscious fashion.

In the women's movement in Lima, we have been discussing these issues openly for several years and are dealing with them by trying out different organizational structures. We have established procedures so that each group can speak for itself, but only an elected core of seven women speak for the movement as a whole. Thus we both try to make our leaders accountable and to provide them with the support necessary to perform leadership tasks. The development of these structures was a discussion open to all women who see themselves as part of the movement, and it has fostered a process of conscious organizing that has helped to cut down a tendency toward structurelessness that prevailed for a while. Half of the core of leaders are elected each year with some rotation in positions so that the process also empowers new leaders to get to know how to use their power in a different way. While the structure is far from being perfect, it provides a way to be open about power and responsibility and to acknowledge existing leaders as well as to train new ones.

Of course these questions of power, leadership, and access to resources which are vital for feminists to address in a world of such overwhelming power imbalances are even more crucial when one works cross-culturally. Over the past four years, I have been part of a cross-cultural team that has worked to see how feminists can build political alliances globally. We realize that in an increasingly interdependent world the challenges that feminism faces demand a global understanding and the development of strategies accordingly. We are looking at how we can

---

* "Del Amor a la Necesidad" (From Love to Need) included in *Memoria del IV Encuentro Feminista Latinoamericano y del Caribe*. Taxco, Mexico, Octubre de 1987.

work across lines created by others to separate us: How can we build strong alliances that take into account our differences but do not necessarily erase them? How can we women from the Third World and from industrialized countries move beyond feelings of anger or guilt that tend to have a paralyzing effect and that do not help us to act politically?

Perhaps the first step is to have respect for others' insights and perceptions of reality. This is only possible when one has developed self-respect and has a political understanding of where one's own view of reality comes from and how it can be broadened by learning from others. No one is to blame for the country, class, or race she was born into: those are givens that we do not have any control over. But one has to take responsibility for that, working consciously to change the aspects of our lives and our countries that are oppressive to others. In working for change we must make the effort to break our stereotypes about people from other cultures and be actively engaged in questioning the biases portrayed by the media and the dominant culture.

For example, in Latin America, this means that we make a distinction between the U.S. government and *gringos* who support and perpetuate its imperialistic domination in the world and those progressive *gringos* and *gringas* who work against such policies and approaches. While there are prejudices and ignorances between feminists in different regions which we must work to overcome, we see the political possibility of alliances in which we work together for change as important.

But in order for us to make such a distinction among *gringos* and create alliances with you, we must first see that you acknowledge and take responsibility for the oppressive consequences of your nation's power in our lives.

Guilt or denial of such a responsibility often interferes with this process of dialogue between our regions. However, the development of global feminist strategies that truly take into account women's diverse needs must be based on such respectful but challenging political discussion. This includes a critique of each other that assumes the potential of a common interest and the possibility of alliances if we engage in such a struggle with each other.

It is urgent that we learn to build such alliances for the sake of women throughout the world today and for the future, not only of women, but of our planet. I find this an exciting challenge and I look forward to engaging in this process with you.

African-American Women and the Black Diaspora

Audre Lorde

Any discussion of the Black women's literary tradition in the African diaspora today requires an active sharing, an exchange. When we speak of ourselves as African-American women, we must encourage ourselves and each other to remember this means we are members of an international community of people of color. More specifically, it means we are women of the Black diaspora, members of a far-reaching and dynamic community which is world-wide and diverse.

Women of the various communities within the Black Diaspora have developed unique and particular aspects of Black women's literary tradition. Those of us in North America must not succumb to the provincial ignorance of other cultures that is a North American legacy. We cannot afford to ignore the literatures of the Black women of Namibia, Trinidad, South Africa, Germany, Vanuatu, Liberia, or Australia. Some recognition and knowledge of their literatures are essential if we wish to understand and connect with the lives and differences of other Black women across the earth who are our sisters, yet whose experiences are different from as well as similar to our own. And if we expect to be recognized as sisters, we must make conscious efforts to support institutions which further the literatures coming out of these various communities.

We need to remember, for example, that the first press owned and run by a woman in South Africa was organized by a Black woman in Soweto, Diane Lefekane. Sechabe Publishers, her press, has published a number of books, including *Women in South Africa,* a collection of short stories.

We need to take note of Sheba Publishers, a London press run largely by Black women both of the African Diaspora and other communities.

And certainly we need to take note of our own Kitchen Table: Women of Color Press, the first press in North America dedicated to the publication and distribution of work by women of color from various communities. The other two presses are Sister Vision Press in Toronto, Canada, and Third Woman Press in Berkeley, California.

A Black women's literary tradition requires that we support those institutions that make that literary tradition available to us. And by support I don't mean simply sitting here and nodding our heads saying isn't it nice they exist. I mean active social and financial support. It's all about privilege—recognizing that we have it and learning how to use it. One of the commonest mistakes of privilege is to sit and absorb without use, without action. This is what Western European/North American education teaches us to do better than anything else. Absorb. Observe. Not take in and act upon, but observe and remain untouched. The essence of a Black women's tradition is that we cannot afford to absorb without reflection and without use. Our survival and the survival of our cultures demand that we support those institutions which give us what we need—a sense of connection between Black women far beyond the geographical constraints of the North American continent.

I have to tell you that what I planned here today was not to talk about the Black women's literary tradition and the African diaspora. I had hoped to bring up here some of the other members of our Black women's literary tradition. There are Afro-German women who were supposed to have been here, one of whom is the publisher of the first anthology looking at racism from a woman's point of view, published in German, which is even now being translated and will be available, hopefully within the next year. One of these women is Katerina Oguntoya, and the other woman is Marion Kraft, who teaches Black women's literature at the University in Balefeld in West Germany. The anthology is *Farbe Bekennen* (*Showing Our Color,* forthcoming, University of Massachusetts Press.) Unfortunately, neither Katerina nor Marion can be here, so I am going to read some excerpts from *A Burst of Light,* which deals with the ways in which I met them, and some of the things that excited me about meeting them. This meeting was an example of the kinds of connections that we need to make between Black women on various continents, and how we need to listen to each other—the similarities in our experiences and the differences.

In the spring of 1984, I spent three months in Berlin conducting a course in Black American women poets and a poetry workshop in English for German students. One of my aims for this trip was to meet Black German women. I'd been told there were quite a few in Berlin, but I had been unable to obtain much information about them in New York.

May 23, 1984
Berlin, West Germany

Who are they, the German women of the Diaspora? Where do our paths intersect as women of Color—beyond the details of our particular oppressions, although certainly not outside the reference of those details? And where do our paths diverge? Most important, what can we learn from our connected differences that will be useful to us both, Afro-German and Afro-American?

Afro-German. The women say they've never heard that term used before.

I asked one of my Black students how she'd thought about herself growing up. "The nicest thing they ever called us was 'war baby'," she said. But the existence of most Black Germans has nothing to do with the Second World War, and, in fact, predates it by many decades. I have Black German women in my class who trace their Afro-German heritage back to the 1890s.

For me, Afro-German means the shining faces of Katarina and Marian in animated conversation about their father's homelands, the comparisons, joys, disappointments, it meant my pleasure at seeing another Black woman walk into my classroom, her reticence slowly giving way as she explores a new self-awareness, gains a new way of thinking about herself in relation to other Black women.

"I've never thought of Afro-German as a positive concept before," she said, speaking out of the pain of having to live a difference that has no name; speaking out of the growing power self-scrutiny has forged from that difference.

I am excited by these women, by their blossoming sense of identity as they're beginning to say in one way or another, "Let us be ourselves now as we define us. We are not figments of your imagination or an exotic answer to your desires. We are not some button of the pocket of your longing." I can see these women as a growing force for international change, in concert with other Afro-Europeans, Afro-Asians, Afro-Americans.

—From *A Burst of Light,* 1987, New York: Firebrand Books, p. 56–7.

I want to tell you parenthetically here that, for example, I have read, and hopefully will be translating, the work of a young Afro-German poet named Ria Lubanefsky, who grew up in East Berlin but who now lives in West Berlin and who is doing with the German language what the early Black poets did with the English language, which is reconstructing it basically so that it reflects not only the emotion of the poem but the actual experience of the person who is creating it. She's a wonderfully exciting poet, who I hope will be more and more available. One of the problems is, we for the most part are very provincial in North America, and we believe that English is the end of all languages. One of the things we need to, I think, start to do as we begin to experience our sisters, and the work of our sisters, is to expose ourselves, open ourselves to learning other languages, so that we can in fact communicate, not only in translations.

> We are the hyphenated people of the Diaspora whose self-defined identities are no longer shameful secrets in the countries of our origin, but rather declarations of strength and solidarity. We are Black Women of the Diaspora, and we are an increasingly united front from which the world has not yet heard.
>
> —From *A Burst of Light*

Breaking the Silence

Miranda Bergman, Susan Greene, Dina Redman, Marlene Tobias

We are four Jewish-American women artists. We were moved by the silences screaming within us. We birthed these silences into action.

As the death toll mounted in the West Bank and Gaza, the need to speak up grew. We were raised to believe in the Talmudic principle: "To be witness to injustice and do nothing is to be an accomplice to the crime." So in early 1989 we searched for a way to break the silence among Jewish people in the U.S. and Israel, who in growing numbers want to declare that neither the Israeli government's occupation of the West Bank and Gaza, nor its supporters in Washington, speak for us. We evolved the idea of the Break The Silence Mural Project.

In our early discussions we decided, for a variety of reasons, that our group would be all women. We wanted to do something as women to join with the women in Occupied Palestine and the women of the peace movement inside Israel, whom we see as the backbone of the struggle against the Occupation. We wanted to make clear that our project was initiated and led by women and to avoid the problems that sometimes arise in a mixed group, where the women members can be seen as subordinate to the men. We wanted the security of a group in which from the beginning we felt an innate sense of equality with each other, to work on any issues of competition and self-esteem. We needed a supportive, collective group that we could depend on in an unpredictable and dangerous situation. Through our work together we wanted to contribute to and participate in building the international movement of women that has so profoundly shaped our lives.

In thinking about the size of the group, we decided that just four women would make the trip, allowing enough hands to complete the work but keeping the logistics as simple as possible. And so our team formed: Miranda Bergman, Susan Greene, Dina Redman, and Marlene Tobias. Two of us were experienced muralists, and two of us were artists new to the mural process. We all had teaching experience in various constituencies. All of us had worked in Central America and for many years in movements in the U.S. We ranged in age from thirty-one to forty-two. Our gut-level need and commitment to take a stand on this issue was the center around which we built our organization. We wanted to find the balance between having a leadership structure, in this case a project director, and at the same time allowing real democratic participation by all. The four of us were already committed to a variety of other activities and leading busy lives, so we were compelled to develop an organizational form that could work directly and efficiently and at the same time encourage personal initiative. The contradiction posed between having defined leadership and the desire to maintain a collective process was sometimes difficult to resolve—it required ongoing discussion that was challenging and sometimes painful. We worked on reconciling the individual need for appreciation and recognition with the desire for group cohesiveness—the formation of a group identity. Our society does little to prepare us for balancing these two necessities.

We constantly tried to deepen our understanding of the political forces in motion and also to pay attention and give validity to the feelings that were unleased during this very intense experience. We learned a lot about working together, about giving and taking criticism, about using all of our strengths to produce a large amount of high-quality work, and about being aware of our weaknesses, individually and collectively. We learned to work together in a loving way.

We started the project with no capital, at first borrowing money to print and send 1,500 letters describing our idea to people we thought might be interested. Then we waited, unsure of what the response might be. We were overwhelmed as letters poured in with contributions and words of encouragement. We also received several small grants, and Margaret Randall gave a benefit poetry reading on our behalf.

When we arrived on the West Bank our entire dynamic was altered dramatically. We were in the middle of a historical uprising, a groundswell of organized resistance to oppression. We saw new examples of the collective process and were able to participate in it to accomplish our projects. We were nourished, educated, and inspired by the work of the Palestinian Women's Committees, the Popular Committees, and the community cohesiveness in the face of occupation. The Popular Committees and many types of cooperatives provide the people ways to participate actively in collective survival through economic self-sufficiency projects, as well as to create new social relationships and organizations that contribute to the infrastructure of a new state. Issues focused with a new clarity. Our work became concrete, serious, and part of an allied effort with our Palestinian hosts. Because we were living under a military occupation, we needed to develop our ability to be flexible, to shift our thinking and adjust our goals as the conditions changed, sometimes quite abruptly.

The Palestinian community welcomed us warmly and wholeheartedly, as Jews, as women, and as U.S. citizens who truly wanted to express our support for a United Nations international peace conference and an independent Palestinian State. We lived with the family of a woman active in the Women's Committee, in a refugee camp, and experienced first hand both the constant threat and terror of living under a violent occupation and the joy, dignity, and hope of a people caring for each other and creating a future. All four of us learned to feel a new pride in ourselves and a more profound understanding of the importance of international solidarity.

Through working daily for nine weeks in alliance with Palestinian artists, and living in the midst of a busy community, we had constant opportunity to share our lives and ideas. Our conversations ranged through many topics. There wasn't much of a language barrier, as many Palestinians speak English in addition to Arabic, and if necessary, there was always someone who could translate for us.

We came to feel poignantly the way racism has been used to demonize the Palestinians; the U.S. media making the words "Palestinian" and "terrorist" almost synonymous. The same racism has been used by the Israeli government, raising the spectre of "murderous Arabs" in a systematic attempt to terrify the Israeli population into silence.

In contrast, we found a serious and coordinated educational campaign by the Palestinian Unified National Leadership of the uprising to differentiate between Jewish people and the policies of the Israeli government. The last communique from the leadership before we left talked about the desire on the part of the Palestinian people to build alliances with Israelis of good will. We were always publicly "out" as Jews, and we were warmly and familially welcomed. We had many opportunities to talk honestly with Palestinian people about their history and feeling for Jewish people and to share our own history with them. We shared many personal stories, and discussed racism and how it works and the similarities, for instance, between racist violence in New York and the West Bank. Through the day-to-day sharing of

time and space, together we built real working alliances, filled with
hope of a future when we can share the richness of each other's cultures,
as cousins, not enemies.

Murals are an art form well suited to a popular uprising like the
Infitada. They are wonderful tools for unlocking creativity, both in
experienced artists and in people who are new to visual art, encouraging
participation from all. They expose and illuminate history and prophesy
visions of the future. Like jazz, they sing of resistance and survival,
and the blossoming of culture. Mural art transforms space and inspires
a community. We were able to complete six murals during our stay,
one major work at The Center For Popular Arts in Al Bireh and five
smaller murals in various schools and cultural centers in the West
Bank and East Jerusalem. To aid in the authenticity and lend depth
to our work, our hosts organized a series of excursions for us at the
beginning of our stay, so that we could better understand the
environment we were to represent. The designs evolved through a
series of meetings discussing theme and developing sketches. Many
people joined in the painting, both accomplished artists and interested
newcomers to the world of paint. Soon people would come by just to
visit and chat, and their lives opened us. Our brushes flew as we
listened to chilling descriptions of imprisonment and torture, the loss
of family members, the loss of the land. And we heard the quiet stories
of love and hope for the future.

Along with the mural painting we were delighted to have the
opportunity to teach both an art class for children and a graphic design
class for adults. Because the Israeli government has ordered the schools
closed for most of the last two years, education has been forced
underground. Many teachers had been jailed. We were happy to fill in.

On every phase of the project we worked in collaboration with
Palestinians. The occupation affected every aspect of our work, from
where and what we could or could not paint, to the safety of those
painting with us. One of the artists who worked closely with us was
picked up in a sweep and taken to prison under "administrative
detention," which meant that he was arrested without charges, was
given no trial, and could spend up to two years in prison.

As women muralists, out there on those walls, up on those scaffolds,
publicly creating, we are being an example of women as capable and
brilliant contributors to communities. As we work together as a team
to produce monumental art, attitudes begin to change as to the roles
and potential of women and men, creating new paths for the children
to walk on. We believe in the historical responsibility of women's
growing role in helping to lead the world in a new direction away
from what Adrienne Rich calls "the arrogance of hierarchy and the
celebration of violence that have reached a point of destructiveness

almost out of control" and into a new age of knowledge of and respect for the interconnectedness and value of all life, where decisions are made from that knowing. In many ways we are at a crossroads. The time is critical—either we will find the way to bring our earth into harmony and justice, or we will destroy the possibility of all life. We believe that we have the potential to positively transform the earth, using the lessons of our past and the visionary creativity and hard work of our present to light the way for our children and all future generations. But the road between here and there is very difficult and unclear. We are living in a time of immense turmoil and contradiction, of people all over the world dreaming and working and struggling for self-determination, justice, and peace. Artists are able to contribute meaningfully to this process, and we believe women artists have a unique and crucial role to play through the integrity and power of our creativity and wisdom embracing the wholeness of life.

Through the process of painting, teaching art, and living with Palestinian people we built real ties. The depth of our experiences created a special quality of relationship among the four of us. We continue as a group and hope to expand into a network of artists for an independent Palestine, continuing to stay in communication and develop joint projects with our friends in the Women's Committees and The Center For Popular Arts. We want to help to build the bridges that connect the different struggles in the world and the different issues in people's lives and help them to see how peace in the Middle East is important to all of us. As symbolized in several of the murals we painted as roots, the lessons go deep and are embedded in who we are. Our visit was more healing, productive, educational, and inspiring than we could have imagined, and we are highly motivated to expand and multiply the gift of our experiences.

Bridge, Drawbridge, Sandbar or Island
Lesbians-of-Color Hacienda Alianzas[1]

Gloria Anzaldúa

La gente hablando se entiende
(People understand each other by talking)
> —Mexican proverb

Buenos dias marimachas, lesberadas, tortilleras, patlaches,[2] dykes, bulldaggers, butches, femmes, and good morning to you, too, straight women. This morning when I got up I looked in the mirror to see who I was (my identity keeps changing), and you know how hair looks when you've washed it the night before and then slept on it? Yes, that's how mine looked. Not that I slept that much. I was nervous about making this talk and I usually never get nervous until just before I'm on. I kept thinking, What am I going to tell all those women? How am I going to present and represent myself to them and who, besides myself, am I going to speak to and for? Last night lying in bed in the dorm room I got disgusted with my semiprepared talk so I wrote another one. I threw that out too. Then I skimmed several papers I was working on, looking for ideas. I realized that I couldn't use any of this material and ordered my unconscious to come up with something by morning or else. This morning I walked over here, picking lint off my shirt, feeling wrinkled, and thinking, Here I am, I'm still the poor little Chicanita from the sticks. What makes me think I have anything useful to say about alliances?

Women-of-color such as myself do have some important things to say about alliance and coalition work. The overlapping communities of struggle that a mestiza lesbian finds herself in allows her to play a pivotal role in alliance work. To be part of an alliance or coalition is to be active, an activist. Why do we make alliances and participate in them? We are searching for powerful, meaning-making experiences. To make our lives relevant, to gain political knowledge, to give our lives a sense of involvement, to respond to social oppression and its debilitating effects. Activists are engaged in a political quest. Activists are alienated from the dominant culture but instead of withdrawing we confront, challenge. Being active meets some basic needs: emotional catharsis, gratification, political epiphanies. But those in an alliance group also feel like a family and squabble and fight like one, complete with a favorite (good child) and a scapegoat (bad child).

The fracture: at homeness/estrangement

I look around me and I see my *carnalas,* my *hermanas,* the other half and halves, *mita' y mita',* (as queer women are called in South Texas), and I feel a great affinity with everyone. But at the same time I feel (as I've felt at other conferences) like I am doing this alone, I feel a great isolation and separateness and differentness from everyone, even though I have many allies. Yet as soon as I have these thoughts—that I'm in this alone, that I have to stand on the ground of my own being, that I have to create my own separate space—the exact opposite thoughts come to me: that we're all in this together, *juntas,* that the ground of our being is a common ground, *la Tierra,* and that at all times we must stand together despite, or because, of the huge splits that lie between our legs, the faults among feminists are like the fractures in the earth. Earthquake country, these feminisms. Like a fracture in the Earth's crust splitting rock, like a splitting rock itself, the quakes shift different categories of women past each other so that we cease to match, and are forever disaligned—colored from white, Jewish from colored, lesbian from straight. If we indeed do not have one common ground but only shifting plots, how can we work and live and love together? Then, too, let us not forget *la mierda* between us, a mountain of *caca* that keeps us from "seeing" each other, being with each other.

Being a mestiza queer person, una de las otras ("of the others") is having and living in a lot of worlds, some of which overlap. One is immersed in all the worlds at the same time while also traversing from one to the other. The mestiza queer is mobile, constantly on the move, a traveler, *callejera,* a *cortacalles.* Moving at the blink of an eye, from one space, one world to another, each world with its own peculiar and distinct inhabitants, not comfortable in anyone of them, none of them "home," yet none of them "not home" either. I'm flying home to South Texas after this conference, and while I'm there, I'm going to be feeling a lot of the same things that I'm feeling here—a warm sense of being loved and of being at home, accompanied by a simultaneous and uncomfortable feeling of no longer fitting, of having lost my home, of being an outsider. My mother, and my sister and my brothers, are going to continue to challenge me and to argue against the part of me that has community with white lesbians, that has community with feminism, that has community with other *mujeres-de-color,* that has a political community. Because I no longer share their world view, I have become a stranger and an exile in my own home. "When are you coming home again, *Prieta,*" my mother asks at the end of my visit, of every visit. "Never, Momma."[3] After I first left home and became acquainted with other worlds, the Prieta that returned was different, thus "home" was different too. It could not completely accommodate the new Prieta, and I could barely tolerate it. Though I continue to go home, I no longer fool myself into believing that I am truly "home."

A few days ago in Montreal at the Third International Feminist Book Fair (June 1988), I felt a great kinship with women writers and publishers from all over the world. I felt both at home and homeless in that foreign yet familiar terrain because of its strangeness (strange because I had never been there). At the conference, and most especially at the lesbian reading, I felt very close to some white lesbian separatist friends. Then they would make exclusionary or racist remarks and I would feel my body heating up, I would feel the space between us widening. Though white lesbians say their oppression in a heterosexist, homophobic society is similar to the suffering of racism that people-of-color experience, they *can* escape from the more overt oppressions by hiding from being gay (just as I can). But what I can't hide from is being Chicana—my color and features give me away. Yes, when I go home I have to put up with a lot of heterosexist bullshit from my family and community, from the whole Chicano nation who want to exclude my feminism, my lesbianism. This I have in common with women-of-all-colors. But what really hurts, however, is to be with people that I love, with you *mujeres-de-todos-colores,* and to *still* feel, after all our dialogues and struggles, that my cultural identity is *still* being pushed off to the side, being minimized by some of my so-called allies who unconciously rank racism a lesser oppression than sexism. Women-of-color feel especially frustrated and depressed when these "allies" participate in alliances dealing with issues of racism or when the theme of the conference we are attending is racism. It is then that white feminists feel they have "dealt" with the issue and can go on to other "more important" matters.

At the Montreal Conference I also felt an empathy with heterosexual women-of-color and with the few men who were there, only to be saddened that they needed to be educated about women-only space. It also made me sad, too, that white lesbians have not accepted the fact that women-of-color have affinities with men in their cultures. White lesbians were unconciously asking women-of-color to choose between women and men, failing to see that there is more than one way to be oppressed. Not all women experience sexism in the same way, and for women-of-color sexism is not the only oppression. White lesbians forget that they too have felt excluded, that they too have interrupted women-of-color-only space, bringing in their agenda and, in their hunger to belong, pushed ours to the side.

Alliance work is the attempt to shift positions, change positions, reposition ourselves regarding our individual and collective identities. In alliance we are confronted with the problem of how we share or don't share space, how we can position ourselves with individuals or groups who are different from and at odds with each other, how can we reconcile one's love for diverse groups when members of these groups do not love each other, cannot relate to each other, and don't know how to work together.

The activist y la tarea de alianzas

Alliance-coalition work is marked or signaled by framing metacommunication, "This is alliance work."[4] It occurs in bounded specific contexts defined by the rules and boundaries of that time and space and group. While it professes to do its "work" in the community, its basis is both experiential and theoretical. It has a discourse, a theory that guides it. It stands both inside (the community one is doing the work for) and outside ordinary life (the meeting place, the conference). Ideally one takes alliance work home.

In alliance-coalition work there is an element of role playing, as if one were someone else. Activists possess an unspoken, untalked about ability to recognize the unreality and game-playing quality of their work.[5] We very seriously act/perform as well as play at being an ally. We adopt a role model or self-image and behave as if one *were* that model, the person one is trying to be. Activists picture themselves in a scenario: a female hero venturing out and engaging in nonviolent battles against the corrupt dominant world with the help of their trusted *comadronas*. There are various narratives about working at coalition, about making commitments, setting goals and achieving those goals. An activist possesses, in lesser or greater degree, a self-conscious awareness of her "role" and the nature of alliance work. She is aware that not only is the alliance-coalition group struggling to make specific changes in certain institutions (health care, immigration laws, etc.) but in doing so the group often engages in fighting cultural paradigms[6]—the entire baggage of beliefs, values and techniques shared by the community. But in spite of all cultural inscriptions to the contrary, the activist with her preconceived self-image, her narrative, and self-reflectivity resists society's "inscribing" cultural norms, practices, and paradigms on her. She elects to be the one "inscribing" herself and her culture. Activists are agents.

In collusion, in coalition, in collision

For now we women-of-color are doing more solidarity work with each other. Because we occupy the same or similarly oppressed cultural, economic space(s) or share similar oppressions, we can create a solidarity based on a "minority" coalition. We can build alliances around differences, even in groups which are homogenous. Because people-of-color are treated generically by the dominant culture—their seeing and treating us as parts of a whole, rather than just as individuals—this forces us to experience ourselves collectively. I have been held accountable by some white people for Richard Rodriguez's views and have been asked to justify Cesar Chavez's political strategies. In classes and conferences I am often called to speak on issues of race and am thereafter responsible for the whole Chicano/Mexicano race. Yet, were I to hold a white woman responsible for Ronald Reagan's acts, she would be shocked because to herself she is an individual (nor is her being white named because it is taken for granted as the norm).

I think we people-of-color can turn this fusion or confusion of individual/collectivity around and use it as a tool for collective strength and not as an oppressive representation. We can subvert it and use it. It could serve as one base for intimate connection between personal and collective in solidarity work and in alliances across differences. For us the issue of alliances affects every aspect of our lives—personal growth, not just social. We are always working with whitewomen or other groups unlike ourselves toward common and specific goals for the time the work of coalition is in process. Lesbians-of-color have always done this. Judit Moschkovitz wrote: "Alliances are made between people who are different."[7] I would add between people who are different but who have a similar conscience that impels them toward certain actions. Alliances are made between persons whose vague unconscious angers, hopes, guilts, and fears grow out of direct experiences of being either perpetrators or victims of racism and sexism.

Feelings of anger, guilt, and fear rose up nine years ago at Storrs, Connecticut, at the 1981 NWSA Women Respond to Racism Conference, when issues of alliances and racism exploded into the open. Along with many women-of-color I had aspirations, hopes, and visions for multiracial *comunidades,* for communities (in the plural) among all women, of *mundos surdos* (left-handed worlds). Cherríe Moraga and I came bringing an offering, *This Bridge Called My Back: Radical Writings By Radical Women Of Color;* it made its debut at that conference. Some of my aspirations were naive, but without them, I would not have been there nor would I be here now. This vision of *comunidad* is still the carrot that I, the donkey, hunger for and seek at conferences such as this one.

At the 1981 conference we laid bare the splits between whitewomen and women-of-color, white lesbians and lesbians-of color, separatists and nonseparatists. We risked exposing our true feelings. Anger[8] was the strongest in/visible current at that conference, as it is at this one, though many of us repressed it then and are still repressing it now. Race was the big issue then, as it is now for us. Race, the big difference. When asked what I am, I never say I'm a woman. I say I am a Chicana, a mestiza, a *mexicana,* or I am a woman-of-color—which is different from "woman" (woman always means whitewoman). Monique Wittig claims that a lesbian is not a woman because woman exists only in relation to men; woman is part of the category of sex (man and woman) which is a heterosexual construct.[9] Similarly, for me a woman-of-color is not just a "woman"; she carries the markings of her race, she is a gendered racial being—not just a gendered being. However, nonintellectual, working-class women-of-color do not have the luxury of thinking of such semantic and theoretical nuances, much less exempting themselves from the category "woman." So though I myself see the distinction, I do not push it.

A large part of my identity is cultural. Despite changes in awareness since the early eighties, racism in the form of, "Your commitment has to be to feminism, forget about your race and its struggles, struggle with us not them" is still the biggest deterrent to coalition work between whitewomen and women-of-color. Some white feminists, displacing race and class and highlighting gender, are still trying to force us to choose between being colored or female, only now they've gone underground and use unconscious covert pressures. It's all very subtle. Our white allies or collegues get a hurt look in their eyes when we bring up their racism in their interactions with us and quickly change the subject. Tired of our own "theme song" (Why aren't you dealing with race and class in your conference, classroom, organization?) and not wanting to hurt them and in retaliation have them turn against us, we drop the subject and, in effect, turn the other cheek. Women-of-color need these and other manipulations named so that we can make our own articulations. Colored and whitewomen doing coalition work together will continue to reflect the dominated/dominator dichotomy UNLESS whitewomen have or are dealing with issues of racial domination in a "real" way. It is up to them *how* they will do this.

Estranged strangers: a forced bonding

Alliance stirs up intimacy issues, issues of trust, relapse of trust, intensely emotional issues. "We seem to be more together organizationally and estranged individually."[10] There is always some, no matter how minimal, unease or discomfort between most women-of-color and most whitewomen. Because they can't ignore our ethnicity, getting our approval and acceptance is their way to try to make themselves more comfortable and lessen their unease. It is a great temptation for us to make whitewomen comfortable. (In the past our lives may have depended on not offending a white person.) Some of us get seduced into making a whitewoman an honorary woman-of-color—she wants it so badly. But it makes us fidget, it positions us in a relationship founded on false assumptions. A reversed dependency of them upon us emerges, one that is as unhealthy as our previous reliance on them. There is something parasitic about both of these kinds of dependencies. We need to examine bondings of this sort and to "see through" them to the unconscious motivations. Both white and colored need to look at the history of betrayal, the lies, the secrets and misinformation both have internalized and continue to propagate. We need to ask, Do women-of-color want only patronage from white women? Do white feminists only need and expect acceptance and acknowledgement from women-of-color? Yet there is an inherent potential for achieving results in both personal and political cross-racial alliances. We could stick to each other like velcro, whose two different sides together form a great bond—the teeth of one fasten onto the fabric of the other half and hold with a strength greater than either half alone.

Though the deepest connections colored dykes have is to their native culture, we also have strong links with other races, including whites. Though right now there is a strong return to nationalist feeling, colored lesbian feminists in our everyday interactions are truly more citizens of the planet. "To be a lesbian is to have a world vision."[11] In a certain sense I share this vision. If we are to create a lesbian culture, it must be a mestiza lesbian culture, one that partakes of all cultures, one that is not just white in style, theory, or direction, that is not just Chicana, not just Black. We each have a choice as to what people, what cultures, and what issues we want to live with and live in and the roles we want to play. The danger is that white lesbians will "claim" us and our culture as their own in the creation of "our" new space.

"Chusando" movidas/a choice of moves

There are many roles, or ways of being, of acting, and of interacting in the world. For me they boil down to four basic ones: bridge, drawbridge, sandbar, and island. Being a bridge means being a mediator between yourself and your community and white people— lesbians, feminists, white men. You select, consciously or unconsciously, which group to bridge with—or they choose you. Often, the you that's the mediator gets lost in the dichotomies, dualities, or contradictions you're mediating. You have to be flexible yet maintain your ground, or the pull in different directions will dismember you. It's a tough job, not many people can keep the bridge up.

Being a drawbridge means having the option to take two courses of action. The first is being "up," i.e., withdrawing, pulling back from physically connecting with white people (there can never be a complete disconnection because white culture and its perspectives are inscribed on us/into us). You may choose to pull up the drawbridge or retreat to an island in order to be with your colored *hermanas* in a sort of temporary cultural separatism. Many of us choose to "draw up our own bridges" for short periods of time in order to regroup, recharge our energies, and nourish ourselves before wading back into the frontlines. This is also true for whitewomen. The other option is being "down"— that is, being a bridge. Being "down" may mean a partial loss of self. Being "there" for people *all the time, mediating all the time* means risking being "walked" on, being "used." I and my publishing credentials are often "used" to "colorize" white women's grant proposals, projects, lecture series, and conferences. If I don't cooperate I am letting the whole feminist movement down.

Being an island means there are no causeways, no bridges, maybe no ferries, either, between you and whites. I think that some women-of-color are, in these reactionary times, in these very racist times, choosing to be islands for a little while. These race separatists, small in numbers, are disgusted not only with patriarchal culture, but also with white feminism and the white lesbian community. To be an island, you have to reject certain people. Yet being an island cannot be a way of life— there are no life-long islands because no one is totally self-sufficient. Each person depends on others for the food she eats, the clothes on her back, the books she reads, and though these "goods" may be gotten from within the island, sequestering oneself to some private paradise is not an option for poor people, for most people-of-color.

At this point in time, the infrastructures of bridge and drawbridge feel too man-made and steel-like for me. Still liking the drawbridge concept, I sought and found the sandbar, a submerged or partly exposed ridge of sand built by waves offshore from a beach. To me the sandbar feels like a more "natural" bridge (though nature too, some argue, is a cultural construction). There is a particular type of sandbar that connects an island to a mainland—I forget what it is called. For me the important thing is how we shift from bridge to drawbridge to sandbar to island. Being a sandbar means getting a breather from being a perpetual bridge without having to withdraw completely. The high tides and low tides of your life are factors which help decide whether or where you're a sandbar today, tomorrow. It means that your functioning as a "bridge" may be partially underwater, invisible to others, and that you can somehow choose who to allow to "see" your bridge, who you'll allow to walk on your "bridge," that is, who you'll make connections with. A sandbar is more fluid and shifts locations, allowing for more mobility and more freedom. Of course there are sandbars called shoals, where boats run amuck. Each option comes with its own dangers.

So what do we, lesbians-of-color, choose to be? Do we continue to function as bridges? Do we opt to be drawbridges or sandbars? Do we isolate ourselves as islands? We may choose different options for different stages of our process. While I have been a persistent bridge, I have often been forced to "draw the bridge," or have been driven to be an island. Now I find myself slowly turning into a sandbar—the thing is that I have a fear of drowning.

Mujeres-de-color, mujeres blancas, ask yourselves what are you now, and is this something that you want to be for the next year or five years or ten? Ask yourself if you want to do alliance-coalition work and if so what kind and with whom. The fact that we are so estranged from whitewomen and other women-of color makes alliance work that much more imperative. It is sad that though conferences allow for short-term alliances, the potential for achieving some feminists' goals are short-circuited by politically correct "performances" by participants instead of more "real" and honest engagement. Choosing to be a bridge, a drawbridge, and a sandbar allows us to connect, heart to heart, *con corazones abiertos.* Even islands come to NWSA conferences—perhaps they come to find other islands.

Terms of engagement

Mujeres-of-color, there are some points to keep in mind when doing coalition work with whitewomen. One is to not be lulled into forgetting that *coalition work attempts to balance power relations and undermine and subvert the system of domination-subordination* that affects even our most unconscious thoughts. We live in a world where whites dominate colored and we participate in such a system every minute of our lives— the subordination/domination dynamic is that insidious. We, too, operate in a racist system whether we are rebelling against it or are colluding with it. The strategies of defense we use against the dominant culture we also knowingly and unknowingly use on each other.[12] Whites of whatever class always have certain privileges over colored people of whatever class, and class oppression operates among us women-of-color as pervasively as among whites.

Keep in mind that if members of coalitions play at the deadly serious and difficult game of making alliances work we have to set up some ground rules and define the terms we use to name the issues. We need to "see through" some common assumptions. One is that there is no such thing as a common ground. As groups and individuals, we all stand on different plots. Sisterhood in the singular was a utopian fantasy invented by whitewomen, one in which we women-of-color were represented by whitewomen, one in which they continued to marginalize us, strip us of *our* individuality. (One must possess a sense of personhood before one can develop a sense of sisterhood.) It seems to me that through extensive coalitions, various "*hermanidades*" may be a created—not one sisterhood but many. We don't all need to come together, *juntas* (total unity may be another utopian myth). Some of us can gather in affinity groups, small grassroots circles and others. All parties involved in coalitions need to recognize the necessity that women-of-color and lesbians define the terms of engagement: that we be listened to, that we articulate who we are, where we have come from (racial past), how we understand oppression to work, how we think we can get out from under, and what strategies we can use in accomplishing the particular tasks we have chosen to perform. When we don't collectively define ourselves and locations, the group will automatically operate under white assumptions, white definitions, white strategies. Formulating a working definition, preferably one subject to change, of alliance/coalition, racism and internalized racism will clear the floor of patriarchal, white, and other kinds of debris and make a clean (well sort of clean) space for us to work in. I've given you my definitions for alliance and coalition. Racism is the subjugation of a cultural group by another for the purpose of gaining economic advantage, of mastering and having power over that group—the result being harm done, consciously or unconsciously, to its members. We need to defy ethnocentrism, the attitude that the whole culture is superior to all others. Ethnocentrism condones racism. Racism is a theory, it is an ideology, it is a violence perpetuated against colored ethnic cultures.

> The intensity of the violence may range from hidden, indirect forms
> of discrimination (housing) through overt forms of ethnocidal
> practices (enforced schooling, religious harassment) to forms of
> physical and direct violence culminating in genocide
> (holocaust). . . . It becomes structurally institutionalized as the
> basis of hegemony, it turns into systematic racism.[13]

Internalized racism means the introjecting, from the dominant
culture, negative images and prejudice against outsider groups such
as people-of-color and the projection of prejudice by an oppressed
person upon another oppressed person or upon her/himself. It is a type
of "dumping."[14] On the phone the other day I was telling my mother
that I'd confronted my neighbor—a Black man who "parties" everyday,
from morning til night, with a dozen beer-drinking buddies—and
demanded that he not intrude on my space with his noise. She said,
"No, don't tell them anything, Black men kill. They'll rape you."
This is an example of internalized racism, it is not racism. Chicanos
as a group do not have the power to subjugate Black people or any
other people. Where did my mother learn about Blacks? There are
very few Black people in the Rio Grande Valley of South Texas. My
mother has internalized racism from the white dominant culture, from
watching television and from our own culture which defers to and
prefers light-skinned *gueros* and denies the Black blood in our *mestisaje*—
which may be both a race and class prejudice, as darker means being
more *indio* or *india,* means poorer. Whites are conditioned to be racist,
colored are prone to internalize racism and, for both groups, racism
and internalized racism appear to be the given, "the way things are."
Prejudice is a "stabilized deception of perception."[15] I call this
"deception" "selective reality"—the narrow spectrum of reality that
human beings choose to perceive and/or what their culture "selects"
for them to "see."[16] That which is outside of the range of consensus
(white) perception is "blanked-out." Color, race, sexual preferences,
and other threatening differences are "unseen" by some whites, certain
voices not heard. Such "editing" of reality maintains race, class, and
gender oppressions.

Another point to keep in mind is that feminists-of-color threaten
the order, coherence, authority, and the concept of white superiority
and this makes some white feminists uncomfortable and assimilated
colored women uneasy. Feminists of color, in turn, are made
uncomfortable by the knowledge that, by virtue of their color, white
feminists have privilege and white feminists often focus on gender
issues to the exclusion of racial ones. After centuries of colonization,
some whitewomen and women of-color, when interacting with each
other, fall into old and familiar patterns: the former will be inclined

to patronize and to "instruct"; the latter to fall into subserviance and, consciously or unconsciously, model herself after the whitewoman. The woman-of-color might seek white approval or take on gradations of stances, from meek to hostile, which get her locked into passive-aggressive to violently reactive states.

But how are you to recognize your *aliada,* your ally in a roomful of people? Coalition work is not a sport where members of a particular team go bare-chested or wear T-shirts that say AMIGA (which stands for an actual organization in Texas). It can get confusing unless you can distinguish each other. And once you identify each other, how will you work together?

When calling a foul, do you harangue the other person in a loud voice? Do you take on a *matador* defense—neglect to guard opposing player in favor of taking the limelight to inflate your ego? Will your organization be a collective or a hierarchy? Should your *modus operandi* be hands on or hands off? Will your offensive strategies consist of nudges, bumps, shoves or bombs? You may have to accept that there may be no solutions, resolutions or even agreement *ever.* The terms *solution, resolution,* and *progressing* and *moving forward* are Western dominant cultural concepts. Irresolution and disagreement may be more common in life than resolutions and agreements. Coalition work does not thrive on "figurehead" leaders, on grandstanding, "leadership always makes you master and the others slaves."[17] Instead, coalition work succeeds through collective efforts and individual voices being heard. Once we focus on coalition/alliance we come to the questions, How long should we stay together? Should we form temporary *carnalaship* of extended family which leads to strong familial and tribal affiliations but which work against larger coalitions?

If you would be my ally

Ideally as allies (all lies), we can have no major lies among us, and we would lay our secrets on the conference table—the ones we've internalized and the ones we propagate. In looking at the motivations of those we are in solidarity with (women-of-color) and those who want to make alliances with us (whitewomen), we not only need to look at who they are, the space(s) they occupy, and how they enter our space and manuever in it, *but* we have to look at our own motivations. Some issues to ponder and questions to ask ourselves: If all political action is founded on subconscious irresolutions and personal conflicts, then we must first look at that baggage we carry with us before sorting through other folks' dirty laundry. Having examined our own motives we can then inquire into the motivations of those who want to be our allies: Do they want us to be like them? Do they want us to hide the parts of ourselves that make them uneasy, i.e., our color, class, and racial identities? If we were to ask white lesbians to leave their whiteness at home, they would be shocked, having assumed that they have deconditioned the negative aspects of being white out of themselves by virtue of being feminist or lesbians. But I see that whiteness bleeds through all the baggage they port around with them and that it even seeps into their bones. Do they want to "take over" and impose their values in order to have power over us? I've had white and colored friends tell me I shouldn't give my energy to male friends, that I shouldn't go to horror movies because of the violence against women in them, that I should only write from the perspective of female characters, that I shouldn't eat meat. I respect women whose values and politics are different from mine, but they do not respect me or give me credit for self-determining my life when they impose trendy politically correct attitudes on me. The assumption they are making in imposing their "political correctness" on me is that I, a woman, a chicana, a lesbian should go to an "outside" authority rather than my own for how to run my life.

When I am asked to leave parts of myself out of the room, out of the kitchen, out of the bed, these people are not getting a whole person. They are only getting a little piece of me. As feminists and lesbians, we need all of us together, *tlan* (from the Nahuatl meaning close together), and each one of us needs all the different aspects and pieces of ourselves to be present and totally engaged in order to survive life in the late twentieth century.

Do they only want those parts of us that they can live with, that are similar to theirs, not different from them? The issue of differences continues to come up over and over again. Are we asked to sit at the table, or be invited to bed, because we bring some color to and look good behind the sheets? Are we there because those who would be our allies happen to have ancestors that were our oppressors and are operating out of a sense of guilt? Does this whitewoman or woman-of-color or man-of-color want to be our ally in order to atone for racial guilt or personal guilt? Does this person want to be "seen" and recognized by us? According to Lacan, every human action, even the most altruistic, comes from a desire for recognition by the Other and from a desire for self-recognition in some form.[18] For some, love is the highest and most intense recognition.

Maria Lugones, a Latina philosopher, a woman who is at this conference, wrote a paper with a whitewoman, Vicky Spelman, "Have We Got a Theory For You: Feminist Theory, Cultural Imperialism, and the Demand for the Woman's Voice,"[19] in which they posit that the only motivation for alliance work is love and friendship. Nothing else. I have friends that I totally disagree with politically, friends that are not even from the same class, the same race, the same anything, but something keeps us together, keeps us working things out. Perhaps Lugones and Spelman are right. Love and friendship can provide a good basis for alliance work, but there are too many

> tensions in alliance groups to dismiss with a light comment that bonds are based on love and friendship. This reminds me of Dill's critique of sisterhood being based on common (white) interests and alikeness.[20]

What may be "saving" the colored and white feminist movements may be a combination of all these factors. Certainly the tensions between opposing theories and political stances vitalize the feminist dialogue. But it may only be combined with respect, partial understanding, love, and friendship that keeps us together in the long run. So *mujeres* think about the *carnalas* you want to be in your space, those whose spaces you want to have overlapping yours.

Ritualizing coalition and alliance building

Speaking and communicating lay the ground work, but there is a point beyond too much talk that abstracts the experience. What is needed is a symbolic behavior performance made concrete by involving body and emotions with political theories and strategies, rituals that will connect the conscious with the unconscious. Through ritual we can make some deep level changes.

Ritual consecrates the alliance. Breaking bread together, and other group activities that physically and psychically represent the ideals, goals, and attitudes promote a quickening, thickening between us.

Allies, remember that the foreign woman, "the alien," is *nonacayocapo* which in Nahuatl means one who possesses body (flesh) and blood like me. *Aliadas, recuerda que la mujer ajena tambien es nonacayocapo, la que tiene cuerpo y sangre como yo.* Remember that our hearts are full of compassion, not empty. And the spirit dwells strong within. Remember also that the great emptiness, hollowness within the psyches of whitewomen propels them to coalition with colored. Oh, white sister, where is your soul, your spirit? It has run off in shock, *susto,* and you lack shamans and *curanderas* to call it back. *Sin alma no te puedes animarte pa'nada.* Remember that an equally empty and hollow place within us allows that connection, even needs that linkage.

It is important that whitewomen go out on limbs and fight for women-of-color in workplaces, schools, and universities. It is important that women-of-color in positions of power support their disempowered sisters. The liberation of women is the private, individual, and collective responsibility of colored and white men and women. *Aliada por pactos de alianzas,* united by pacts of alliances we may make some changes—in ourselves and in our societies.

After reading this paper consider making some decisions and setting goals to work on yourself, with another, with others of your race, or with a multiracial group as a bridge, drawbridge, sandbar, island, or in a way that works for you. *En fin quiero tocarlas de cerca,* I want to be allied to some of you. I want to touch you, kinswomen, *parientas, compañeras, paisanas, carnalas,* comrades, and I want you to touch me so that together, each in our separate ways, we can nourish our struggle and keep alive our visions to recuperate, validate, and transform our histories.

Notes

Rather than discussing anti-Semitism, a dialogue I choose not to take on in this paper for reasons of length, boundaries of topic, and ignorance on my part of all its subtleties (though I am aware that there is a connection between racism and anti-Semitism I am not sure what it is), I've decided not to take it on nor even make a token mention of it. I realize that this is a form of "If you don't deal with my racism I won't deal with yours," and that pleading ignorance is no excuse.

1. This is an elaboration and reworking of a speech given at the Lesbian Plenary Session, "Lesbian Alliances: Combatting Heterosexism in the 80's," NWSA, June, 1988. *Quiero darles las gracias a,* I want to thank Lynet Uttal for her generous critical reading of this text. I also want to thank Jaime Lee Evans, Helen Moglen, Joan Pinkvoss, Lisa Albrecht, Audrey Berlowitz, Rosalinda Ramirez, and Claire Riccardi for the various ways they encouraged and helped me writing of this paper.
2. The words *marimachas* and *tortilleras* are derrogatory terms that *mujeres* who are lesbians are called. *Patlache* is the Nauhtl term for women who bond and have sex with other women. *Lesberadas* is a term I coined, prompted by the word *desperado.*
3. Gloria Anzaldúa, "Never, Momma," a poem published in *Third Woman,* Fall, 1983.
4. The concept of framing metacommunication was articulated by Gregory Bateson in *Steps to an Ecology of Mind.* New York: Ballantine, 1972.
5. Ibid.
6. For a definition of cultural paradigms see: Kuhn, T.S., 1970. *The Structure of Scientific Revolutions.* Chicago: University of Chicago Press.
7. Judit Moschkovich.
8. This was documented by Chela Sandoval, "Women Respond to Racism," A Report on the National Women's Studies Association Conference held in Storrs, Connecticut, 1981 in *Making Face, Making Soul/Haciendo caras: Creative and Critical Perspectives by Feminists-Of-Color,* ed. Gloria Anzaldúa (San Francisco: Spinsters/Aunt Lute, 1990. See also Audre Lorde, "The Uses of Anger: Women Responding to Racism," in *Sister Outsider: Essays and Speeches* (Trumansburg, NY: The Crossing Press, 1984, 145–175).
9. Monique Wittig. 1981. "One is Not Born A Woman," *Feminist Issues,* Vol. 1, no. 2, Winter.
10. Lynet Uttal, from commentary notes of her reading of this text, February 1990.
11. Elana Dykewomon. Talk given in June, 1988, in Montreal at the Third International Feminist Book Fair for a panel on Lesbian Separatism.
12. See Anzaldúa's, "En Raport, In Opposition: Cobrando cuentas a las nuestras." In *Making Face, Making Soul/Haciendo caras: Creative and Critical Perspectives by Feminists-of Color,* ed. Gloria Anzaldúa (San Francisco: Spinsters/Aunt Lute, 1990). The essay first appeared in *Sinister Wisdom* 33, Fall 1987.

13. *Minority Literature in North America: Contemporary Perspectives*, ed. Wolfgang Karrer and Hartmut Lutz, unpublished manuscript.

14. Gail Pheterson defines internalized domination as "the incorporation and acceptance by individuals within a dominant group of prejudices against others." "Alliances Between Women: Overcoming Internalized Oppression and Internalized Domination," in this collection.

15. Alexander Mitscherlich's definition of prejudice in *Minority Literature in North America: Contemporary Perspectives*, ed. Wolfgang Karrer and Hartmut Lutz, 257.

16. See my introduction to *Making Face, Making Soul/Haciendo caras* cited above. My rationale for hyphenating *women-of-color*, capitalizing *Racism*, and making *whitewomen* one word is in this introduction.

17. Maria Lucia. 1986. Santaella, "On Passion as (?)Phanevou (maybe or almost a phenomenology of passion)." *Third Woman: Texas and More*, Vol. III, Nos. 1 and 2, p. 107.

18. Lacan, Jacques. 1977. *Écrits, A Selection*, trans. Alan Sheridan. New York: W.W. Norton.

19. Maria Lugones and Elizabeth V. Spelman. 1983. "Have We Got A Theory for You! Feminist Theory, Cultural Imperialism and the Demand for 'The Woman's Voice'." *Women's Studies Int. Forum*, Vol. 6, No. 6, pp. 573–81. Reprinted in *Making Face, Making Soul/Haciendo caras: Creative and Critical Perspectives by Feminists-of-Color*, ed. Gloria Anzaldúa (San Francisco: Spinsters/Aunt Lute, 1990).

20. Lynet Uttal, from commentary notes of her reading of this text, February 1990. Uttal refers to Bonnie Thornton Dill, 1983, "Race, Class, and Gender: Prospects for an All Inclusive Sisterhood." *Feminist Studies* 9:131–48.

APPENDIX

Global Networking in Women's Studies

Virginia J. Cyrus

Global networking has become a central concern of feminist educators and scholars. A comprehensive list of all relevant projects and groups would include almost every feminist activity during the past three decades. Instead, the following listings are highly selective, omitting one-time or ad hoc enterprises and including only on-going, formally institutionalized educational programs and interdisciplinary research organizations that operate on a global or at least multinational level.

The selected resources fall into four broad categories: (1) international meetings that focus on the education of and research about women; (2) periodicals that provide an interdisciplinary perspective on education and research about women around the world; (3) multinational research centers; and (4) Women's Studies programs operating internationally or explicitly designed to serve a multinational clientele.

International meetings

During the past two decades there have been a number of international meetings which have enabled Women's Studies educators, researchers and activists to network across national boundaries. These would include those focused on particular disciplines or fields, such as the 1976 Wellesley Conference on Women in Development and the 1986 International Conference of Women's History. Others have been one-time interdisciplinary events such as the Tribune and Forums held in conjunction with the United Nations Decade for Women, the 1976 International Tribunal on Crimes against Women or the 1982 Simone de Beauvoir Institute. Both of these kinds of meetings are central to global networking; however, the listings below include only regularly recurring meetings.

An explicitly scholarly feminist forum is the triennial free standing conference, the **International Interdisciplinary Congress on Women: Women's Worlds.** The first Congress, subtitled "The New Scholarship," was held at the University of Haifa, Israel, in 1981; the second, "Strategies for Empowerment," in Groningen, the Netherlands, in 1984; the third, "Visions and Revisions," at Trinity College in Dublin, Ireland, in 1987; and the fourth, "Realities and Choices," at Hunter College in New York in 1990. The fifth Congress will be held in 1993 in Costa Rica.

The **International Feminist Book Fair** provides an opportunity for feminist publishers, writers, librarians and scholars to explore and acquire feminist publications from all over the world. The first was held in London, England, in 1984; the second in Oslo, Norway, in 1986; the third in Montreal, Canada, in 1988; and the fourth in Barcelona, Spain, in 1990. For information about future fairs, contact Carol Seajay, Editor, Feminist Bookstore News, 456 14th Street, Suite 6, P.O. Box 882554, San Francisco, CA 94188, U.S.

In the United States, the **National Women's Studies Association Annual Conference** has become a forum for international Women's Studies. The International Task Force, the African and African-American Task Force and the Asian and Asian-American Task Force all present sessions that provide a global perspective. NWSA also is committed to the inclusion of international perspectives in all sessions and plenaries. For further information, contact NWSA, University of Maryland, College Park, MD 20742, U.S.; telephone 301-454-3757.

International periodicals

Change International Reports (P.O. Box 824, London, SE24 9JS, England) provides research and consultancy services to other non-governmental organizations and maintains a research and information archive. Reports and publications cover such varied subjects as prostitution, militarism, women in various nations, violence, homework and refugees.

Connexions: An International Women's Quarterly (People's Translation Service, 4228 Telegraph Avenue, Oakland, CA 94609, U.S.) is devoted to making available women's writing generally unavailable in the U.S. in order to contribute to the growth of a world-wide network connecting women working on similar projects.

ILIS Newsletter (International Lesbian Information Service, Centre Femmes, 5 Blvd. St. Georges, CH-1205 Geneva, Switzerland).

International Women's News (International Alliance of Women, B.P. 355, Valetta, Malta) is concerned with women's participation in public forums and elective office.

The **International Women's Tribune Centre** (777 United Nations Plaza, New York, NY 10017, U.S.; telephone 212-687-8633) was founded following the 1975 United Nations Women's Year Non-Governmental Organizations Tribune in Mexico City. It produces thematic newsletters on a variety of topics from housing, food production and violence to credit and small business. It also maintains a collection of books, slides, periodicals and organizations.

ISIS International Women's Journal and *Women in Action* (ISIS Italy, Via S. Maria dell'Anima 30, 00186 Roma, Italy, or ISIS Switzerland, Case Postale 50 [Cornavin], CH-1211 Geneva 2, Switzerland). ISIS is an international women's information and communication service founded in 1974 to facilitate global communication among women and to gather and distribute materials and information produced by women and women's groups. ISIS has a network of 10,000 contacts in 130 countries and produces periodicals, newsletters, pamphlets, books, films, and information about project groups in such areas as health, media, education, nutrition, violence against women, employment, and technology. It also publishes topical monographs and resource guides on a variety of subjects in English and Spanish.

WIN News (Women's International Network, Fran Hosken, Editor, 187 Grant Street, Lexington, MA 02173, U.S.), a quarterly published since 1975, focuses on international information about women and women's groups. Each issue covers such areas as peace, human rights, development, environment, health, media, etc., as well as reports from the various regions of the world. WIN also publshes some books on international women's topics.

Women at Work (International Labor Office, 1750 New York Avenue N.W., Washington, D.C. 20006, U.S.) focuses on Europe and the Third World.

The price is right for *Women of Europe* (Commission of the European Communities, Directorate—General Information Communication Culture, Women's Information Service, Rue de la Loi 200, B-1049 Brussels, Belgium). This free bimonthly publication reports on women's issues and activities in the European Community and Parliament as well as in the twelve countries which make up the EC. It lists books, studies and meetings of particular interest to or impacting on European women. It also periodically publishes monographs on single themes or issues.

Women's International Forum (Pergamon Press, Fairview Park, Elmsford, NY 10523, U.S.), published bimonthly, includes scholarly articles on interdisciplinary themes, book reviews, and most usefully, the "Feminist Forum," a comprehensive listing of conferences and other announcements, calls-for-papers, and brief listings of new books, films, etc.

The Women's Studies Quarterly and International (Feminist Press, City University of New York, 311 East 94th Street, New York, NY 10128, U.S.) provides descriptions of Women's Studies activities in countries around the world, of courses including or focused on international women's issues regardless of where they are taught, and of pedagogical resources and strategies.

Multinational research centers

In most regions of the world, feminist scholars and researchers have formed associations to encourage research and activism on behalf of women. Listed here are only those centers with the mission of investigating women's isssues beyond national borders.

International

International Research and Training Intitute for the Advancement of Women, INSTRAW (Avenida Cesar Nicolas Penson 102-A, P.O. Box 21747, Santo Domingo, Dominican Republic; telephone 809-685-2111; or Room 2914F, United Nations, New York, NY 10017, U.S.; telephone 212-754-5682.) Following the recommendation of the International Women's Year conference, the U. N. General Assembly established INSTRAW to provide training for women and to undertake research and information collection and exchange in order to promote women's advancement and integration into the development process.

Africa

Association of African Women for Research and Development AAWORD (B.P. 11007, CD Annexe, Dakar, Senegal).

Asia

Asian and Pacific Centre for Women and Development (Pesiaran Duta, P.O. Box 2224, Kuala Lumpur, Malaysia).
  Asian Women's Research and Action Network (Philipina, P.O. Box 208, Davao City, 9510 Philippines).
  Research Center for Asian Women (Sook Myung Women's University, 53-12, 2-KA Chungpa-Dong, Yongsan-ku, Seoul, Korea).

Europe

Aegean Women's Studies Institute (San Jose State University, San Jose, CA 95192, U.S.).
  Centre for Research on European Women, CREW (22 rue de Toulouse, 1040 Brussels, Belgium) publishes a newsletter, CREW Reports.
  European Network on Scientific and Technical Cooperation on Women's Studies (Ministry of Education and Science, Helen

Hootsmans, Postbus 25000, 2700 L2 Zoetermeer, the Netherlands) is sponsored by the Council of Europe—seventeen European countries including Turkey.

Mediterranean Women's Studies Institute, KEGME (Eleni Stamiris, Director, 192/B Leoforos Alexandros, Athens, Greece GR 115).

Middle East

Institute for Women in the Arab World (Julinda Abu Nasr, Director, Beirut University, P.S. Box 13-5053, Beirut, Lebanon; telephone 811968).

Western hemisphere

International Center for Research on Women (1717 Massachusetts Avenue, N.W., Suite 501, Washington, D.C. 20036, U.S.; telephone 202-797-0007) funded by United States Agency for International Development to advise on and evaluate the agency's policies and programs in regard to their impact on women.

Institute for Central American Development Studies (P.O. Box 145450, Coral Gables, FL 33114, U.S.; or Apartado 3 Sabanilla, 2070 San Jose, Costa Rica).

U.S.-based **National Council for Research on Women** (Sara Delano Roosevelt Memorial House, 47-49 East 65th Street, New York, NY 10021, U.S.) is organizing linkages among the 200 existing centers and organizations world-wide, which represent over 2000 researchers, policy planners and practitioners.

Opportunities for international study

International Women's Studies Institute (1230 Grant Avenue, Box 601, San Francisco, CA 94133, U.S.) is a summer program dedicated to the study of women's issues in a cross cultural perspective. It offers a chance for exchange between scholars, students, professionals and activists from various countries in order to explore commonalities and differences.

Institute for Central American Development Studies (Apartado 3 Sabanilla, 2070 San Jose, Costa Rica) is a study abroad program for undergraduate and beginning graduate students that focuses on women, economic development, and agriculture and the environment.

Institute for Study in Salzburg (Sigrid Stadler, Director, Institute for Study in Salzburg, Johannes-Filzer Strasse 26-55, A-5020 Salzburg, Austria) is an annual seminar intended to coordinate international research projects and professional exchanges with researchers working on similar projects and to establish cross-connections in research.

National Women's Studies Association International Task Force (NWSA, University of Maryland, College Park, MD 20742, U.S., telephone 301-454-3757) sponsors no international study programs, but the Task Force is compiling a catalog of international Women's Studies opportunities in higher education.

The **Women's International Studies Exchange (WISE)** (Dr. Tobe Levin, Martin-Luther Strasses 35, 6000 Frankfurt Am Main 60, Germany; or Jalna Hamner, University of Bradford, Bradford, West Yorkshire, England 7BD 1DP; or University of Maryland European Division, APO New York, NY 09102, U.S.) is organizing to facilitate international exchanges of under- and post-graduate students as well as lecturers and researchers in Women's Studies among institutions participating in the consortium. They want to offer Women's Studies students from all over the world the opportunity to experience feminist institutions in a foreign country, to encourage an international perspective in Women's Studies instruction and to strengthen ties among women scholars around the world.

Women's Studies in Europe (Women's Studies Term in Europe, Antioch University, Yellow Spring, OH 45387, U.S.) In cooperation with European feminists, Antioch University International offers an opportunity for graduate and undergraduate students to examine international feminist issues, combining experience and research in the context of comparative Women's Studies.

Women's Studies Summer Institute at the University of London Institute of Education (CREG, Institute of Education, Bedford Way, London WC1H OAL, England) offers a variety of courses each year.

Ford Foundation Mainstreaming Minority Women's Studies Project
Summer 1989

Barnard College
The Barnard Center for Research on
  Women
Project Director: Temma Kaplan
3009 Broadway at 117th Street
New York, NY 10027

University of California, Los Angeles
Center for the Study of Women
Project Director: Karen E. Rowe
236 A Kinsey Hall
University of California
Los Angeles, CA 90064

Duke University/
University of North Carolina
Center for Research on Women
Project Director: William Chafe
207 East Duke Building
Durham, NC 27708

University of Arizona
Southwest Institute for Research on
  Women
Project Director: Myra Dinnerstein
Douglas Building 102
Garden Level
Tucson, AZ 85721

Memphis State University
Center for Research on Women
Project Director: Elizabeth
  Higginbotham
College of Arts and Sciences
Memphis, TN 38152

George Washington University
Women's Studies Program and Policy
  Center
Project Director: Phyllis Palmer
Stuart Hall, Room 203
Washington, DC 20052

City University of New York
Graduate School and University Center
Project Director: Sue Rosenberg Zalk
33 West 42nd Street
New York, NY 10036

Columbia University
Institute for Research on Women and
  Gender
Project Director: Martha Howell
763 Schermerhorn
New York, NY 10027

Metropolitan State University
Project Director: Marsha Neff
Suite 121, Metro Square Building
121 Seventh Place East
St. Paul, MN 55101-2189

University of Oregon
Center for the Study of Women in Society
Project Director: Barbara Corrado Pope
Eugene, OR 97403

University of Wisconsin–Madison
Women's Studies Research Center
Project Director: Janet Shibley Hyde
209 North Brooks Street
Madison, WI 53715

Contributors' Biographies

Lisa Albrecht is an Assistant Professor in the General College of the University of Minnesota, where she teaches writing to underprepared students. She also teaches in the Women's Studies Department and is affiliated with the Center for Interdisciplinary Studies of Writing. She is currently editing *The Third Wave: Feminist Perspectives on Racism,* with Norma Alarcon, Jacqui Alexander, Sharon Day, and Mab Segrest, to be published by Kitchen Table: Women of Color Press in 1991. She also is a managing editor of *Evergreen Chronicles: A Journal of Gay and Lesbian Writers.*

Davida J. Alperin is a graduate student in the Department of Political Science and the Center for Advanced Feminist Studies at the University of Minnesota. She completed her Masters at the Humphrey Institute of Public Affairs in 1986 and is currently working on her dissertation about political relations between Blacks and Jews in the United States. Her interest in alliances goes back to when she worked as a community organizer with a number of different coalitions in New York City and the Twin Cities.

Gloria Anzaldúa is a Chicana tejana lesbian-feminist poet, fiction writer and cultural theorist. She is co-editor of *This Bridge Called My Back* and author of *Borderlands/La Frontera: The New Mestiza.* Forthcoming: *Making Face, Making Soul/Hacienda Caras: Creative and Critical Perspectives by Feminists-of-Color* (San Francisco: Spinsters/Aunt Lute, 1990) and *Prietita Tiene Un Amigo/Prietita Has a Friend* (San Francisco: The Children's Book Press, 1991).

Miranda Bergman was born in St. Paul, Minnesota, in 1947 and was raised in San Francisco. She is an activist and artist who has been painting and designing public art since 1970, stretching from West Oakland to Nicaragua. She was a founder and editor of *Community Murals Magazine* and is an arts administrator and teacher.

Beth Brant is a Bay of Quinte Mohawk, lesbian, mom and grandmother. She is the author of *Mohawk Trials* (Firebrand Books, 1985) and the editor of *A Gathering of Spirit: Writing and Art by North American Indian Women* (reprinted by Firebrand Books, 1987). She is currently completing a book of short stories, *Food and Spirits,* to be published by Firebrand Books (U.S.) and Press Gang (Canada) in the near future.

Rose M. Brewer is an Associate Professor of Afro-American and African Studies at the University of Minnesota. She also has appointments in the

Department of Sociology and the Department of Women's Studies. Her research and writings are in race, class, gender, the Black family, social stratification, and Black feminism. She is completing a book manuscript: *Race, Gender and Political Economy: The American Case Since the New Deal*.

Charlotte Bunch, feminist author, organizer, teacher and activist has been a leading figure in the women's movement for over two decades. The first woman resident fellow at the Institute for Policy Studies in Washington, DC, she was a founder of DC Women's Liberation, of The Furies, and of *Quest: A Feminist Quarterly*, which she edited during the 1970s. She served on the Board of Directors of the National Gay and Lesbian Task Force for eight years. Her writings have appeared widely, and she has edited seven anthologies, including *Lesbianism and the Women's Movement, Learning Our Way: Essays in Feminist Education*, and *International Feminism: Networking Against Female Sexual Slavery*. Her latest book is a collection of her essays from 1968 to 1986 entitled *Passionate Politics: Feminist Theory in Action* (St. Martin's Press, 1987). Currently she is the Director of a new Center for Global Issues and Women's Leadership at Rutgers University.

Roxanna Carrillo is a Peruvian activist and organizer and one of the founders of Centro de la Mujer Peruana Flora Tristan and of Centro de Documentación y Información sobre la Mujer. She is currently working on her Ph.D. in Political Science with a focus on women and politics in Latin America at Rutgers University.

Virginia J. Cyrus, Associate Professor and Director of Women's Studies at Rider College, Lawrenceville, NJ, was National Coordinator of the National Women's Studies Association from 1982–1984. In 1984, she founded NWSA's International Task Force. She served on the Advisory board for the Second and Third International Interdisciplinary Congresses on Women.

J. Michele Edwards is an associate professor of music and Director of the Women's/Gender Studies Program at Macalester College (St. Paul, MN). Her recent scholarship on women making music includes a review essay in *NWSA Journal* and "Women and the American Orchestral Institution," presented at the 1989 College Music Society meeting. She is currently working on contributions to a new textbook, *Women and Music: A History*, edited by Karin Pendle (forthcoming from Indiana University Press). Edwards also conducts Harmonia Mundi, Twin Cities' woodwind and piano ensemble, which regularly perform works by women composers.

Rita Giacaman is an instructor at Birzeit University.

Rayna Green is a writer, scholar, folklorist, cultural historian and activist, and a member of the Cherokee Nation of Oklahoma. She is currently the

Director of the American Indian Program at the National Museum of American History, Smithsonian Institution. Her most recent books are: *That's What She Said: Contemporary Poetry and Fiction by Native American Women* (Indiana University Press, 1984), and *Native American Women: A Contextual Bibliography* (Indiana University Press, 1983).

Susan Greene was born in New York City in 1958. She has been painting community murals for the past ten years. Currently she is leading mural workshops for homeless people and has taught muralism to several disenfranchised constituencies.

Nora Hall is the founder and director of the Leadership for Black Women program at the University of Minnesota in Minneapolis. She also teaches communication, women's studies, and human relations seminars. She has a Master's degree in Journalism from Southern Illinois University in Carbondale, a B.S. degree in Mass Communication from Jackson State University in Mississippi, and is completing a doctorate in Mass Communication at the University of Minnesota. Her professional experience includes more than fifteen years of work in broadcast and print media production. She has also worked with service agencies, both profit and nonprofit, to develop communication strategies and programs. Hall has served in various management capacities for more than ten years and is on the boards of several organizations.

Chi-Kwan A. Ho is a Ph.D. candidate in Human Development at the University of Maryland, College Park. She is currently writing her dissertation on gender role socialization among three generations of Chinese-American women. Chi-Kwan is a founding member of the Association for the Advancement of Feminism (AAF) in Hong Kong and Coordinator of the National Women's Studies Association (NWSA) Asian and Asian-American Task Force. This article is based on a presentation delivered at the NWSA conference: Leadership and Power: Women's Alliances for Social Change, University of Minnesota, Minneapolis, June 1988.

Penny Johnson lives in Ramallah, works in the public relations department of Birzeit University and is a contributing editor of *Middle East Report*.

Audre Lorde now lives in St. Croix, U.S. Virgin Islands, where she is working on a novel and a new collection of poems and continuing to make trouble.

Judith McDaniel lives and writes in Albany, New York, but her writing and solidarity work have taken her to Nicaragua, Big Mountain, and other places far from the Adirondack mountains. *Sanctuary: A Journey* and *Metamorphosis, Reflections On Recovery,* both published by Firebrand Books, are records of those travels.

Michelle Parkerson is a writer and independent filmmaker. She is the author of two books of poetry and short fiction, *Waiting Rooms* (Common Ground Press, 1984) and *Public Love* (manuscript-in-progress). Currently a lecturer at Howard University's Department of Radio, TV and Film, she is also at work on a film about lesbian poet/activist, Audre Lorde.

Gail Pheterson, born and educated in the United States, has lived in Europe since 1975. She has been Associate Professor of Psychology and Women's Studies at the University of Utrecht and Guest Professor at several universities in the Netherlands, France, and the U.S. She is editor of *A Vindication of the Rights of Whores* (Seal Press, 1989), and co-director of the International Committee for Prostitutes' Rights.

Dina Redman, who was born in New York City in 1952, currently works as a freelance designer and illustrator in San Francisco. She has also lived and worked extensively in Nicaragua, teaching at the School of Fine Arts and designing children's books.

Janice L. Ristock is Associate Professor of Women's Studies at Trent University, Peterborough, Ontario. Her research interests include feminist collectives, community organizing, violence against women and burnout. She is currently co-editing, with Jeri Dawn Wine, a volume on feminist community organizing in Canada. The book is being published by the University of Toronto Press and will be available in the fall of 1990.

Marlene Tobias, born in Washington, D.C., in 1950, currently lives in Berkeley, California. From 1975–86, she was a collective owner/operator of an offset print shop in San Francisco that served the progressive community in the Bay Area and in particular, the Solidarity Movement with Central America. She now makes her living as a freelance graphic artist.

Guida West has been an activist in the welfare rights movement for twenty-five years. She taught sociology at Rutgers University for ten years and was also Special Projects Administrator at the Rutgers Institute for Research on Women in New Brunswick, New Jersey. She is currently Director of Policy, Advocacy and Research at the Federation of Protestant Welfare Agencies in New York City. She is the author of *The National Welfare Rights Movement: The Social Protest of Poor Women* (Praeger, 1981), and co-editor, with Rhoda Lois Blumberg, of *Women and Social Protest* (Oxford University Press, 1990). She is at work on another book, *Protest Leadership Outcomes,* about welfare rights leaders, which will be published by Praeger.